Conservatives the party of the poor **TV**
cess while social mobility plummets The
ng classes **Your local community café is**
e world Plus-size models are idolised by
ar **As consumers are told they are more**
nudge politics and product placement
America, black people are worse off by
zling' is the new feminist empowerment
tion sports a grass roof and a vegetable
photos, books and information will soon
erates. But no fear: according to Yahoo,
ours' A culture that worships scientific
in labour **In an age of unprecedented**
Brothers proudly display their chastity
and individuality... which is why a billion
P's 'Beyond Petroleum' ad campaign is
g the Alberta tar sands for oil Slumdog
ild poverty rockets in the real Mumbai
stressed enamelled dishes Cutting-edge
s but girls really do prefer pink' Edinburgh
e to sponsor schoolchildren to plant five
e economy hits rock bottom A slice of
he salt as a packet of Walkers crisps **As**
the world, the global media is enchanted
a 'commoner', so that's OK) At a time of
enborough becomes a national treasure
consciences by paying a carbon-offset
ss on prime-time TV while sales of ready
Gaga is h-il--- ist icon Amidst
curious gatherers

GET REAL

ELIANE GLASER

Get Real

How to Tell it Like it is in a World of Illusions

FOURTH ESTATE • *London*

First published in Great Britain in 2011 by
Fourth Estate
An imprint of HarperCollins*Publishers*
77–85 Fulham Palace Road,
Hammersmith, London W6 8JB
www.4thestate.co.uk

1

A catalogue record for this book is
available from the British Library

ISBN 978-0-00-741681-3

Typeset in Minion by
G&M Designs Limited, Raunds, Northamptonshire
Printed and bound in Great Britain by
Clays Ltd, St Ives plc

MIX
Paper from
responsible sources
FSC
www.fsc.org
FSC® C007454

FSC™ is a non-profit international organisation established to promote
the responsible management of the world's forests. Products carrying the
FSC label are independently certified to assure consumers that they come
from forests that are managed to meet the social, economic and
ecological needs of present and future generations,
and other controlled sources.

Find out more about HarperCollins and the environment at
www.harpercollins.co.uk/green

For Adam

CONTENTS

Introduction   xi

1 Ideology's Second Life   1
2 Soft Power   35
3 Token Gestures   53
4 Electric Dreams   67
5 Smokescreens   89
6 An Office Romance   111
7 The Age of Consent   125
8 Science Fiction   147
9 Baloney   171
10 Greenwash   189

Afterword   207
Acknowledgements   210
Further Reading   211
Index   217

A poet's work is to name the unnameable, to point at frauds, to take sides, start arguments, shape the world, and stop it going to sleep.

SALMAN RUSHDIE, *THE SATANIC VERSES*

INTRODUCTION

It's a sunny Sunday morning and I'm popping out to the corner shop with my little son in his pushchair. We are both in a carefree mood. But then I pass a BP petrol station, and I can't help noticing that it's bright green. How strange, I think to myself, to see a purveyor of pollution decked out in such an eco-friendly shade. Once inside the shop, I scan the shelves for a nice healthy treat. I'm tempted by tubs of Rachel's Organic yoghurt, but then remember that they're made by Dean Foods, the largest dairy company in America; and by Seeds of Change chocolate bars, inconveniently owned by Mars. You'd never know that, I note rather irritably, from the naturalistic, folksy packaging. And as I look for a newspaper to buy I see that the *Times* front page is sporting the headline 'Cameron to Give Power to the People'. Is he now, I say to my slightly startled son. That's a strange way to dress up public-spending cuts. My son's eyes widen. He's not yet used to my impromptu political rants. But I have always looked at the world like this. And I've always felt a bit critical, as though I was giving the world too much of a hard time. But the way things are going now I feel worryingly justified.

The world I see around me is one in which oil giants advertise their environmental credentials, mass-produced brands are marketed as artisanal and ethical, and a multi-millionaire Old Etonian proclaims the Conservatives the party of the poor. A world in which TV talent shows stage spectacles of against-the-odds success while rates of social mobility drop to pre-1970s depths, Hugh Fearnley-Whittingstall catches wild sea bass while sales of ready meals reach an all-time high, and plus-size models are celebrated by the world's media while rates of anorexia soar. We have sleepwalked into a world where nothing is as it seems; where reality, in fact, is the very opposite of appearance.

I keep hearing proclamations that we have entered a revolutionary era: of grassroots people power, a new politics, transparency and technological transformation. And of course, in some ways, our world has changed for the better in recent years. There are plenty of grounds for optimism. Across the Arab world, people of all ages and backgrounds have taken to the streets to fight oppressive regimes. WikiLeaks has exposed the machinations of global political elites. Phone-hacking revelations have put a media multinational on the back foot. And yet at the same time, those brave new world fanfares simply do not ring true.

Is it just me, or does it seem as if new remedies are everywhere, but they're often symptoms of a deeper malady? That despite our obsession with reality, we're also in the grip of a massive sleight of hand? That we know there is something wrong, but we seem to have lost the intellectual language we need in order to articulate what's happening?

So many game-changing moments turn out to be fleeting or merely symbolic. Just as people are challenging the power of elites, those elites are speaking the language of people power in order to make even greater advances. World-altering progress is becoming increasingly hard to distinguish from the rhetoric of marketing. Like the Vodafone ad 'Our Power', that claimed credit for the Arab Spring, when in fact the company had caved in to Egyptian government demands to shut down its network during the protests there. Vodafone was roundly criticised and denied it had commissioned the ad; but this kind of thing goes unremarked all the time.

I was checking my email recently when Windows Explorer popped up. There was the familiar list of my directories and programs, but several of them were flashing up with those dreaded red crosses. My computer was infected with a virus. The screen was instructing me to download a virus protection program that would solve the problem. But when I Googled the name of the program, I found that it was itself a virus, something called spyware. It had snuck into my computer and replicated my Windows Explorer page; and downloading the program would make things even worse. I went searching on the internet for a genuine anti-spyware program, but how could I be sure that any of those weren't themselves viruses? Since nobody knows how computers work any more, none of my friends could help. It was like being in a hall of mirrors from which there was no escape: the solution had turned out to be the problem in disguise. I recognised this sensation from somewhere, but I couldn't quite put my finger on it. Until I realised that I recognised it from the whole of modern life.

Right now the potential for change seems overwhelming, and yet real change has also never felt less possible. At a time of such trumpeted progress, it feels as if genuine advances have slipped out of our grasp. Despite all the momentous events of recent years – the rise of the internet, the near-collapse of finance capitalism, the Arab Spring – I do not have a sense of radical empowerment. In fact, I am puzzled, and increasingly angry; not just at the injustice of it all, but at the sense that something huge is being swept under the carpet. Liberal commentators are cheerleading the new revolution. But where I'm standing that revolution, as *Gavin and Stacey* would have it, is not occurring. We seem to be living our lives under the spell of a mass cognitive dissonance, and everyday existence has taken on a frustratingly unreal texture. We need to get real. And that is what made me want to write this book.

I aim to provide a spotter's guide to the delusions we live by – from L'Oréal advertisements to the Obama effect; from the natural childbirth movement to iPhone apps. As the philosopher John Gray has noted, 'There are very few books that really help us understand the present.' This book is an attempt to do just that. I believe that it's time to hold up for scrutiny the increasing gap between the appearance and the reality of our lives, and to demonstrate why it really matters, right now. I believe that we can be optimistic about progress in the world, but for me that optimism lies in critique. Because how can we solve problems if we deny their existence; if we disguise them by highlighting sparkly exceptions? How can we improve the world if we're constantly buying into fake solutions, confected by the marketing operations of powerful elites, determined to preserve their status? Our assumptions of choice, opportunity and accessible information lead us to consent, over and over again, to the illusions we are sold. But it doesn't have to be that way.

So what has turned our world upside down, replacing reality with topsy-turvy mirage? In part I blame the spin, PR, marketing and rhetoric that has found its way into every nook and cranny of our lives. But we are familiar with that story, and in a sense it hides an even deeper deception. Because this is an age of apparent authenticity and realism, embedded reporters and user-generated content, HD, 3D and unbranded 'community personality' Starbucks cafés. Fake authenticity makes delusions doubly difficult to spot. And this is also an age in which we have swallowed the corporate line that the consumer is king, that we are savvy, self-aware and self-determining as never before. The notion that we may be duped and self-deluded, that we may be in the grip of false consciousness, is nowadays deeply taboo. But as I'll be arguing in this book, that just leaves us even more vulnerable to deception, 'nudge' politics and soft power, forms of manipulation that are on the rise and do not necessarily have our best interests at heart. We're caught in a trap, as the King would have it. And we need suspicious minds.

And there's another factor at play. With the melting away of conflicts between East and West in the Cold War and Right and Left in our politics, the big ideologies have been consigned to history. The influential political scientist Francis Fukuyama hailed 'the end of history' and the triumph of capitalist democracy. But this book argues that agendas never really disappeared. They just began to operate undercover, leaving us with a looking-glass world in which reality is spun and vested interests appear in disguise. Politicians now regard the word 'ideology' as an insult, but they are driven by ideology nonetheless. It's now a covert form of ideology that's at work, and that we ignore at our peril. This book puts ideology back at the heart of the problem, but also of the potential solution.

Because if we want to improve our world – indeed, with the environmental challenges we face, to save it – we need not only to identify hidden agendas, but also to have explicit aspirations. We need not to be afraid to say what we mean and what we mean to do. If we're too credulous in some ways, we also don't believe in enough. We need to debunk delusions and reclaim ideology as positive idealism, otherwise people power and revolution will remain empty ciphers that serve to obscure the lack of real agency and real change.

There are some who might find the claim that we live our lives under the spell of pervasive and self-defeating delusions somewhat paranoid. Are we in fact perfectly clear-sighted, yet impotent? Or just comfortably apathetic? So what if technological innovation doesn't solve world poverty, but allows us to have a bit of fun? Is it so wrong to download an app onto your mobile phone which causes it, when moved on a flat surface, to fart? Some of the illusions we live by are helpful, even pleasant; they help us get out of bed on a Monday morning, and allow us to indulge in a little couch-potato escapism. Sometimes – I will admit it – I feel a bit like a crazed conspiracy theorist. But then I read that David Cameron has welcomed Simon Cowell's idea for a 'political *X Factor*' in which hot topics are debated and voted on by the British public, and has launched a competition to 'develop an online platform that enables us to tap into the wisdom of crowds to resolve difficult policy challenges', and an amended version of that famous aphorism pops into my head: Just because you're paranoid, it doesn't mean they're not out to con you.

The delusions I'll be talking about in this book are sustained by a seamless blurring of deception and collusion. When people talk about conspiracy theories, the assumption is that there are evil agents doing the conspiring. But the conspiracies I'm interested in are really diffuse. We are both agents and victims, and our compliance with soft power comes about through unconscious creeping cooperation. It's in the drinking water.

I am, however, passionately committed to the idea that decoding delusions can help us to loosen their limiting grip on our lives, and take action to improve our world for real. Because it's these whitewashed problems and illusory solutions that are responsible for our curious sense of paralysis. But we can see through them if we look hard enough.

I'll start, in the first chapter, with the story of how ideologies went underground. Then in the chapters that follow, I'll take a polemical pop at how hidden agendas and topsy-turvy illusions operate today: in relation to politics, equality, new technology, the media, work, freedom, science, food, and the environment. In each chapter, I'll highlight one rule of covert ideology's lying game: a trick of the trade for you to recognise when you're going about your illusion-spotting day. The idea is that bit by bit, the powerful elites in our societies that thrive on deception will be forced to play their hand. Game on.

ONE

Ideology's Second Life

Ideology is dead

I sometimes feel as if I was born in the wrong era. I'd like to have been a socialist cabaret queen in Weimar Germany, or an anarchist squatter in 1970s New York, or at least to have been around at a time when having an ideology was cool. Back in the sixties, seventies and even eighties, students wore their isms like the badges on their second-hand tweed coats. But in the early nineties, ideology fell out of fashion. The generation that has grown up since the resignation in 1990 of Margaret Thatcher, the last British prime minister not to be embarrassed about her political allegiance, thinks that Left and Right are so, like, over. And thus it is that today's politicians, ever keen to get with the programme, would never commit the uncool style crime of actually having political beliefs.

In a speech to the Chicago Economic Club in 1999, Tony Blair declared that 'The political debates of the twentieth century – the massive ideological battleground between left and right – are over.' Along with his transatlantic counterpart Bill Clinton, Blair pioneered the very un-ideological Third Way. David Cameron, likewise, declared in 2009 that he 'will not be the prisoner of an ideological past', and that he doesn't do 'isms'. This is the era of oxymoronic cross-party combos like 'Red Toryism' (espoused by the writer and commentator Phillip Blond), 'Blue Labour' (advanced by the academic Maurice Glasman) and 'progressive conservatism' (developed by the Demos think tank). In a 2005 article for *The Economist*, José Manuel Barroso,

1

president of the European Commission, wrote that Europe was now focusing less on 'ideology' and more on 'results'. And in a speech in Philadelphia in 2009, Barack Obama proclaimed that 'What is required is a new declaration of independence ... from ideology.'

To call a policy ideological now is the most damning of criticisms. You hear it levelled at politicians on all sides. While in opposition, the then shadow education secretary David Willetts advised education minister Alan Johnson to break free from his party's 'ideological arguments'. The shadow business secretary John Denham accused the government's plans to treble tuition fees of being 'not financial, but ideological'. Republican protesters against Obama's proposed healthcare reforms cast them in extreme ideological terms, as 'socialist', 'totalitarian' and 'fascist'. One man at a Pennsylvania town hall meeting yelled, 'I don't want this country turning into Russia, turning into a socialised [sic] country.' To subscribe to an ideology these days is denounced as either naïve or sinister: like getting too involved in student union politics, or joining the Hitler Youth.

And along with 'ideology', 'divisive' is another new dirty word. This turn of events is most peculiar. Since when is it a bad thing for politicians to have political principles that are different from those of other politicians? To be, in short, idealistic? But according to this way of thinking, we now live in a virtuous, non-divisive, post-political age in which our leaders pursue a pragmatic agenda of cooperative consensus; of 'getting the job done'. Politicians around the world, from Angela Merkel to Nick Clegg, Barack Obama to Joe Lieberman, have embraced the non-partisan, cross-party centre ground. If they come up with any policies at all, they are the result of consulting you, dear voter.

There's another kind of enemy that's now condemned with the label of ideology: 'Islamist terrorists'. Since September 2001, Muslim people who attempt to blow up planes or trains or passers-by are assumed to have been driven by a coherent set of ideas, to have been 'radicalised'. The possibility that they might be some lone nut, or have particular, individual reasons for doing what they do is not considered. A week after the planes struck on 9/11, George Bush declared that the enemy in the war on terror was 'heir to all the murderous ideologies of the twentieth century … follow[ing] in the path of Fascism, and Nazism, and Totalitarianism'. Christopher Hitchens started using the term 'Islamo-fascism'. What Islamists share with Nazis and Communists, it's suggested, is a hatred of 'freedom'. As with the Western attitude to Communism, it's the other side who are brainwashed by ideas, not us. Freedom is not an ideology, we are told; it is a value.

But claims that ideology is either dead or evil are themselves supremely ideological. Those who purport to be free from bias; who claim the absence of any tendentious motive; who talk about politics, in short, as if it were like plumbing, are disguising their political goals in order to evade critique. It's the enemy that is driven by partisan intentions, they say. We are simply doing what works. This is not only a strategy, it's a concealed strategy, and much more effective as a result. It's politics – and big ideas – in hiding. I promised I'd identify the ten rules of ideology's lying game; and the first rule is to claim to be ideology-free.

So my heart sank when I read that veteran firebrand Shirley Williams congratulating the 2010 coalition government on their pledge to 'work together in the national interest'. 'The generation I belong to, steeped in ideology and partisan commitment, is passing away,' she wrote. 'My own vision was one of equality and social justice advanced by state action. The new politics is pragmatic, innovative, suspicious of state power, and holds to values rather than dogmas.' Williams commended a new spirit of 'cooperation' over 'the safe, long-established confrontation'. I thought, come on Shirley, stick to your guns! Don't dismiss political principle and party loyalty as aggressive tribalism; it's what democracy is all about. Sure, we can all love each other and agree all the time, but that's called totalitarianism. I want my politicians to make a case, to argue their position, to try to persuade me that their vision is best. I want frank and passionate argument, sharply divided debate, and clearly delineated alternatives. Post-ideological politics is being sold as 'the new politics', but I think it's an empty scam.

Broadsheet think-pieces and intelligent magazines keep telling me that this is an age of big ideas – whether about new forms of political agency or technological revolution. In fact, those are empty rhetorical gestures, and big ideas are the great taboo of our times. This helps to explain why the initial optimism of the Arab Spring protests evaporated so quickly: in each country the overthrow of the existing order provided a genuinely exciting sense of freedom, but there was no clear vision of what kind of society the protesters wanted to put in its place. It also helps to explain the apparently nihilistic character of the English riots in August 2011, and the baffled attempts to understand them. The riots were political all right, even though it was branches of Foot Locker rather than town halls that were being attacked. They were about racism, economic inequality and the mismatch between austerity and consumerism. But overt ideology was absent from both the riots and the commentary, leaving everyone dissatisfied. There was a 'March for the Alternative' against public-spending cuts in Britain earlier that year, but what the alternative actually consisted of was not spelled out. Francis Fukuyama's 'end of history' thesis, which linked the fall of Communism with the solution of all the world's problems, was rightly derided as cartoonish. But his claim that the triumph of liberal democracy signalled the end of the world's big ideological battles has become the mainstream view.

Take a look beneath the hype, though, and it's clear that it's not just me who longs for good old-fashioned idealism. Just look at the Martin Luther King-esque rhetoric, the Che Guevara T-shirts and the shouts of 'Yes we can' that accompanied the election of Barack Obama in 2008. That political enthusiasm was touted as a sign of a new era, but it was actually really retro. And that's why Obama has so far proved to be such a disappointment. Because while his campaign evoked a time when ideology was alive and well, his tenure has been pragmatic, centrist, anti-ideological. Progressive proposals – from closing Guantánamo to providing commitments on climate change – have been weakened or quietly shelved. The healthcare reforms in which liberals invested so much hope were watered down in the face of opposition from the pharmaceutical and insurance industries. Laissez-faire economics still rules Wall Street. This is not just about political compromise: it's about moving beyond politics altogether. Left-wing critics lament Obama's inaction; but his inaction, or rather his lack of a political project, is precisely his selling point. The psychoanalyst Robert Stolorow wrote in The Huffington Post in 2009 that it is 'reassuring that President Obama is ... for the most part capable of resisting the coercive grip of ideology ... he has shown himself to be able to transcend the false dichotomies and polarities ... that have traditionally divided us'. Obama has been described admiringly by an aide as a 'devout non-ideologue'. But to me that's not only a contradiction in terms, it's a sign of a deep malaise.

When politicians are asked to explain why young people are so uninterested in politics these days, they invariably give the same answer. We are 'out of touch' with the new generation, they say. We need to 're-engage'. But re-engage how? Young people are a mystery, politicians think, with their masonic Facebook habits and specialised footwear. We must learn their strange ways. So time and again, this re-engagement is imagined in the form of *X Factor*-style face-offs, appearances on YouTube, and votes via text message. But the real reason why young people don't turn out to vote is not that they have transformed themselves into an opaque new species. It's perfectly straightforward and rational: now that there's no difference between political parties, why on earth should they bother?

Our attitude to politics is in a muddle. Since we regard political division as something to be avoided, we do not identify the absence of political choice as a factor in voters' disaffection. 'They're all the same' is the refrain of bored non-voters; and yet we want sameness in the form of non-ideological politics. Although I'm always reading commentators hailing the return of 'big ideas' in politics, that isn't going to happen if any real big ideas are dismissed as either hopelessly romantic or as dogma. You're not supposed to believe in a politician who believes in anything. There isn't much idealism in this Massachusetts senatorial address: 'I'm Scott Brown. I'm from Wrentham. I drive a truck.'

From the bland, managerial prime ministership of John Major in the 1990s to New Labour's triangulations, from the hair-splitting policy distinctions of the 2004 Bush–Kerry election to Angela Merkel's explicit desire to transcend party politics and be a 'mother to the nation', political principles have been abandoned in favour of a rush to the electoral centre. As if that mythical place exists anyway. Politicians, stop sniffing around, trying to second-guess the middle ground: lead us to your own promised land! Just look at how Israel's political centre has shifted to the right in recent years. The political mood is up for grabs, so get off the fence! But – yawn – it's cross-party cooperation that's now applauded, with initiatives such as the Transpartisan Alliance and the Liberty Coalition springing up in the US. Senator Joe Lieberman wears his independence as a badge of honour, which is easy to do as independents are the fastest-growing group of voters in America. And since the expenses crisis in the UK a new generation of independent MPs has followed white-suited Martin Bell's 1997 example. Party membership and loyalty are collapsing in 'democracies' around the world.

And people, if cooperation in politics is really overrated, not to mention dangerous, so too is pragmatism. In the UK there are more and more calls for MPs to spend time 'on the ground' in their constituencies, resolving boundary-wall disputes and getting zebra crossings repainted. That's no way to start a revolution. And with the rise and rise of economics, the ultimate politics of pragmatism has evolved: politics as budget management. Policy decisions have been reframed as fiscal decisions, and everything is now given a monetary value in order to be deemed important, or even to exist at all: from the cost of prisoner reoffending to the economy, to the 'bio-credits' system which assigns financial value to endangered species (we can't just save them for their own sake). I'm all for not wasting money, but it's getting to the point where nothing in our public or private lives escapes monetary analysis: you can see this tendency in popular economics books like Steven Levitt and Stephen Dubner's *Freakonomics* or Eduardo Porter's *The Price of Everything*. Even the massive oil spill in the Gulf of Mexico in 2010 was at times, surreally, assessed via the fluctuations in BP's share price. In the absence of political projects, the only way we have of articulating value is through price. What the writer and theorist Mark Fisher astutely refers to as 'capitalist realism' now stands in for political idealism. Politicians' speeches are judged by the reaction of the markets, the hard-headed bottom line, imposing 'realistic' limits on politics as the art of the possible. But what could be more skittish or fantastical than the derivative-driven dreamworld of Wall Street and London's Square Mile? And in a beautiful irony, despite politicians' apparently down-to-earth references to 'the public purse', the use of audit to make the intangible real just spawns another, virtual reality: public servants routinely spend as much time representing their work – through box-ticking and report-writing rituals – as doing the work itself. This is government as trusty housekeeper, as technocratic bank manager. Reducing politics to ways of spending money is the perfect way of draining it of ideas.

That doesn't mean those ideas have actually disappeared. Politicians often talk about what they can 'afford'. But that's whitewash: it's all about political choices. They can cut their fiscal cake as they wish, apportioning more funds to defence or education. And they can make their cake bigger by raising more taxes. The new realism in politics is just another way to portray subjective intentions as objectively inevitable. When the coalition government announced massive public-spending cuts to reduce Britain's budget deficit, the Institute for Fiscal Studies analysed the proposals and showed that they would disproportionately affect the poor. I love these tell-tale glimpses of ideology that shine through the haze of rhetoric when the numbers are actually crunched. Economics is useful when it's politically revealing.

Sure, there is a mash-up element to modern politics: it is possible to be both green and Tory. But no matter how many times I hear that Right and Left are over, I still have a clear sense of what they mean. The Right is about tradition, nationalism, free trade, a small state, individualism, family values, support for employers, and liberty over equality. The Left is about society, taxation, a big state, human rights, multiculturalism, support for workers, and equality over freedom.

But governments no longer articulate their project, and sweeping changes of national importance slip by while the media pick over minutiae, isolated incidents, fringe policy details. The public no longer joins the dots. Politics is fragmenting into 'culture wars', single-issue interest groups and identity allegiance. And although both Right and Left are in the ideological closet, one side is more frequently outed than the other. It's the Right that has in recent years been identified as ideology-free. Conservatives criticise the progressive world view, but progressives nit-pick over technicalities. The Right is regarded as pragmatic and the Left as a dreamy luxury we can't afford. But why isn't the Right just as much of a luxury as the Left? Cutting rich people's taxes is after all rather expensive.

What about capitalism, you may be thinking. Isn't that the dominant ideology now? If so, what effect did the financial crash have on its pre-eminent status? Well, you might think that because it's got an 'ism' on the end, capitalism would be regarded as a particular belief system. And it's true that for an extraordinary moment in 2008, the financial system was indeed thrown into relief as a belief system, and a pretty eccentric one at that. Old-school ideology seemed to be making a comeback. Marx was cool again, and commentators dusted off their Keynes. For the first time in ages, there seemed to be alternatives, different isms to pitch, one against the other. But despite the fact that the entire world economy was on the brink of total meltdown, that window of ideas was only open for about three weeks. Then it was business as usual, the capitalist show was back on the road, and British bankers paid themselves £50 billion in bonuses in January 2010. Nobody came up with any viable alternative to free-market capitalism. In fact, it was more enthusiastically applied.

The reason why the crash came as such a shock to the Right, and why the Left still can't come up with a different way of doing things, is that aside from that brief moment of crisis, capitalism succeeds in presenting itself as not a belief system at all. Even just uttering the word 'capitalism' marks you out as not only anti-capitalist, but also as living in a dream world. As with contemporary politics, capitalism is an ideology of no ideology. It purports to be about hard facts rather than belief. During a speech at the Edinburgh Television Festival in 2008, News Corporation's James Murdoch compared free-market economics to Darwinian evolution. The analogy pointed to an assumption that is everywhere. Capitalism is regarded, by its critics as much as by its proponents, as being as transparent and inevitable as a force of nature. So it's become impossible to imagine any alternatives, because that would seem like finding an alternative to gravity. The crash was initially represented as a mortal blow to capitalism. But very quickly, influential commentators like Nassim Nicholas Taleb, author of *The Black Swan*, started presenting it as simply the latest in a series of periodic collapses: part of capitalism's natural, intrinsic fabric. Critique was contained. That explains why all the 'lessons' of the crash have been calls for more regulation: we cannot imagine different forces of nature, so all we can do is attempt to control their worst excesses. But the notion that free-market capitalism is a force of nature is a myth. It's a system that is consciously chosen and artificially maintained. And we need to remember that in order to have any chance of imagining different ways of organising society.

How convenient for politicians, and political power in general, to avoid the messy business of laying oneself open to explicit discussion and democratic challenge. The refusal to take a position in today's political culture – centrism, cross-party cooperation, the embrace of pragmatism, politics as economics, and the culture wars – all these developments provide fertile conditions for agendas to advance in secret. And this matters not only because elites are allowed to privately get their way, and not only because political culture is impoverished. It matters because the rejection of ideology is the rejection of idealism, of visions to improve our world.

I want the ideas that overtly set out the kind of world we'd like to live in to be regarded not as naïve and unworldly, but as the object of genuine choice and aspiration. My own ideological position, as you've probably gathered by now, is to the left of the main political parties. And it's true that in the remainder of this book I will spend a fair amount of time targeting the illusions that deny and sustain inequality. But at the same time, I would love to see a world in which modern

Conservatives and Republicans didn't feel the need to be mealy-mouthed about their allegiance to proper, right-wing ideology. If the Left has given up on grand narratives, the Right has lost its nerve. It would be great if they ditched the tedious new waffle about 'ethical', 'responsible' or 'philanthropic' capitalism, 'the green economy', 'social entrepreneurship' and so on; if they dispensed with the Converse trainers and baseball caps and came out proud in their belief in capitalism with claws. To spend my time bashing the right-wing establishment would be to miss a trick, in any case. The illusions that shape our lives, after all, don't only come from the neoliberal economics of the Chicago School; or from Enron, Halliburton and McDonald's. They also come from the groovy, liberal world of Google, Apple and Whole Foods.

Long live ideology!

Go into a dark room on a bright day, cover a window with sheets of paper, and make a small hole in one of the sheets. Then turn around. On the opposite wall you will see a perfect image of the world outside – in full colour and movement – but upside down. That is the magical effect produced by the camera obscura, a device which was employed by the astronomer Johannes Kepler and the painters Vermeer and Canaletto, and which became a popular seaside tourist attraction in Victorian Britain. In 1845, Karl Marx and Friedrich Engels used the device as a metaphor in a rather different context. They wrote that 'In all ideology men and their circumstances appear upside-down as in a camera obscura.' Most people, when asked, would say that the word 'ideology' means a set of overt political beliefs, like Communism, Marxism, or free-market economics. But here we're starting to see a meaning of the word which is the very opposite of that: something much more contradictory, subtle, and even unconscious. Marx and Engels turned the meaning of the word on its head. What they were describing is the curious effect that this form of ideology produces, where reality is the opposite of what it appears to be. In this upside-down world, powerful elites project an inverted version of reality

10

which serves to uphold their own interests: that success is always the product of hard work, for example, or that the American dream is within everyone's reach. According to this alternative definition, ideology means saying one thing, and meaning the exact opposite. Producing the appearance of action, while doing nothing at all. Creating the cosmetic impression that everything is fine, when it is not. And pretending that partisan arguments are actually universal facts.

You don't hear this meaning of the word ideology very often nowadays. But my claim is that it's this version of ideology that now defines our age. At the end of the Cold War, politicians rejected big ideas, and as the new millennium approached, they were driven underground. We began to deny that our lives were shaped by these big ideas, and as a result we failed to recognise that we live in an age in which our agency is being discreetly stripped away. Only by recognising how the world is distorted can we see how to put it right. We live according to delusions, covert assumptions, norms of behaviour and shaping forces that pass under the radar precisely because we deny their existence. And they don't just govern the world of politics: they permeate every corner of our everyday lives, from work to leisure, from food to sex.

If we're to understand contemporary politics and culture, we need to restore the lost world of Marx and Engels' camera obscura: the secret life of ideology which produces a distorted image of society in which inequality is downplayed and social harmony prevails. It's a fascinatingly paradoxical and mercurial concept which we have lost sight of today at a cost: because it describes the world we live in even better than the one in which it was first developed. Improving our world begins with rediscovering overt ideology's lost value; but analysing our predicament begins with rediscovering covert ideology's lost meaning.

When I was a teenager, I had a brief flirtation with Orthodox Judaism. I went to study the Bible at a yeshiva in Jerusalem. At the yeshiva, I asked the rabbi why it was that women were not expected to take part in religious rituals like going to the synagogue and

reciting morning prayers, especially since those rituals were so important and prestigious in the community. The rabbi told me that women
didn't need to take part, because women were so much more holy
than men. It was a textbook ideological manoeuvre: portraying power
relations as the opposite of what they are in reality in order to keep
the status quo in place. My flirtation slightly cooled after that.

For Marx and Engels, ideology was not just an intellectual concept,
a set of abstract ideas. Capitalist exploitation meant that people were
actually living a lie. In order to maintain their privilege, the ruling
classes had pulled off a cunning trick. They had got the workers to
internalise the upside-down belief that they weren't really being
exploited at all. The interests of the powerful were legitimated at the
expense of ordinary people, but with ordinary people's consent. We
tend to think of Marxism nowadays as having about as much subtlety
as a Five-Year Plan. But Marx and Engels' ideas were complex and
elegant: this was no cartoon battle between virtuous labour and evil
capital. They argued that the dissemination of ideology was not just
about deliberate manipulation by the ruling classes; it also involved
unconscious self-deception on the part of the workers, who came to
regard the dominant ideology as their own. Ideology is not simply the
work of PR men: it's also made up of diffuse information that cannot
be traced to a specific source. It's unspoken cultural norms, 'the way
things are', the social equivalent of an odourless gas.

Marx and Engels' theory of ideology as a wily, dissembling force
was developed by a series of subsequent thinkers, from the French
philosopher Pierre Bourdieu's colourful analysis of polite and civilised behaviours (such as knowing which cutlery to use for each
course) as forms of ideology which alienate the uninitiated, to the
Italian Marxist philosopher Antonio Gramsci's notion of ideology as
'hegemony': the cultural tricks which the ruling classes use to persuade
everyone else to accept their subordinate status. Gramsci described
the subtle and pervasive ways in which power relations are diffused
through the habits of everyday life, woven into the fabric of culture
and normalised as social rituals: from school to work to weddings.
Gramsci showed how power and control are achieved not only

through brute force but also through consent and the evolution of shared 'common sense'.

Covert ideology is also at work in that defining characteristic of modern authority, soft power. The phrase was coined by the international-relations guru Joseph Nye (who is also credited with inventing neoliberalism). He defined soft power as co-option rather than coercion. You get what you want not through the imposition of force, but by cultivating a sense of legitimacy around your project. America is a global empire not because it has the most bombs, but because it promotes enlightened democratic values around the world. If Joseph Nye was down with this kind of thing, the psychologist and social theorist Erich Fromm was more critical. He contrasted overt authority, which is strict but upfront, with anonymous authority, which pretends that it is not exerting force, that everything is being done with the individual's consent. 'While the teacher of the past said to Johnny, "You must do this. If you don't, I'll punish you,"' Fromm explains, 'today's teacher says, "I'm sure you'll like to do this." Here, the sanction for disobedience is not corporal punishment, but the suffering face of the parent, or what is worse, conveying the feeling of not being "adjusted", of not acting as the crowd acts. Overt authority used physical force; anonymous authority employs psychic manipulation.' Now, I know caning is brutal, but at least it's an exercise of power without the pretence of benign liberalism.

To see the two meanings of overt and covert ideology in action, take the example of David Cameron's 2011 public-spending cuts. They were frequently denounced by critics as motivated by ideology. This is the first, overt meaning of the word. But in a key speech to defend the cuts, Cameron said, 'We are not doing this because we want to, driven by theory or ideology. We are doing this because we have to.' Here we can see ideology at work in its other, covert form. The cuts were indeed driven by a right-wing ideological intent: you could see that in the enthusiasm with which cheering Tory back-benchers waved their order papers as each set of 'austerity measures' was unveiled. But claiming that the move was simply a matter of necessity ensured that this intent remained largely hidden. One

Conservative politician commented: 'Voters know there have to be cuts, it's the realism of working people.' What a great way to advance iniquitous policies under the cover of expediency, and with the apparent blessing of the people who will be hurt the most. These appeals to necessity and realism enable elites to do what they want. But they also leave us with a lack of agency, a curious sense of paralysis. Without a clear sense of what leaders stand for, what their principles are, what direction they want to take the country in, we're faced with the sense that we just have to accept what happens, because it's the plain truth, a matter of unavoidable fact.

I find it fascinating that ideology is a word with two meanings, one directly opposed to the other. Like propaganda, it means something obvious and something underhand at the same time. Covert ideology is not about labels or badges or isms. It's about ruses, hidden agendas and delusions. It's into this shady underworld that I'd now like to delve.

The fake's progress

In the new world of covert ideology, subliminal deception has taken over from explicit argument and overt persuasion. So I don't think it's a surprise that we've forgotten ideology's covert meaning, because that enables the deception to pass unnoticed. The twentieth century saw the evolution of myriad beguiling techniques in advertising, marketing and PR. And gradually, those techniques were applied to all areas of our public and private lives: from political campaigns to adverts for condoms.

Wasn't it ever thus, you might ask. How new is this covert form of ideology, and where in the world is it most powerful? To attempt some kind of answer, let's go back to 1948 and George Orwell's *Nineteen Eighty-Four*, a novel which seems – on the face of it – to be relevant to our age. George W. Bush's Clear Skies Act of 2003 actually relaxed the rules on air pollution, rather like *Nineteen Eighty-Four*'s Ministry of Peace, which keeps Oceania in a state of perpetual war. But Orwell retained a powerful faith in the impervious soul of human beings. The state ideology of *Nineteen Eighty-Four* may be clever, and it may be powerful, but it 'can't get inside you'. Fast forward to Western liberal democracies in the early twenty-first century and quite a lot has changed. Today's consumer-citizens are focus-grouped, market-researched and second-guessed; and policies and product-desire are designed to slip undetected into our minds and homes without awakening hostile antibodies. Who needs Big Brother when we're complicit in our own subjection? Orwell did not predict the subtle ideology of democratic, rather than totalitarian, states. He did not predict this age of consent.

While there were elements of covert ideology in the historical past, the virus has mutated into a more insidious strain. That's why the focus of this book is on the developed world, primarily the UK and the US, from the 1990s onwards. Contemporary Burma – or any regime which uses violence to impose its policies on its population – is, like Stalinist Russia, heavily ideological. But those regimes are ideological in a brutally overt sense of the word: they employ external force to implement their ideas. There's a paradox, a trap here. The more developed and mature the democracy, the more susceptible its citizens are to thinking that everything is fine, and to willingly internalising covert forms of ideology which may not be in their best interests. Of course, it's important to try to improve society and politics. But it's also important to watch out for the corollary of that improvement: the perils of resting on one's developed-world democratic laurels.

So how has this First World fakery evolved? Take for example the father of public relations, Edward Bernays. Bernays was a nephew of Sigmund Freud, and he applied his uncle's insights into individual psychology to the mass marketing of consumer goods. 'We are governed, our minds moulded, our tastes formed, our ideas suggested largely by men we have never heard of,' he wrote in his frankly titled book *Propaganda*, published in 1928. 'In almost every act of our lives, whether in the sphere of politics or business, in our social conduct or our ethical thinking, we are dominated by the relatively small number of persons … who understand the mental processes and social patterns of the masses. It is they who pull the wires that control the public mind.' For Bernays, this kind of control wasn't a bad thing. He had lived through war and revolution, and he shared his uncle's unease about the chaotic and aggressive human impulses that civilisation held in check. He fretted about the huge social changes brought about by urbanisation and universal suffrage, which had left traditional hierarchies in disarray: 'The steam engine, the multiple press, and the public school, that trio of the Industrial Revolution, have taken the power away from kings and given it to the people.' As Stuart Ewen notes in his excellent *PR!: A Social History of Spin*, and filmmaker Adam Curtis in his seminal documentary series *The Century of the Self*, the role of PR was therefore to persuade people not only to buy things they needed, but also things they could be made to want. Consumer dissatisfaction was a great new way to control the unruly herd. 'If we understand the mechanisms and motives of the group mind,' Bernays wrote, 'is it not possible to control and regiment the masses according to our will without their knowing it?' For Bernays, commercial manipulation was the best way to manage that dangerous devil, democracy.

Or take the example of another early PR man, Ivy Lee, who fretted that 'The crowd is now in the saddle. The people now rule. We have substituted for the divine right of kings, the divine right of the multitude.' Business had to control the masses, but by stealth, by worshipping them on the false pedestal of the enlightened consumer. 'Courtiers' were required to 'flatter and caress' the 'enthroned' crowd (Vodafone's 'Power to You' slogan comes to mind). And for the journalist and political commentator Walter Lippmann, it was essential that 'the public be put in its place', so that 'each of us may live free of the trampling and the roar of a bewildered herd'. In his 1922 book *Public Opinion*, Lippmann made a case for 'the manufacture of consent', anticipating Bernays's 1947 pamphlet 'The Engineering of Consent' (as well as Noam Chomsky's 1988 critique, *Manufacturing Consent*). Since public opinion was an 'irrational force', Lippmann rejected what he called the 'original dogma of democracy' as a mistaken Enlightenment belief in human rationality. He looked to Hollywood, what he called the 'dream factory', to create 'pseudo-environments' that would shape the public will by deploying powerful symbols that appealed to their unconscious. 'We must breathe into the allegory the breath of life,' he wrote. 'We have to merge the public's fantasy life with the sense of what is possible.' It was a way of replacing overt ideology – 'the sense of what is possible' – with covert ideology – 'the public's fantasy life'.

Or take the 'depth boys', a group of advertisers in the mid-twentieth century who also borrowed insights from Freudian psychoanalysis. The depth boys pioneered the use of 'motivational research' to understand not just what we buy but why we buy it: how consumer behaviour is swayed by the deeply buried drives of the unconscious. Instead of making an explicit case for why customers should buy this deodorant over that one, the depth boys designed deodorant bottles that looked like penises. It was motivational research that spawned that darling of the modern commercial and political world, the focus group. Like motivational research, focus grouping pushed selling underground. This wasn't about asking consumers (or indeed voters) what they wanted. This was about asking them about their hopes, their dreams, their fears; and then pushing those buttons. The modern consumer (and as we'll see later on, the modern voter) was a product not of conscious choice but of subconscious manipulation.

Focus-grouping was pioneered by the psychologist and marketing expert Ernest Dichter, whose book *The Strategy of Desire* appeared in 1960. Dichter was famous for focus-grouping housewives to work out how to sell them guilt-free instant cake mixes (his solution: 'add an egg'). These underhand psychological techniques are still very much in use: when *The Strategy of Desire* was reissued in 2002, one reviewer noted that 'It is astonishing that so much of what Dichter explored as early as the late 1930s has come back into vogue.' And it's these techniques that have created so much of the curiously topsy-turvy, oppositional culture we inhabit today.

Take the example, if you will, of Femfresh 'natural balance' feminine wipes. I was always told that the problem with feminine hygiene products is that they wreak havoc with one's natural balance. They kill off the benign bacteria that maintain a healthy ecosystem. That would mean that the name of the product is the name of the thing the product destroys. This is not about simple deception: I'm sure Femfresh products have been properly tested. There's something more subtle and profound going on. The idea of good bacteria is already counter-intuitive. And the marketing of Femfresh taps right into our psychology through its play on the close association between solution and problem. Sigmund Freud wrote that the human subject, the ego, is acted on by the superego and the id. When we enter civilisation and become a member of society, we repress our id, our desires. Through that act of repression, those desires are sublimated into the superego: the internalised demands of the outside world that make us conform to social expectations. We tend to think that our desires and our self-control are diametrically opposed; but they're not. The superego and the id are intimately connected. That's why when you're on a diet all you can think about is cake, why strippergrams often dress up in police uniform, and why pious tabloids are so obsessed with scandal. The problem, the desire, is bound up with the solution, the repression.

The kind of ideological culture we've developed today is all about authenticity, transparency and participation. As the writer and cultural commentator Thomas Frank describes in *The Conquest of Cool*, advertising has adapted to anti-corporate critique by incorporating the symbols of that critique into its own lexicon. Problem and solution have become inextricably entwined. Just as mass-market consumerism co-opts countercultural individuality, advertising has become anti-advertising. This helps to explain why we now live in a world that seems on the one hand to be full of lightning innovation and the latest underground trends, but on the other to be curiously static and paralysed: any potential challenge is seamlessly absorbed. You can see this kind of thing in action in Saatchi & Saatchi's 'viral' advertising campaign for T-Mobile, featuring an apparently spontaneous 'flashmob' dance-a-thon in Liverpool Street Station and a public 'singalong' in Trafalgar Square. Crowds of ecstatic participants film the spectacle on their mobile phones, either unaware of or unbothered by the fact that the event is being orchestrated by a company. The ads are truly an image for our times: a corporate simu-lacrum of 'alternative' festival fun. And a million suckers (me included, but for research purposes, obviously) have watched them on YouTube, happy to collude in the creation of a mass internet sensation.

Even if you're not into DIY you're probably familiar with the slogan for the wood preservative Ronseal: 'It does exactly what it says on the tin.' In a way, it's the opposite of Femfresh's 'natural balance': it cele-brates plain speaking. And Ronseal wood preservative does do what it says on the tin. But the slogan encapsulates a kind of 'honest guv' realism that is now rife in our culture. An appeal to realism, what you might call the Ronseal effect, is the best card in the pack. You can see it everywhere, from John Major's 'back to basics' politics to the justi-fication of market capitalism as a force of nature to evolutionary explanations for male dominance. It's why a senior aide accounted for one of ex-PR man and arch smoothie David Cameron's diplomatic gaffes by saying, 'What you see with David is what you get. He has always spoken his mind and told it exactly as it is.' And it's why Nick Clegg introduced his ingenious redefinition of the word 'fairness', when the coalition's public-spending cuts were revealed by the Institute for Fiscal Studies as having a disproportionate impact on the poor, by saying, 'I think you have to call a spade a spade.' (Clegg went on to elaborate in a very obscure and unspade-like manner about fairness being about public-service use as well as tax and benefits.) These new realist ruses are a kind of 'veil of obviousness', to borrow a phrase from the Austrian-American psychologist Fritz Heider. I don't know about you, but whenever I hear someone say 'To be honest,' I instantly start to mistrust what they're saying. The Ronseal effect is to disguise illusions as apparent down-to-earth reality, while dismissing idealism and overt ideologies as illusions.

In 2006, the PR maestro Harold Burson admitted in an interview for *Der Spiegel* that 'Most of the things we do today were identified by Bernays eighty years ago.' But today those tactics are disguised by a collective delusion of egalitarian empowerment and corporate candidness. 'The bedrock of effective PR', writes Amanda Barry in *PR Power: Inside Secrets from the World of Spin* (2002), is 'honesty and trustworthiness'. 'It is never OK to step beyond the line of reality,' she says. 'People want participation, not propaganda,' writes David Meerman Scott in his book *The New Rules of Marketing and PR: How to Use Social Media, Blogs, News Releases, Online Video, and Viral Marketing to Reach Buyers Directly* (2007). 'People want authenticity, not spin.' PR today is all about a 'conversation' with active consumers and corporate social responsibility. Unlike advertising, PR isn't salesmanship: it's 'information'. If you can see its work, it's failed.

In her anti-corporate bible *No Logo*, Naomi Klein describes how – particularly during the nineties – companies turned their attention from producing products to producing brands. It was part of a general trend in modern life for everything solid to melt into air: for political organisations to become front groups, governments to become contractors of outsourced services, and money to become futures and derivatives. But for companies as well as for humans, this created a problem. Since brands were confections, spun out of nothing, they were vulnerable to unfavourable associations, like the allegations of child labour that tainted Nike's former superbrand during the 1990s. Klein quotes David D'Alessandro, president of John Hancock Mutual Life Insurance, complaining in 1999: 'It can take a hundred years to build up a good brand and thirty days to knock it down.' Marketers were flummoxed. They described consumers as 'paradoxical', 'incomprehensible' and 'unpredictable'. Just like the fickle modern voter, consumers had become impossible to read. But this wasn't a mystery at all: it was simply that brands, like modern political parties, no longer had any distinguishable substance. Faced with the radical choice of Coke v. Pepsi, it was no surprise that loyalties could shift so easily.

The solution, as the French journalist Christian Salmon describes in *Storytelling: Bewitching the Modern Mind*, appeared in the form of good old-fashioned stories. From around the turn of the millennium, marketing departments started to fill out the empty ciphers of their brands with compelling, made-up narratives. Like that of Aleksandr Orlov, meerkat star of comparethemarket.com's viral campaign. Aleksandr currently has over 750,000 Facebook fans and over 40,000 followers on Twitter, and his memoir – a tale of love, heroism, immigration and entrepreneurship – has become a huge bestseller, outselling Tony Blair's *A Journey*. The hip new ad world of 'immersive' guerrilla marketing, word-of-mouth and online buzz seems a world away from 1920s German psychology professors; but it's a more insidious form of the same sleight of hand. Because this time it's supposedly ironic and tongue-in-cheek, engaging with active and knowing customers. The vision of the enthroned crowd has become a widely shared delusion. We've become pretty familiar with the empty con of brands: it's the mock authenticity of participatory marketing narratives we need to watch out for now.

Modern focus-group politics, too, is about selling an enthralling story to voters. As Salmon puts it, 'politics, as currently practised, is no longer the art of the possible, but the art of the fictive. Its aim is not to change the world as it exists, but to affect the way it is perceived.' In a 2006 report entitled 'Reconnecting the Prime Minister', a focus-group company called Promise Corp recounted their work with Tony Blair in the run-up to the 2005 general election. New Labour had shifted from being a 'Product-Oriented Party', 'which argues for what it stands for and believes in', to a 'Sales-Oriented Party', employing 'the latest advertising and communication techniques to persuade voters that it is right', and finally to 'a Market-Oriented Party', 'driven by frequent and intimate contact with voters, the party's customers'. 'A market-oriented party designs its behaviour to provide voter satisfaction,' the report explained. 'It uses market intelligence to identify voter demands and then designs its product to suit them.' The same shift, in other words, from overt to covert ideology; but disguised with the rhetoric of 'intimate contact' with voters, with the myth of participation and engagement.

The report outlined the problem for New Labour: that it was perceived by the public as a 'premium', 'high cost, high service' brand like British Airways or Mercedes, whereas the Conservatives were regarded as a 'value for money' brand like Tesco or Ryanair. Under the heading 'Analysis – Freud, Klein and the Mechanism of Splitting', it went on to describe how Promise Corp deployed focus-group exercises that 'allow as many unconscious motivations as we can invite into the group's work'. Melanie Klein's theory of the 'good and bad breast', corresponding to the nurturing or the withholding mother, was invoked to throw light on the focus groups' perceptions of the 'good' and 'bad' Tony Blair. I would like to have seen Blair's reaction when presented with that aspect of the research.

The problem with the focus group is that although it purports to listen carefully to what voters say, it doesn't actually listen at all. Like a kind of patronising counsellor, it assumes people are essentially irrational, so it tries to read between the lines. 'Most pollsters know what voters *think*,' said an article in a 1994 edition of the trade magazine *The Polling Report*. 'But too few understand how voters feel.' The goal of a focus group was 'to gain access to private, non-communicable, unconscious feelings and emotions'. An effective focus group will 'draw out the "motivational factors" behind the "top of mind" opinions – which is critical to understanding what is driving public opinion'. Personally, I would rather be asked for my views. But most of all, I'd like my politicians to do their job: to come up with ideas of what they would like to do. Focus-grouping voters is not about asking people what they want and then putting it into action. It's about getting under their skin in order to get more power. For example, focus-grouped voters often say they feel scared of violent crime. That fear is usually not the result of experience, but rather of reading tabloid newspapers. Politicians respond by promising tougher sentencing. But in fact, violent crime has fallen in recent years. Appealing to emotions rather than conscious views turns the world upside down.

Just as new-generation advertisers get modern online consumers to do their work for them in the name of empowered participation, focus-grouping is a way for voters to actively collude in their own manipulation. The focus-group politics that emerged under Clinton and Blair was couched in terms of listening, of responding, of authenticity; but although spin and consulting voters were presented as opposites, they are actually the same thing. What would be genuinely different is taking the lead, taking a position, making difficult decisions, prioritising competing concerns. But oh no, that's old, 'tribal' politics, and we don't want to go back there.

Well, why not? We drink out of mugs saying 'Keep Calm and Carry On', our politicians call for a revival of traditional community values, old-fashioned church weddings are back in vogue, influential *New York Times* political commentator David Brooks resurrects David Hume, Edmund Burke and Adam Smith as policy guides for today, and soul singer Duffy looks and sounds straight out of the sixties. We're more than happy to use elements of the past when it suits us: the point is, it's a choice. The modernising 'imperative' is once again a way of disguising particular ideological agendas.

Delusion in denial

'The vast majority of advertisers are truthful and honest,' according to the Advertising Standards Authority in Britain. And consumers, for their part, are 'savvy and enthusiastic recipients of advertising, who enjoy its entertainment value and make use of the information it provides … self and co-regulation continues to be the best and most effective way to secure high standards in advertising'. How reassuring that the body that's supposed to regulate advertising is leaving it up to corporations themselves. But of course that's fine, if we consumers are now wise to the tricks of the trade. According to the Australian marketing company Orangehammer, today's consumers are 'more intelligent, more sophisticated, more media savvy, more brand aware, and more aware of the ploys of marketing communication'. 'The Indian consumer is more sophisticated, discerning and … more demanding,' says India's *Economic Times,* and Chinese consumers are getting more 'savvy and sophisticated', says the *European Business Review.* My favourite little example comes from a report by Allegra Strategies, the corporate-strategy consultants working with those coffee chains currently homogenising our high streets. 'The rise of artisanal independents and the new "Third Wave" of coffee culture is having a significant impact on what the major branded chains are doing in their businesses to create the necessary authenticity required by today's more sophisticated and savvy consumers,' they say. 'We will see much better "crafted" coffee emerging as a result.' I love this reasoning. Initiatives like those 'local community' Starbucks cafés are an attempt to fool increasingly sophisticated and savvy consumers with fake authenticity. But that's OK, because consumers are increasingly sophisticated and savvy.

This mantra of the rational, discerning consumer is accompanied not only by psychological manipulation, but also by a lack of general awareness that psychological manipulation is still rife. And that's because our faith in consumer sophistication is accompanied by a rejection of Freudian psychoanalysis. A *Time* magazine cover in 1993 asked 'Is Freud Dead?'. A Channel 4 film screened in the same year was entitled *Bad Ideas of the 20th Century: Freudism*. A slew of books shunning Freud's legacy was published in the nineties, including *Seductive Mirage* by Allen Esterson and *Why Freud was Wrong* by Richard Webster. That decade also saw the rise of cognitive neuroscience and an increase in the use of drug treatments for mental illness.

At the same time that psychological marketing is enjoying an undercover revival, there's little public discussion of these techniques. Marketers have become publicly coy about their manipulative techniques, and the public has lost its radar. We believe that Freud has been proved wrong, so we don't realise that psychological techniques are still very much in use. We've ceded psychoanalysis to advertisers and PR strategists who use it against us, and we no longer have the means to critique what's going on. Fascinatingly, Bernays helped to arrange the publication of his uncle's books in America. He did the PR on Freud, creating the popular persona of 'Uncle Siggy'. It meant that the antidote was released alongside the poison. But now, although it's commonplace to acknowledge how influential Freud has been, we're actually intensely hostile to psychoanalytic interpretations. We have swallowed the corporate line that we are in fully conscious control: that the consumer is king. When in fact the savviness rhetoric is a cover for the deception. We can be savvy, but that means spotting the subtext, what's really going on.

In 1957, an American journalist called Vance Packard published *The Hidden Persuaders*, an exposé of motivational research and other insidious advertising techniques. It explored 'a world of psychology professors turned merchandisers', and revealed 'what makes us buy, believe – and even vote – the way we do', 'why men think of a mistress when they see a convertible in a shop window', and 'why your children like cereals that crackle and crunch'. *The Hidden Persuaders* stayed at the top of the US bestseller list for a year, was translated into twelve languages, and by 1975 had sold three million copies. But where are the Vance Packards of the twenty-first century?

When I studied English at university in the early nineties, I was introduced to the work of a sexy group of cultural critics who analysed the world in smart and surprising ways, from Jacques Derrida to Antonio Gramsci, Louis Althusser to Theodor Adorno. Don't take the world at face value, they argued; it's full of traps and tricks. But the influence of that way of thinking was soon on the wane. There was a turn away from the world and into the dusty archive, and big ideas seemed to give way to micro-history and byzantine identity politics. The study of covert ideology faltered just as the phenomenon itself really began to take hold in ways that these academics could only dream of.

Part of the reason the cultural critics turned away was because, like the good post-modernists they were, they denied the existence of an objective, concrete reality that ideology could obscure. Everything was, to some extent, an illusion. I think it's wrong to stereotype post-modernists as cartoonish relativists who say that white is black and black white. But I do subscribe to the common-sense observation that of course there is a reality, and in the dream factories of contemporary culture it is increasingly mis-sold. Those cultural critics would have their work cut out in the era of Facebook, Twitter, 3D TV and augmented-reality computer games; of ever more sophisticated spin, PR and viral advertising campaigns; of image and spectacle and confected sincerity. But where are they now, when we really need them?

We are in the grip of a very modern pincer movement. Just at the moment when we're most reluctant to acknowledge our own credulousness, more resources than ever before are being poured into the business of deceiving us. And the ruse-mongers are making full use of this denial, in their faux-egalitarian flattery that the people know best. But how could we, when everything means the opposite of what it says on the tin? I'm not saying people have become more stupid – quite the opposite. The illusion-spotting abilities of the average citizen have been sharpened to a fine point through living in a world of surfaces. But illusion-mongering is super-well-organised, and its practitioners are really smart.

I went out the other day to buy a winter coat, and found myself in the grip of something called false consciousness. The same thing happens every October. As soon as there's a nip in the air, I take one look at last year's winter coat and feel compelled to replace it – despite the fact that the price of winter coats puts them in the once-every-three-years garment category. There was nothing really wrong with last year's coat – it was just a bit bobbly and not on trend. But although I knew that rationally, it didn't stop me looking for a new one. And down in the ear-splitting, nerve-jangling basement of Topshop, this unnecessary raid on my bank account wasn't even fun. What I thought was good for me wasn't good at all.

Although Freud never wrote explicitly about ideology and false consciousness, his ideas help to explain how it works. Psychoanalysis solves the problem of how on the one hand we can be sentient beings, consciously perceiving the world, and on the other hand be utterly in the grip of delusions, often at moments – such as in our own age – when we feel most in control. Freud explains that we are not coherent, unified beings straightforwardly encountering the world around us. Instead, my ego is undercut by the unruly desires of my id, wanting to escape down the pub when I've got loads of work to do. But my internalised superego is also my own worst enemy, niggling me about a non-urgent task when I'm trying to relax on a Sunday.

Freud's insights account for how covert ideology can exist as an underground, unconscious phenomenon; and how it involves self-deception, not just getting the world wrong. Once we get our heads around the fact that we internalise the demands and expectations of society, and that these get bound up with our innermost desires, we can start to see how psychoanalysis gets us beyond the false opposition between coercion and consent. We are constrained by delusions, but we are also oddly attached to deluding ourselves. Call it political emancipation or call it therapy: Freud can still help us to unpick ideology's tight grip.

It was Marx and Engels who developed the idea of false consciousness as a political phenomenon. They wrote about how capitalism leads the working classes unwittingly to conspire in their own subjection by adopting one of two bogus beliefs: either that this is an inevitable state of affairs, or that they have a realistic shot at upward mobility. For the next hundred years or so after Marx, philosophers and political theorists had fierce debates about false consciousness. If the working classes were being oppressed, why didn't they join forces and overthrow their rulers? Why did they seem content to remain downtrodden, even regarding their 'betters' (royal weddings come to mind) with admiration?

But towards the end of the twentieth century, an acute squeamishness set in about the entire relationship between ideology and social hierarchy. Who is doing the duping, and are some people more duped than others? As the pernicious rhetoric about 'people power' illustrates, ideology serves to benefit the rich and powerful. But does this mean that those at the top of the tree are consciously and deliberately duping those at the bottom? And are those at the bottom more gullible than those at the top? So powerless and downtrodden, in fact, that they've become blind to their own situation? Is it patronising to expect these people to think and act in a certain way – isn't it up to them to decide if they are downtrodden or not?

It's true that political and corporate leaders have more resources at their disposal. They can pay the PR man to disseminate messages that consolidate their advantage. The Indian writer Arundhati Roy is right to ask: 'Isn't there a flaw in the logic of that phrase – speak truth to power? It assumes that power doesn't know the truth. But power knows the truth just as well, if not better, than the powerless know the truth.' I think it's right to question why it is that the poor in our societies are not demonstrably angrier than the rich. If you've got less money and power, if you're being screwed over, then surely you have more of a stake in kicking up a stink. It's difficult not to conclude that those at the lower end of the socio-economic scale are often complicit in their subjection, that they believe in the elites that ventriloquise the voices of ordinary people. We might be happy to say that the Zimbabweans who vote for Robert Mugabe do so because they are traumatised by the effects of colonial rule, but what about the working-class Italians who adore Silvio Berlusconi?

Over the last twenty years, the language of equality of opportunity has created a bizarre marriage of get-on-your-bike Thatcherism and political correctness by pretending that people are fully in control of their fate and not constrained by their circumstances. In their desire not to patronise the working classes, many liberals deny the pervasive influence of power.

But at the same time, the problem of false consciousness affects the affluent as well as the poor. The G20 leaders and the directors of Google are not free agents, self-consciously exercising absolute power. A highly-paid barrister might be more in thrall to the seductive ideology of work than a pub landlord, and a government minister more under the sway of myths about society than a retail assistant. Even the demonised bankers spend their days – I'm sure of it – in thrall to competitive self-doubt, exhaustion and a creeping sense that their lives are defined by the phrase 'Money can't buy you love.' A confident sense of enlightenment can leave you vulnerable to self-delusion.

Ultimately, ideology and false consciousness affect different people in different ways: for some, it's a matter of material gain; for others, quality of life. To the question of whether I count myself among the ranks of the duped, I would answer a resounding Yes. But if ideology-spotting abilities are not determined by status or money, they can be improved by developing greater awareness. At least I am having a go. And I believe that everyone else can too. That is not to deny that these are complex and knotty questions which are not easy to answer. They cut to the heart of our attitudes towards class, control, education, democracy, the media, and the very issue of consciousness itself. And as a society, we have stopped asking them.

When the British government recently caved in to the demands of commercial broadcasters to allow product placement in TV programmes, the only concerns raised were about children buying more sweets and crisps. Why? Because we imagine ourselves to be media-literate and discerning, consciously in control of our perceptions and our lives. To admit that we are duped and deluded, that our lives are shaped by illusions that we are scarcely aware of, let alone able to control, is nowadays highly controversial.

Debates about false consciousness just aren't being had any more, and the phrase has become *verboten*. It's a taboo that unites the grad-student table-dancers who protest that what they are doing is empowering and the Americans without health insurance who lobbied hard against the provision of a state safety net. Thomas Frank is one of the few contemporary commentators who has mentioned it: as he puts it in *What's the Matter with Kansas?*, 'it's like a French Revolution in reverse in which the workers come pouring down the street screaming more power to the aristocracy'. To utter the words 'turkeys', 'voting' and 'Christmas' in the same sentence tends to produce outrage across the board. No one is allowed to suggest that people don't always know what's best for them. But who of us can really say we do, all of the time? And as we're about to see, our reluctance to face false consciousness results in rich rewards at the top.

Nudge back

The notion of false consciousness might be a massive public blind spot, but to the elites in our society, it's a perfectly obvious reality. In 1957, Vance Packard quoted *Advertising Age* declaring that 'In very few instances do people really know what they want, even when they say they do.' And in 2005, the late Steve Jobs said: 'You can't just ask customers what they want and then try to give that to them. By the time you get it built, they'll want something new.' In a direct contrast to all the rhetoric about consumer savvy, the modern corporate world is built on this assumption of false consciousness; and so is modern politics. In the nineties under New Labour, it was known as focus-grouping. In the twenty-first century, it's known as 'nudge'. The 2008 book *Nudge* by the economist Richard Thaler and the legal scholar Cass Sunstein was given a rapturous reception by Barack Obama, David Cameron and policy wonks around the world. Cameron set up a Behavioural Insight Team, dubbed the 'nudge unit', run by Tony Blair's former strategy adviser David Halpern. Halpern was the co-author of a Cabinet Office Paper entitled *Mindspace: Influencing Behaviour Through Public Policy*. The nudge unit has reported to a high-level team including Steve Hilton, the PR man turned director of strategy for Cameron. Britain's Department of Health is issuing 'guidance on the most effective behaviour change techniques'. The Royal Society has launched a 'Brain Waves' project to investigate neuroscience's implications for politics and society. And the French government has established a Centre for Neuroscience, Behavioural Research and Policy in its Centre for Strategic Analysis.

What's the link with brain science? Well, nudge politics was spawned from research in neuroscience and behavioural economics. This research goes hand in hand with the rejection of Freudian psychoanalysis. Its proponents argue that it is the wiring and firing of our brains, rather than our superegos and ids, that really make us who we are. Now it does seem at first sight that these new ways of thinking share with psychoanalysis a belief that human beings are driven by irrational forces beyond their control. Buzzy new popular science and politics books – from Daniel Goleman's *Social Intelligence* to David Brooks's *The Social Animal* to Dan Ariely's *Predictably Irrational* – argue that we're not as rational as we think we are. Thaler and Sunstein challenge traditional economics' naïve belief in the rational individual, arguing that we don't always act according to our best interests. We put off paying into pension plans and eat chicken nuggets.

But nudge politics has no interest in encouraging people to be more rational. Its interest lies in allowing an elite group of scientists, politicians and corporations to spot patterns in our irrational behaviour and steer our choices accordingly. Thaler and Sunstein would protest that nudging preserves free will intact, because the range of choices is still there. But that doesn't wash, because free will is trumped by the art of persuasion. The one big factor that is left out in all this is power: the fact that some people are in a better position to make advantageous decisions than others, and the fact that nudging allows some people to manipulate others. 'We are not exactly lemmings,' Thaler and Sunstein write, 'but we are easily influenced by the statements and deeds of others.' Too right. But they regard this as a creepy opportunity rather than a prompt for critique. I find it amazing that there's not more condemnation of nudge politics; but that's because we don't see it as shot through with power dynamics. And in its weird validation of irrationality, it legitimates the reality deficit that pervades modern life. Instead of enabling policy-makers to exploit the fact that people's lives are shaped by covert ideology, I want you and me, dear reader, to identify the multiple ways in which covert ideology stops us being free.

Like focus-group politics, the politics of nudge is another step away from offering explicit priorities for people to choose between; away from overt ideology and the democratic tussle to achieve the good society. This kind of politics appeals to subconscious drives rather than conscious minds. According to David Halpern's *Mindspace* report, much of our behaviour takes place 'outside conscious awareness'; so 'providing information *per se* often has surprisingly modest and sometimes unintended impacts' (unintended for whom, I wonder). Government should, therefore, 'shift the focus of attention away from facts and information', and towards 'automatic processes' and 'altering the context in which people act'. It should become, in fact, a 'surrogate willpower'. How ironic that in this technological 'information age' people should no longer be making informed, rational decisions; that instead they should be subliminally corralled into behaving in a way that is 'best for them'. And who decides what is best for them? Political and corporate elites. So 'best for them' actually means 'best for elites'.

As we'll see later, in the chapter on food, corporate lobbying against informative labels on processed foods is the deliberate *withholding* of information. In 2010 Britain's Food Standards Agency, a governmental regulatory body equipped with scientific experts working in the public interest, had its powers stripped and replaced with a set of 'responsibility deal networks' shifting the emphasis from 'top-down lectures' to 'voluntary codes' and 'personal responsibility' (there's a fascinating slippage here between companies and individuals). Regulation of business has to be 'light touch' in order not to 'patronise' consumers, leaving those businesses free to manipulate the bundles of irrational drives they assume consumers to be. The Behaviour Change Network working on public health was to operate with the new 'nudge unit', bringing together 'experts in behavioural science with those from businesses'. And there we have it: we are not being nudged towards 'wellbeing', but towards being compliant and serviceable consumers.

All this hype about consumer savviness is a smokescreen designed to conceal the fact that we're being nudged. We've forgotten how to deploy the vital analysis of covert ideology, because of the modern belief that we are rational, conscious individuals, free to make choices about the lives we lead. Because even though those popular-science books keep telling us we're irrational, I believe that their real message is the opposite. They are actually telling us that unlike the unruly Freudian unconscious, we now have the chance, thanks to cutting-edge science, to master the mysteries of the human mind. Oh, except that this mastery is in the hands of a select few.

False consciousness has become taboo at the precise moment that it's being used to consolidate elite power. It's not just that there's a continuity in the subconscious techniques used by politicians and marketers in the early twentieth century and now. It's that – especially with the spotlight on neuroscience – they are now being applied subconsciously. We have false consciousness about false consciousness. While we're getting up in arms about being patronising or patronised, elites are quietly exploiting those paradoxes in order to shore up their status. We need to detect these manipulations. But we also need to face up to the fact that we are not always in conscious control, and not just about what we buy at the supermarket; but about persuasion and freedom, politics and power. In a sense the whole of our culture is structured like a Freudian human mind. There's an obvious, face-value level, and then a subtext that you need to decode. It's only modern consumerist Freud-hating culture that denies there's a deeper level. But it's that very culture – with its unprecedented deceptions – that has made the subtext even deeper.

Freud himself thought it was impossible to do away completely with covert ideology, delusions, false consciousness, whatever you want to call it, because it's part of being human in a civilised society. Marx was more revolutionary: he looked forward to the brave new Communist world when there would be no illusions, no subtext, and everyone would be master of their own destiny. Communism didn't turn out quite like that, as we know. But Freud believed in a more realistic kind of progress. Psychoanalysis is not about the elimination of the unconscious. It's about the resolution of a problematic relationship between our conscious and unconscious minds. It's about moving from a state of being 'neurotically unhappy', to paraphrase Uncle Siggy, to being 'normally unhappy'. We can't strip away covert ideology completely, as Marx had hoped. But we can be inspired by his incisive analysis to expose its cracks and flaws, and that's essential if we really want to tell the truth about power. As the German philosopher Jürgen Habermas argued, the opposite of ideology is not truth, but emancipatory critique. That critique can enable us to become self-aware, self-determining and idealistic once more.

I'm optimistic that we can become more aware and more rational if we try: that we have the capacity as well as the right to decide what kind of society we want to live in. Unlike the nudgers, I don't believe that false consciousness is an unchanging fact of life, an inevitable consequence of cognitive hard-wiring; and I don't believe it's an excuse for governments and corporations to become our 'surrogate willpower'. In an age when PR has taken over politics, let's bring the credo back into style. Now that psychological techniques are more prevalent than ever, let's fight back with Freud. In a virtual, airbrushed world saturated with PR and marketing, let's recognise 'authenticity' – those false calls to 'get real' – as the smartest ruse of all. We can be sceptical and optimistic at the same time; critique the world but also change it. We can be less credulous about the covert ideology that is distorting our world, and believe once more in the overt ideology that's the first step to transforming it. It's time to see through modern illusions and restore our ideals.

TWO

Soft Power

We're all familiar with the scourge of political spin. They're all corrupt, they're all the same, they're all lying through their teeth. *Yes Minister, The West Wing, Spin City* and *The Thick of It* dramatise politicians' two-faced machinations. One 2009 study found that politicians – along with estate agents – are trusted least out of all professions in Britain, behind bankers, journalists and lawyers. But what if authenticity were even scourgier? What if the politicians you really had to watch out for were the ones who rolled up their sleeves, bared their souls and spoke from the heart? What if the rotten core of contemporary politics wasn't rhetoric, persuasion, or the copious use of spin doctors, but candour, sincerity, acting on genuine conviction? And conviction politics is what we have today. Of course, conviction is itself a product of spin – but it appears to have nothing to do with it.

I first noticed conviction politics in action on 28 March 1992, on a pedestrianised shopping street in Luton. Things were not going well for Prime Minister John Major. It was less than two weeks before the general election, and the Conservative Party were facing almost certain defeat. Major was being jostled and heckled by angry Labour voters. Suddenly, he appeared to be gripped by a spur-of-the-moment inspiration. Climbing onto a soapbox, he picked up an old-fashioned megaphone, and began to argue back. But the soapbox was not actually a soapbox at all: it was a Central Office document box, apparently tested by Special Branch to make sure it would not collapse when 'Honest John' stepped up onto it.

David Cameron had his own soapbox moment just before the 2010 general election. He was being heckled by apprentices at a further education college in south London. Dressed in a plain white shirt, with the sleeves rolled up and – of course – no tie, Cameron seemed suited down to the ground by the apparent unruliness of the moment. 'This is what politics should be like,' he said. 'This is what you are going to get from me at this election: not a script, not a lectern, not surrounded by a bunch of hand-picked people. But proper, live public meetings where actually you can argue about the future of our country and then together we can decide. Right?' Putting his PR training to good use, Cameron spun audience hostility and his resulting wobble into the gold of authenticity. After all, in 2007, amid speculation that Gordon Brown was about to call a snap general election, Cameron had given an hour-and-a-half-long speech to the Tory party conference without autocue; a speech 'from the heart'. 'It might be a bit messy,' he'd warned his audience, 'but it will be me.'

Contemporary politics is like a shabby-chic wardrobe, or a pair of distressed jeans. It's not that cracks don't appear. It's that they are recruited to the task of making the surface of modern politics even smoother. Critique is incorporated into the edgy mix. It's Walter Wolfgang, the septuagenarian socialist peace activist ejected from the 2005 Labour Party conference for heckling Jack Straw, converted into the conference mascot. It's Peter Mandelson turning Gordon Brown's woodenness in front of the cameras into an asset: 'Look, you know he's not a sort of TV personality. He's not sort of Terry Wogan or Des O'Connor.' It's Tony Blair's sincerity over Iraq; Michelle Obama's mirthful revelations about her husband's dirty socks; the Tea Party town-hall meetings; Sarah Palin as hockey mom. Over the last two decades, this fake authenticity has taken over political discourse, and we have come to believe in proclamations of a new politics, people power, and grassroots revolution. I'm not saying people aren't wise to a lot of this: the leaders' wives' disclosures about their husbands' domestic habits were dubbed the 'my imperfect hero' strategy. And I'm not saying that all politics and all protest is the product of PR. But authenticity and political activism have become symbolic tokens which are marketed to the public, concealing deeper deception and widening imbalances of power. The next rule of ideology's lying game is saying one thing, and doing the exact opposite. And so to the forty-fourth President of the United States, Barack Obama.

'People power'

'One of the reasons I ran for president,' Obama confided in a post-election address, 'was because I believed so strongly that the voices of everyday Americans, hardworking folks doing everything they can to stay afloat, just weren't being heard over the powerful voices of the special interests in Washington.' And yet now Obama and big business are the chummiest of chums. If we're all so cynical about politicians now, what was it with all the hope that surrounded Obama's election? I mean, I know a lot of it was about the fact that he was black. But people's faith in him as a genuine political leader contrasted sharply with the words of Obama's former White House social secretary Desirée Rogers, who told the *Wall Street Journal*'s magazine, 'We have the best brand on earth: the Obama brand' (as Naomi Klein has noted, she got rapped over the knuckles for revealing the marketing behind the image). *Advertising Age* was able to explain more fully: 'Mr Obama somehow managed to be both Coke and Honest Tea, both the megabrand with the global awareness and distribution network and the dark-horse, upstart niche player' (in a lovely irony, Coca-Cola bought a 40 per cent stake in Honest Tea in 2008). That captures it perfectly: the Obama brand is both too everyday and too authentic to look like a brand. And the Obama brand is both Main Street and street-cred: both ways of suggesting he's down with the people. When in fact he's really down with Wall Street.

Obama's not alone. The Republican House of Representatives Speaker John Boehner has promised to 'give government back to the people'. The Tea Party's adopted style is feet-on-the-ground populism. Back on this side of the pond, Gordon Brown promised to 'put more power where it belongs – in the people's hands'; Nick Clegg announced that the Liberal Democrats were 'giving power to people and communities'; and David Cameron pledged to 'restore real people power' through a radical redistribution of power from Westminster to 'the man and woman in the street'. 'We are the radicals now,' Cameron elaborated, in one of his many variations on this Alice-in-Wonderland theme, 'breaking apart the old system with a massive transfer of power, from the state to citizens, politicians to people.' Over the last decade, British politicians on all sides have been tuning in to 'the wisdom of crowds': the Labour Party had their 'Big Conversation' in 2003; in 2009 the Conservatives launched their own internet version in the form of a £1 million competition to come up with a 'large-scale crowdsourcing platform'. After all, explained the then shadow culture secretary Jeremy Hunt, 'The collective wisdom of the British people is much greater than that of a bunch of politicians or so-called experts.'

I am heartily sick of having the people power thing sold to me all the time, of being told that this is a shiny new era of engagement with voters, the open scrutiny of decision makers, the public consultation, the citizens' assembly, the parliament for minorities and the independent public inquiry. In his book *The Life and Death of Democracy*, the political scientist John Keane praises these new forms of 'deep', 'direct' or 'monitory' democracy: 'All these devices have the effect of potentially bringing greater humility to the established model of party-led representative government and politics.' After the expenses crisis that engulfed British MPs in 2009, the constitutional expert Vernon Bogdanor declared that 'Our constitutional future is about to be rewritten, and it will be rewritten not by the politicians but by those whose servants they are.' But far from enhancing the democratic representation of the British people, the expenses crisis resulted in a situation where no one in their right mind would choose to become an MP, other than a millionaire or a martyr.

Remember the 2010 election campaign, that 'thrilling', 'electrifying' and 'transformative' contest that 'really caught people's imaginations' and 'engaged them as never before'? What seemed at the time to be a bona fide, over-to-you affair was in fact the most stage-managed and hollow campaign there's ever been. The machinery of actual democracy was replaced by the tokens of fake democracy. The traditional morning press conference, where leaders used to be challenged on the nitty-gritty of their manifestos, was abandoned. Instead there was man-of-the-people Nick Clegg's first-name encounters with individual voters, 'decent' David Cameron's all-night communion with 'the bakers, the brewers, the fishermen landing their catches', and Gordon Brown's prostration before Gillian Duffy, a pensioner from Rochdale. Everything seemed so genuine; and yet one thing was missing: actual policies. The leaders ignored several huge elephants in the living room: Afghanistan, Iraq, climate change, and exactly how they would deal with deepening financial crisis. This was an *X Factor* campaign in which Nick Clegg enjoyed for a time the popularity of Joe McElderry, and Mrs Duffy had her fifteen minutes of being Susan Boyle. But we were left with the least legitimate and most covertly ideological government I've ever seen. I don't want authenticity or humility in politics, I just want politicians to make a case for what they want to do.

It's a cliché of modern politics that voters have become cynical, but the reality is that we bounce between cynicism and wild optimism, neglecting all-important critique. We may dismiss Cleggmania now as a passing fad, but if we don't understand it we won't be able to cure our ailing politics. The key to Clegg's precipitous rise and fall was his lack of overt ideology. Those who liked him weren't clear what the Lib Dems actually stood for, and when his star began to fall, he had no political principles to hold on to.

A lot of the people-power hype is associated with new technology. Democracy is no longer about tedious little details like manifestos and voting. It's about whizz-bang online engagement and getting your hands on information. As Joe Trippi, Howard Dean's presidential campaign manager, puts it in his book *The Revolution Will Not be Televised: Democracy, the Internet, and the Overthrow of Everything*: 'The power is shifting from institutions that have always been run top down, hoarding information at the top, telling us how to run our lives, to a new paradigm of power that is democratically distributed and shared by all of us.' In 2007, American presidential hopefuls took part in a democratic 'experiment' hosted by CNN and YouTube. Members of the public were to submit their videoed questions via the internet for the candidates to answer live. The presenter, Anderson Cooper, was excited. 'This is something we've never done before,' he said. 'The candidates on this stage don't know how it is going to work ... and frankly we think that's a good thing.' The performance exemplified modern politicians' enthusiasm for being subjected to regular bouts of techno-charged 'direct democracy'. The Number 10 website in the UK is an elaborate portal for e-feedback. There's a 'Meet the PM' section, webchats, blogs, a Twitter feed, a YouTube channel, and e-petitions. Cameron has put forward a 'revolutionary' project to publish the 'business plans' of government departments online. The White House website boasts the Open Government Initiative, promoting 'transparent, participatory, and collaborative government'. 'The Administration is empowering the public – through greater openness and new technologies – to influence the decisions that affect their lives.' Each US government department has its own website, with its own feedback 'opportunities'. I am tired of all this guff, all these polling consultants and web gurus coming up with meaningless do-gooding phrases. We are drowning in it, and the reality of just how represented we are politically is being ever more obscured. The Open Government Initiative was set up by Obama's director of communications, Daniel Pfeiffer. There it is in a nutshell, with that weasel word 'communications': this 'transparent, participatory, and collaborative government' is, quite literally, PR.

Jeffrey Levy, one of the architects of 'Government 2.0', has described in an article on the White House website how proud he is that even negative comments get posted on the site. 'I think you gain credibility by showing you're willing to take some criticism ... we welcome everybody's comments,' he said. This sign of open government is shared by the supreme leader of Iran, Ayatollah Ali Khamenei. In 2009, a twenty-five-year-old maths student, Mahmoud Vahidnia, captivated the world's media when he upbraided Khamenei in person for being an inaccessible idol that nobody was allowed to criticise. Intriguingly, however, Vahidnia's tirade was reproduced on

Khamenei's own website, along with the cleric's calm response. 'Don't think that I'll be unhappy to hear such statements,' he said. 'No, I would be unhappy if such statements are not made.' I'm not implying that the US has the same democratic deficit as Iran. But I find it interesting that the two countries share the same mock-humility bullshit. The masochism strategy is the political trope of our times.

Take the new vogue for public apologies. In February 2009, the four bankers most to blame for Britain's financial meltdown prostrated themselves before the Treasury Select Committee. Or did they? Lord Stevenson, the former chairman of HBOS, said: 'We are profoundly and, I think I would say, unreservedly sorry at the turn of events' (the word 'unreservedly' invariably signals an underlying reservation). Andy Hornby, the former chief executive of HBOS, said he was 'extremely sorry for the turn of events that's brought it about'. And Fred ('the shred') Goodwin, the former CEO of RBS, issued an 'unqualified apology for all of the distress that has been caused'. Caused by whom? Or rather, by what? It seems it was the 'turn of events' wot done it. Rather like that ubiquitous 'I am not a racist/ sexist, but I apologise if others happened to take offence' formula, so much is said, and so little meant.

Or take David Cameron's 'listening exercise' after his plans for the reorganisation of the NHS were comprehensively slammed amid talk of a supposed 'humiliating U-turn', or Rupert Murdoch's pledge to make Sky News independent while bidding for full control of BSkyB, or his subsequent decision to close the *News of the World*. These performances of compliant submission make me think of Shakespeare's *Henry IV* and Stephen Greenblatt's theory of subversion and containment. In an essay entitled 'Invisible Bullets', the influential Renaissance literature scholar argued that far from undermining Prince Hal's royal status, the Falstaffian revelry of his rebellious years actually consolidates it. Monarchy thrives on dissent; it needs subversion and apparent weakness to appear truly strong. Sometimes it even produces subversion – the *agent provocateur*. This is power as theatre, as display rather than brute force, invisible rather than real bullets. It's power that is perfectly suited, Greenblatt notes, to an Elizabethan government with no standing army; and it's also just the ticket for a polite, mature democracy like modern-day Britain or America. It's an answer to the oft-repeated question of how Elizabethan plays that appear to stick two fingers up at the monarchy could be put on in an absolutist state: because they weren't really subversive at all. Of course, not all subversion is containment: it's more up for grabs than that. And there's also a fair amount of brute force around, too. But the theory of subversion and containment helps to explain why modern politics is so exasperating: because all this apparent weakness is actually a form of soft power. Once you start spotting examples, you see them all over the place: at the height of the phone-hacking scandal Cameron called a press conference in which he told reporters, 'The truth is, we've all been in this together.' This seemingly blanket admission was simultaneously the exact opposite – a ploy designed to diffuse the focus of blame.

The people-power rhetoric fits right in with a broader delusion. Politicians and the public alike are colluding in a collective act of worship at the inverted altar of the underdog. This is the age of the utopian belief in Twitter and Facebook, the public adoration of ordinary heroes, fictional and semi-fictional: the Susan Boyles, Billy Elliots and Slumdog Millionaires; and Antony Gormley's 'democratic' art project, *One & Other*, which placed 2,400 ordinary people on the pedestal of Trafalgar Square's empty fourth plinth. Bring on the bonfire of the vanities: those ivory-tower universities that value educational excellence, the avant-garde exhibitions that don't cater for school parties, and the professional establishment – those doctors and lawyers who dare to follow their own codes of conduct, to exercise independent discretion, to claim specialised expertise. Down with the professional literary critic: step forward Devon-based health visitor Lynne Hatwell, courted by magazines and chat shows, whose blog champions 'the voice of the people'.

After the financial crash none other than the former head of the Soviet Union Mikhail Gorbachev proclaimed that 'Today, as we sit among the ruins of the old order, we can think of ourselves as active participants in the process of creating a new world.' I heard a hundred pronouncements that these 'active participants' would no longer tolerate the telephone-number salaries and lavish bonuses of the Square Mile and Wall Street. But those warnings are looking more and more like a containment strategy to me. Yes, there were protests against the subsequent public-spending cuts in the UK, but they were dwarfed by the large-scale uprisings in the Arab world, and also by the million-strong crowd that gathered in central London in April 2011 to celebrate Kate and Wills' wedding. And the fascinated mixture of horror and glee with which spectacles of disorder are represented is a sign of just how rare they are. During the student protests against tuition fees in 2010, the cameramen far outnumbered the window-smashers. The scale of the coverage served to contain the protest by overplaying its extent. The demonstrations didn't exactly enjoy widespread public support, either. On my favourite mood-of-the-nation phone-in programme, caller after caller ticked off those 'feral thugs' bent on destroying private property. On the eve of the cuts' implementation, a poll revealed that 57 per cent of the British public supported them; 29 per cent thought they should go even further. The destruction of Ireland's economy by casino bankers hardly created a winter of discontent. The line about all sectors of society needing to 'share the pain' of the recession seemed to go down well enough. Blitz-spirit austerity chic was everywhere. Since we were 'all in it together', we had to 'pull together'. We'd been abusing our TK Maxx storecards like there was no tomorrow, and this strong fiscal medicine would do us good. David Cameron even 'consulted' the public on which cuts they 'wanted': a performance which the SDLP MP Mark Durkan termed 'the axe-factor'. And the City minister Lord Myners was able to get away with a *Guardian* article on bankers' bonuses with the maddeningly patronising headline: 'You are Right to be Angry'. This apparent kowtowing was a smokescreen for the reinstatement of the old global financial order.

The real outrage is that our unquestioning belief in the new grassroots revolution goes right alongside a massive reduction in the political will exercised by ordinary people. People power is a figleaf for the real power deficit. The worthy parade of the institutions of 'monitory democracy' is a sop to genuine accountability, a compensatory gimmick to plug the hole left by the decline of representative democracy. Focus-group politics is power-seeking dressed up as voter empowerment. Public inquiries are sham. Regulatory bodies are toothless. Complaints procedures and ombudsmen sound great on paper, but try to use them in practice and you'll quickly find yourself in a Kafka-esque world of box-ticking and the virtual keeping up of appearances. There's a procedure for everything, but none of them has bite. The British Parliament is increasingly a rubber-stamp exercise controlled by the whips. Parties now routinely ignore their election pledges, the most recent and most brazen culprit being the coalition government of 2010, whose long list of broken promises includes an end to 'top-down reorganisation of the NHS', followed by an attempt at the biggest top-down reorganisation the NHS has ever seen. The role of prime minister is becoming more and more presidential. Governments appear to lop their own limbs off in the name of small-state localism, but this just ends up consolidating elite control. Because the state doesn't just impose power; it's a mechanism for implementing the people's will. Despite the displays of humility, political leaders seem to be able to get away with anything: after the débâcle of Iraq, it's not clear what would now constitute a resignable offence. The phone-hacking scandal that flared up in 2011 revealed yet another cognitive dissonance: all the cant about modern transparency was shown to be plainly at odds with the reality of the corruption infecting a huge media empire, the police, and successive governments.

In addition to being intimidated by media tycoons, politicians are ultimately beholden not to the electorate but to the financial markets. After the announcement of massive public-sector spending cuts, an economist at BNP Paribas bank said that 'If the austerity measures had not been delivered the markets would have gone mad.' Everywhere, corporate and financial lobbies influence politics on an unprecedented scale: for all the talk of protecting what's left of British industry, the government didn't stop the sale of Cadbury to Kraft, or prevent Diageo closing the Johnnie Walker plant at Kilmarnock. And in the US, the Supreme Court has reversed a century-old ban on companies funding political campaigns, ensuring even greater corporate clout. The privatising demands of credit-ratings agencies trump Greece and Portugal's national democracies. Just as capitalism hides the reality of powerful, deadening monopolies behind the fiction of the bustling marketplace, modern politics is the art of disguising top-down as bottom-up.

Yes, the protests across the Arab world were inspiring. But the challenge is to have real people power that lasts for more than a second. As I write this, none of the protests has gone anywhere decisive, or anywhere particularly good. For the most part that's because of the reassertion of hard rather than soft power: of military force rather than covert ideology. But the transience of those events has also demonstrated the dangers of getting too mesmerised by the spectacle of demonstrations and Facebook campaigns, and of not concentrating on long-term overt ideological vision: on the kind of societies people want to create.

The wholesale rejection of ideological contestation has left a vacuum into which has leapt the rhetoric of people-power marketing that surrounds us today. As far as the West is concerned, politics used to be a relatively straightforward business of cause and effect. First work out what you believe in; then support a party that stands for those beliefs and will put them into action. Now that's considered 'tribalism'. The only hope for voters seems to lie with process and technique, with electoral reform and new media gimmicks for staging electoral contests. But changing the system is pointless without distinct options to choose from.

Because it echoes Communism, 'people power' sounds like a political project. But since parties are too scared to set out their stalls, it has no political meaning. We're left with the hollowed-out post-Fukuyama tokens of Communist idealism. People power may be back in style, but there's a curious lack of substance. Glastonbury may ape Woodstock, but we're a world away from Black Power or the birth of Women's Liberation. Politicians make use of the rousing connotations of Communism, but the idealism inherent in that project is gone. People power sounds left-wing, but as the Tea Party has shown, it can very easily blur into right-wing populism; just as the language of liberation can easily be recruited to the cause of free-market capitalism. In fact people power has become associated not with Communism but with its rejection: Berlin in 1989, the Tiananmen Square protests and the 'colour revolutions' that followed across Eastern Europe. Because people power is an empty signifier, it can be co-opted by a range of political ideologies. Political affiliation, on the other hand, has the advantage of being real.

The rhetoric of people power does in fact perform a political purpose, but it's the opposite of what it seems. It denies and therefore preserves inequality by claiming that the masses are now in charge; and if you do not succeed in life, well, it's nobody's fault but your own. This is a gift to those who would like to preserve their wealth and status undisturbed. The result is a world where citizens have less and less influence, but where there's a constant, craven and ultimately empty pandering to a symbolic populace; a world full of the false belief that everything has changed, everyone is equal, and our destiny is in our own hands. It's a dream-like world where we are given a platform from which to speak, but the words don't come out. I'm not sure whether we've become passive or just powerless. It could be that people know perfectly well what's going on, they're just unable to do anything about it. But what's clear is that although a lot of left-wing ink has been spilt bemoaning the erosion of political accountability, all that outrage somehow fails to capture the surreal and paradoxical quality of the situation. It's surreal because at the very moment our power as citizens is draining away, we're being told that we've never had it so good.

Astroturf

Those who conceal their influence through fictional deferral to the public now have a handy new trick at their disposal. 'Astroturf' campaigns – fake grassroots movements – were developed in the nineties by tobacco firms keen to create the impression of widespread resistance to smoking bans. In 1993, the PR giant Burson-Marsteller created the National Smokers Alliance, a manufactured smokers' rights group, on behalf of Philip Morris, the home of Marlboro. The rest of the commercial world was quick to adopt this radical alternative to traditional advertising, and the theatre of artificial activism was soon populated by a cast of 'sock puppets' and 'meat puppets': fictional personas enlisted to big up your own products, or do down the competition. Employees of Sony, L'Oréal and Walmart have all posed as puppets; and even the CEO of Whole Foods, John Mackey, has found time to lurk pseudonymously on online messageboards.

As co-editors of PR Watch John Stauber and Sheldon Rampton describe, politicians caught on too. At a 1994 conference called 'Shaping Public Opinion: If You Don't Do It, Someone Else Will', John Davies, CEO of Davies Communications and one of the earliest astro-turfing experts, explained how his political letter-writing campaigns worked. 'We handwrite it on little kitty-cat stationery if it's an old lady. If it's a business we take it over to be photocopied on someone's letterhead. [We] use different stamps, different envelopes ... Getting a pile of personalized letters that have a different look to them is what you want to strive for.' Feather Larson & Synhorst, a telemarketing company which was Scott Brown's 'partner' in his campaign to become Massachusetts' senator, offers a similarly retro-authentic 'letter desk' service. Its website assures potential clients that 'personal letters from constituents are proving to be increasingly effective in swaying legislators' opinions on hot issues. FLS can economically generate hundreds or thousands of letters on your behalf ... each letter is personalized, individually signed and often includes a handwritten postscript from the constituent.'

Today's astroturfers still use snail mail when they want that grubby tang of authenticity, but the internet provides the perfect artificial ground for fake grass. A service called DomainsByProxy camouflages political and corporate identities online, and a plethora of books teach the art of building 'bottom-up' and 'viral' campaigns: from Steven Holzner's *Facebook Marketing: Leverage Social Media to Grow Your Business* to Joel Comm and Ken Burge's *Twitter Power: How to*

Dominate Your Market One Tweet at a Time. 'There are some campaigns where it would be undesirable or even disastrous to let the audience know that your organisation is directly involved,' explains an article on the website of a PR firm called the Bivings Group with the rather ominous title 'Viral Marketing: How to Infect the World'. 'In cases such as this, it is important to first "listen" to what is being said online ... once you are plugged into this world, it is possible to make postings to these outlets that present your position as an uninvolved third party.'

The fresh green lawns of political activism are being replaced by plastic grass. In 2009, the then deputy prime minister John Prescott launched an online campaign to galvanise popular protest against bankers' bonuses. It looked like a real Robin Hood initiative, with liberal use of the phrase 'power to the people'. Prescott himself, the archetypal Northern working-class man, gave a series of rousing, iconoclastic media interviews. But what the coverage neglected to mention was that the campaign was hosted by GoFourth.co.uk, an organisation set up with the aim of helping to return the Labour government to a fourth term in office, and run by the party's comms chief Alastair Campbell. Prescott is a vocal fan of Twitter, and has regularly emphasised the endearing irony of himself as a former trade-union leader who can't type but is *au fait* with new technology. But he has seamlessly merged his shop-floor pedigree with being down with the kids. This is highly skilled image management, not ramshackle incongruity. Prescott's 'Tweets' were in fact co-written by his son David, the director of Gamechanger, a digital PR agency. From David Prescott to David Cameron to David Axelrod – Obama's top adviser and an astroturfing supremo – PR men with an ear for the demotic have wormed their way into the heart of government.

And although America has been transfixed in recent years by the incongruous spectacle of a right-wing street-protest movement, all is not as it seems. In fact, the town-hall meetings and Tea Party demonstrations against public health insurance and climate-change legislation have been carefully orchestrated from above. Thomas Frank has described how the American Right has deliberately engineered a shift in public attitudes, so that the traditional association between Republicans and blue-blood elites has switched to liberal Democrats. The Republicans are now associated with salt-of-the-earth ordinary folk. Astroturfing gives this fairy tale a new twist. This time it's medical insurance companies and energy firms that have been pulling the strings alongside Republican hard liners. And the theatricals are more sophisticated. The Republican candidate in the 2010 West Virginia US Senate race, right-wing businessman John Raese, presented himself as being on the side of workers, although he opposed the minimum wage. His election ads were peopled by actors pretending to be real voters. 'We are going for a "Hicky" Blue Collar look,' read the talent agency's casting call. 'These characters are from West Virginia so think coal miner/trucker looks.' As Sourcewatch, the brilliant PR-spotting portal, has shown, America's Health Insurance Plans, the multi-million-dollar lobbying company for the health-insurance industry, mobilised 50,000 employees to press Congress to scupper the healthcare reform bill. The town-hall meetings were coordinated by Americans for Prosperity (AFP), which helped run the Tea Party protests along with the conservative organisation FreedomWorks (in 2004, the 'single mom' from Iowa who was a key cheerleader for George W. Bush's plans to privatise Social Security turned out to be FreedomWorks's Iowa state director). In Taki Oldham's film *(Astro)Turf Wars*, a convener of the annual AFP 'Defending the American Dream' conference reports revealingly on efforts to fight healthcare reform: 'We hit the button and we started doing the Twittering and Facebook and the phonecalls and the emails.' A PR company called Bonner & Associates, funded by the coal industry, forged the signatures of local ethnic minority and elderly people on letters opposing a Bill to regulate greenhouse gases. Energy firms linked to the American Petroleum Institute hired an events-management company to bus in employees to 'Energy Citizen' rallies against climate-change legislation. Many such performances are brought to you care of Charles and David Koch, the multi-billionaire brothers who bankroll simulated bottom-up support for crony capitalism.

Some astroturfers, such as the aforementioned John Davies and Feather Larson & Synhorst, are surprisingly frank about what they do. But although they advertise their techniques, they don't tend to identify their areas of operation. It took considerable sleuthing by the *Wall Street Journal* to discover that the DCI Group, a sister company of FLS, was behind the deliberately amateurish YouTube video 'Al Gore's Penguin Army', which satirised Gore's film about climate change *An Inconvenient Truth* (DCI has ExxonMobil on its client list). The Tea Party is deliberately decentralised: there is no HQ or manifesto to state its ideology. It's anti-state and ostensibly anti-political, but it has a covertly political corporate agenda. When pushed, many astroturfers become coy. 'I've never been to a Tea Party event,' David Koch assured *New York* magazine. And in a *Guardian* interview, John Silk, the creative director of Lewis PR in the UK, described how clients new to online PR will often ask the question, 'Can't we just anonymously post positive comments?' On the contrary, he tells them; they have to be more subtle than that: 'Positive sentiment takes time to build. You wouldn't try to make friends at a party by going up to strangers and telling them how great you are.' You can manipulate people, in other words, but it's gauche to admit it.

When instances of astroturfing come to light the response is something of a legal and ethical muddle. Insiders dismiss them as 'bad apple' exceptions: Jack Bonner, founder and chief executive of Bonner & Associates, accounted for its fake letter-writing campaign by blaming it on 'a rogue temporary employee'. Likewise, governments and law-makers believe they can ring-fence individual offences: the EU called for astroturfing to be made illegal in 2007, and the US government passed the Lobbying Disclosure Act in 1995 and the optimistically titled Honest Leadership and Open Government Act in 2007; all to no avail. There are vociferous opponents of astroturfing amongst the online 'community', but they rarely acknowledge that it thrives on the very culture of the grassroots that they so enthusiastically nurture. There is a certain naïvety to these attempts to sort the good PR from the bad, because astroturfing is taking over the commercial and political worlds. But there's a broader, crucial question about discernment here. In a 2009 YouGov survey, more than 40 per cent of British shoppers admitted that they were not aware that online 'consumer reviews' may not be genuine, and a report by the American marketing-research company Nielsen in the same year found that 70 per cent of online consumers trust recommendations from strangers. If the trappings of new technology create the fiction that the consumer is king, political astroturf allows power to masquerade as the popular will. We need to get wise to fake grassroots politics, counterfeit authenticity, bogus people power, the masochism strategy and the dynamics of subversion and containment. These techniques are axiomatic of the false promises of empowerment which are sold every day to ordinary people, and which in the absence of overt ideologies we are only too ready to believe.

THREE

Token Gestures

How surreal it is to find that the brave new world of the twenty-first century is an age of unprecedented inequality. Here are some stats to prove it. In the US, the top 1 per cent own 40 per cent of the national wealth. The share of the national income taken home by the top 0.1 per cent has quadrupled since the seventies; for the top 0.01 per cent it has quintupled. Meanwhile, incomes for middle and bottom earners have fallen in real terms. In Britain we are returning to Victorian levels of wealth inequality: the richest 10 per cent are now nearly a hundred times richer than the poorest 10 per cent. Salaries for FTSE-100 chief executives are rising twice as fast as salaries for shop-floor workers. Meanwhile, there's a new backlash against gender equality, a new alienation of minority religious groups, and non-whites in Britain and America are falling behind according to nearly every social and economic indicator.

But I'll tell you what I find even more surreal: and that's the parallel universe created by a culture which celebrates role models, pays lip service to minorities, and revels in illusions of economic success and social mobility. Did you zone out while reading those stats just now? I don't blame you. Because the images of Michelle Obama and Oprah Winfrey, Michael Jordan and Alan Sugar are just so much more compelling. Call me a killjoy, but whenever I hear people talk about role models or exceptional success, I'm thinking, what good does it do, really? If you hold up an example of someone who has made it, how do people actually get from here to there? I detect a defensiveness in these exhortations to celebrate; an unwillingness to face the reality.

I even suspect that these exemplars actually make things worse, by creating the very visible impression that there isn't a problem after all. This chapter is about how real inequalities – of economics, class, race, gender and religion – have come to be ignored in favour of prominent, visible archetypes that can be used to make things appear just fine. These archetypes are a great example of covert ideology, which creates the upside-down impression of a world where anyone can make it if they just try hard enough.

Although I've started to see a recognition of reality – in epidemiologists Richard Wilkinson and Kate Pickett's *The Spirit Level*, say, an exposé of the impact of inequality on everyone; or in human geographer Danny Dorling's *Injustice: Why Social Inequality Persists* – equality has almost totally disappeared as a political issue. We need to turn again to our old friend, overt ideology. Because once we've noted the stats, the debate seems to falter. It's as if we've forgotten even the most elementary ideological language for discussing the issue. We've been struck ideologically dumb. And that stops us being able to do anything about it.

In the days before right- and left-wing politics became taboo, inequality was the main dividing line. It's amazing to think that, pre-nineties, Tories claimed openly that a certain measure of inequality was right and proper – that those who were more talented or hard-working should be able to reap rewards. Labour, on the other hand, argued that inequality was detrimental to society as a whole, so those who were less able to advance up its ranks should be given extra help. That included those who were less talented, as well as those who were disadvantaged materially. Call me nostalgic, but how refreshing it is to swim about in the clear blue water of political difference! But all of that has gone. As actual inequality has increased, parties of every persuasion have come up with strategies for sweeping it under the carpet. Right-wingers make copious use of populist rhetoric because they are too squeamish to declare their real allegiance to what they used to call justified inequality. David Cameron has proclaimed the Conservatives the real party of the poor, and in his election-night speech in Massachusetts, the wealthy Republican Scott Brown reminded his audience that he had won 'the people's seat': 'When I first started running, I asked for a lot of help, because I knew it was going to be me against the machine,' he said. The Labour Party and the Democrats, meanwhile, now talk only of equality of opportunity, not equality of outcome. They dismiss redistributive policies as unpopular, and maintain the pretence that aspiration works. This is all great news for those at the top, whose privilege is now both unchallenged and unanalysed. Everyone else is supposed to make do with an ineffectual combination of symbolism and euphemism.

A class act

In 1990, the newly installed prime minister John Major announced that 'In the next ten years we will have to continue to make changes which will make the whole of this country a genuinely classless society.' In 1999, Tony Blair told the Labour Party conference: 'My friends, the class war is over.' In the US, the American dream has turned into the myth of the classless society: George W. Bush scoffed at Al Gore during the 2000 presidential campaign for resurrecting the canard of class. Politicians brazenly attempt to spirit class away by denying its existence; and they appear to be getting away with it. As the middle class becomes increasingly squeezed in Britain and America, more and more people identify as – you guessed it – middle-class, which is a way of obfuscating disparity. A 2011 survey by the opinion consultancy BritainThinks found that 71 per cent of Britons identify themselves as middle-class, 24 per cent as working-class, and a revealing zero as upper-class. Debates about socio-economic inequality have given way to the 'culture wars': noisy rows about abortion and same-sex marriage that divert attention from more significant divisions. David Brooks advised readers of *Atlantic Monthly* in 2001 not to regard American society as structured like a hierarchy; the correct model is a high-school cafeteria, divided into 'nerds, jocks, punks, bikers, techies, druggists, God Squadders' and so on. 'The jocks knew there would always be nerds, and the nerds knew there would always be jocks … that's just the way life is.' This focus on cultural allegiance is the perfect cover for discrepancies in power. Let's not forget, David, that the jocks beat up the nerds.

As well as being distracted by the culture wars, people are buying into the notion that inequality is somehow natural. The Protestant work ethic and the idea of the undeserving poor have made a come-back, and success is increasingly associated with virtue. Naked greed is clothed in metaphors of hard graft and productivity. Structural explanations for inequality now seem redundant, because to be poor is the result of poor choices. A study conducted in 2009 by the Joseph Rowntree Foundation found that 69 per cent of respondents agreed with the statement: 'There is enough opportunity for virtually every-one to get on in life if they really want to. It comes down to the indi-vidual and how much you are motivated.' And in her book *Smile or Die: How Positive Thinking Fooled America and the World*, the American writer Barbara Ehrenreich identified a strong force in American culture that 'encourages us to deny reality, submit cheer-fully to misfortune and blame only ourselves for our fate'. We all want to avoid the really big issue, the enduring influence of socio-economic disadvantage as a factor in people's lives. You can see this in the cross-party emphasis on parenting style over economic background in determining social outcomes; on 'warmth not wealth'. The assump-tion of meritocracy neutralises anger about bankers' outrageous 'compensation schemes': they are supposedly our country's 'brightest and best'. And since class is now widely assumed to be a matter of self-determination, the working classes are fair game for satire: we can all laugh with impunity at *Little Britain*'s 'chav' Vicky Pollard.

In our topsy-turvy world, the highlighting of exceptional triumph has become the public way we deal with inequality. Susan Boyle's success was described by Piers Morgan, one of the *Britain's Got Talent* judges, as 'a wonderful testament to the powers of persistence, positive thought, and living a dream'. But her apotheosis illustrated the pious doublethink of the millions of viewers who found themselves able, through the redeeming vision of the 'hairy angel', to feel better about every other working-class, middle-aged woman who is left in society's gutter. *The Apprentice*, *The Secret Millionaire* and *Ladette to Lady* stage seductive pageants of Thatcherite aspiration, and the impression that success is within everyone's reach sanctions the ubiquity of affluence and aristocracy in our media. 'Kirstie [Allsopp] and Hugh [Fearnley-Whittingstall] are posh. They know that. We know that,' says Andrew Jackson, who has commissioned their shows for Channel 4. 'Maybe in the past they would have hidden it … But over the past two or three years [posh] presenters have become less ashamed.' That wink-wink assumption is a useful get-out: 'They know that. We know that.' It's 'know your place' passing as post-modern public awareness. And it points to the extraordinary complicity between citizens, their leaders, and the manufacturers of popular culture to forgive or even celebrate the gap between the haves and the have nots. The country-house drama *Downton Abbey* becomes wildly popular at the height of the economic downturn (is the title really a coincidence?), and its writer Julian Fellowes enters the House of Lords. As post-recession cuts to public services hit the headlines, the world is captivated by news of a royal engagement. But lest we become too aware of our forelock-tugging reverence, the match is billed as busting traditional hierar-chies: 'Kate Middleton's "commoner" status stirs up Britons' old class divide' is the *Washington Post*'s headline, and affectionate TV docs leading up to the big day show Wills cleaning a toilet on a gap-year 'expedition' to Chile (message: he's a down-to-earth kinda guy). The Oscar-winning, box-office record-breaking film *The King's Speech* epitomises this containment strategy, this worship of status in the guise of critique. The King's Australian speech therapist Lionel Logue is initially shown refusing to call His Majesty anything other than Bertie, lending the film an irreverent air; and Colin Firth's lionisation as King, as hero of the British film industry, as all-round alpha-male dish, is legitimised by his stammer.

Model politicians

Our culture has displaced its concerns about inequalities of money, power and status onto a futile power struggle between people and politicians. There's a muddle in modern politics that we might call the pedestal paradox. Citizens want their leaders to be just like them, not to have airs and graces, to be genuine and ordinary. But at the same time, they also desperately want their leaders to be, as it were, perfect parents: to be people they can look up to, who never make mistakes, change their minds, stumble or hesitate for a moment in an interview. This helps to explain the outrage unleashed by the leaking of MPs' expenses in 2009: it was directed at their arrogance and presumption, but also at the fact that they had slipped up so badly: at their gross failure as household managers. It also helps to explain the otherwise inexplicable willingness on the part of the British electorate to accept the coalition government's deep cuts to public services: at least they're getting the family finances in order. We seem to want political leaders who are in perfect control of everything, but who also hand over their power to the people. And that is why we are content with a juvenile, empty cipher called 'people power' that promises everything but, in reality, delivers nothing. It's also why politicians are too scared to be proper figures of authority and responsibility, to state their political position and choose between difficult alternatives.

Instead of trying to persuade our politicians to deal with broader iniquities in society, we're obsessing over our childish iconoclasm towards the politicians themselves. We're not complaining about the democratic deficit, but about claims for 88p bath plugs and whether or not MPs should employ cleaners. The expenses row was such a displacement of proper debates about money and power. Heather Brooke, the glamorous freedom-of-information campaigner, became the heroic subject of a film, and MPs flagellated themselves in public. The *Guardian* ran a 'groundbreaking "crowd-sourcing" exercise', in which readers were encouraged to go online and sift through embarrassing revelations about MPs' expenses: 'The response has been enormous, the results intriguing and, thanks to the efforts of many thousands of readers, not one MP who has put in a dodgy expenses claim can think about relaxing just yet.' How convenient for those bankers and CEOs who could get back to accumulating their capital undisturbed.

This compelling psychodrama between politicians and the public means that instead of coming up with fairer policies, politicians just make themselves appear humble. More and more attention is focused on politicians themselves as symbolic role models: from where they go on holiday to where their children go to school. It's not what politicians do that matters; it's what they represent. One of David Cameron's opening gambits in the 2010 election campaign was a well-publicised proposal to end subsidies for MPs' food in the House of Commons restaurant. In a speech entitled 'Cutting the Cost of Politics', the multi-millionaire leader bemoaned the fact that 'in the restaurants on the parliamentary estate, you can treat yourself to a "lean salad of lemon and lime marinated roasted tofu with baby spinach and rocket, home-roasted plum tomatoes and grilled ficelle crouton" for just £1.70. That's all thanks to you – taxpayers' cash subsidising a politician's food and drink.' Eric Pickles, the Tory John Prescott, was the perfect choice as ambassador for delivering the deepest cuts to the most impoverished councils in Britain in 2011: in an earlier speech Cameron had described him as 'leading the most radical shift in power that this country has seen in decades'. With his working-class Northern roots, Pickles was 'public chum number one. The big man on the side of the people.' From Tony Blair's glottal stops to Cameron's hair shirt, politicians are increasingly fond of 'leading by example'; but this is often just a way for them to send out 'messages' that are diametrically opposed to their real agenda. Behind the scenes of the theatre of lifestyle and personality, the real politics happens without scrutiny. And while the faux-humble posturing is often ridiculed, it is not recognised as part of a broader trend. MPs' expenses, bankers' bonuses, Scott Brown's truck: all swirl around on a merry-go-round of empty iconography. Crucial issues of wealth, class and social justice are endlessly epitomised but never properly addressed.

With today's politicians it's all about identity and personal stories, until it comes to the matter of class, and then – hey presto! – it suddenly doesn't matter at all. The one aspect of politicians' lives that does mean something – their backgrounds, and by implication the ability of ordinary non-elites to attain political success and representation – is the one aspect whose importance is denied. 'What people are interested in,' David Cameron insisted in 2009, 'is not where you come from but where you're going.' Most of the current cabinet went to private schools and Oxbridge, and three quarters of them are millionaires. The proportion of privately-educated MPs in Parliament is on the rise. But class does not play well in today's political theatre. In a by-election in 2008, the long-standing Labour stronghold of Crewe and Nantwich, home of railway workers, fell dramatically to a millionaire Conservative candidate, Edward Timpson, after a Labour campaign to portray him as a 'toff' – featuring local activists dressed in top hats and tails – backfired. Local voters apparently felt 'patronised'. The government's Olympics Minister Tessa Jowell said in the wake of the episode: 'I don't think anybody is impressed by "toff talk" … this is an old-fashioned way, for our young voters, for people to talk.' Injustice is so 1970s. Oh, except that the 1970s were more equal than now.

In 2009, when Gordon Brown jibed that David Cameron's tax policies had been 'dreamed up on the playing fields of Eton', the backlash was instant and universal. The editor of the *Spectator*, Fraser Nelson, put it thus: 'I write a column for the *News of the World* read by the type of people who tend to decide British elections. I have received all manner of letters about their likes and loves … But never a complaint that Cameron and Osborne are toffs and don't understand ordinary people.' Class still divides our societies and determines the pedigree of our leaders, but no one wants to admit it. So when it comes to the genuinely important class gap between ordinary citizens and our leaders, we are oddly content to put aside the fighting talk and let them off the hook.

Face value

For politicians and a public who are united at least in preferring not to face inequalities of economics and class, it's convenient that gender, race and religion have become the new priorities. The architects of New Labour in the 1990s found 'diversity' a convenient substitute for class struggle. And in the US, identity politics has inflected the political mainstream. But identity politics is all about symbolism. In 2002, when Halle Berry became the first black woman to win the award for Best Actress at the Oscars, history was made. 'This is for every nameless, faceless woman of colour who now has a chance after tonight because this door has been opened,' she cried. But with Berry's tears of gratitude, a generation of producers and directors breathed a sigh of relief, because they could finally close the book on the problem of race in Hollywood. Role-model schemes have become obligatory in equal-opportunity policy, crime-prevention initiatives, human resources, and educational projects. To take just one example, in 2007 the British government unveiled with great fanfare the 'Black Boys' National Role Models' programme. But there is no point in showcasing exceptions unless the conditions that set the rules are changed. What is needed is more attention paid to the bottom of the hierarchy, not the top.

The role-model model diverts attention from exploring the real, root-and-branch reasons why people from ethnic minorities may not simply follow the good examples offered to them. Role models are the entrepreneurs of race relations, following a Thatcherite template of self-motivated success. They function as PR for those who would like racism to cease to be an issue in a world that is still profoundly racist. When the *New Nation* newspaper published its 'Power List' of a hundred black role models in 2007, the *Daily Mail* announced that this 'explodes the myth that African Caribbeans are not achieving success'. The election of Barack Obama was in some ways a giant leap forward for race relations: I myself cried seeing him walk out with his family on that stage in Grant Park, Chicago. But there was a weird slippage in the way that people talked about race after his victory: as if we'd now entered a post-racial era, and could everyone stop talking about how black people are disadvantaged, please, because we've got one in the White House. After Obama came to office, as the journalist and writer Gary Younge has noted, unemployment among black Americans continued to rise: it currently stands at almost twice the rate for white people. Rates of mortgage foreclosures increased twice as fast as for white people. This was not really Obama's fault. The wealth gap between black and white households in America has widened massively since the mid-1980s: white families are typically now five times as rich as their black counterparts. But I didn't like the way he avoided the topic of race and declined to offer material support to the black underclass, while silently capitalising on his own exceptional appearance. Role models fit perfectly into a world where symbols rule: Disney's black princess Tiana, star of the 2009 animated film *The Princess and the Frog*, was unveiled with the kind of hype that ought to greet the appointment of a new Secretary-General of the United Nations. But the almost gleeful media circus that greeted golfer Tiger Woods's speedy fall from grace illustrated how easily praise for minority role models flips over into condemnation when they fail to perform the ideal parts assigned to them. These fairy tales are really flimsy.

'Choice'

As the L'Oréal slogan 'Because You're Worth It' illustrates, anti-feminism now appears in feminist disguise. Expensive and time-consuming hair-dyeing treatments are the new 'me-time' empowerment. The bonds of sisterhood are forged in pole-dancing classes. The guru-cum-drill-sergeant Gok Wan shouts 'Go, girlfriend!' as his makeovers squeeze into tummy-tuck pants. And a patriarchal culture is let off the hook via the media's delighted emphasis on all the little women-friendly exceptions. The overwhelmingly male World Cup fever that grips England every four years – when every pub is filled with roaring blokes and every white van sports a St George's flag – is offset by newspaper images of female fans sportingly daubed with tribal face paint. The archaic assumption that every girl's ultimate dream is a fairy-tale wedding is legitimated by Kate Middleton's well-publicised omission of the word 'obey' from her wedding vows. Ideology does its work through the thousands of 'size zero' models who are so ubiquitous as to be virtually invisible. But it does even more work through the 'plus size' models whose rare appearances are beamed around the world.

If any woman can make it, either pencil-thin or plump, then whether she does so or not becomes a matter of choice. Choice feminism is like socio-economic 'opportunity': failure becomes your fault. And choice has replaced structural change as the sign of liberation. If women spend their time roaming the aisles of Primark or working in a lap-dancing club, then that is their decision. It is not the result of unfavourable circumstances or cultural pressures. And just as the free-speech argument is often invoked to allow a platform for right-wing extremism, it's telling that the choice argument is most commonly invoked in order to justify conservative choices. Like that moment in *Sex and the City* when Charlotte is challenged by her careerist friend Miranda on why she's taking her husband's advice and leaving her prestigious art-gallery job. 'I choose my choice! I choose my choice!' she cries, before explaining that 'The women's movement is supposed to be about choice, and if I choose to quit my job, that is my choice.'

During the 1980s, feminist writers such as Catharine MacKinnon and Andrea Dworkin were conducting lively debates about false consciousness in relation to rape, domestic violence and pornography. Now the very idea of false consciousness is shocking. The anonymous author of the Happy Feminist blog admits that 'like a lot of Americans, I automatically recoil when I hear the term "false consciousness". It sounds authoritarian.' But since women have still not achieved parity with men, while at the same time they are supposed to be empowered and self-determining; since they still wear six-inch-heel Louboutins but do so now 'because they want to', the potential for false consciousness is surely greater than ever. The ideology of freedom obscures the fact that women's lives are constrained by a thousand tiny insinuations which nobody is allowed to identify any more. Particular paradigms of feminine behaviour are covertly but insistently promoted by the media and popular culture. If women are free, then why are we all supposed to conform to the same ideal; namely, to be baking Nigella's cupcakes while wearing a Cath Kidston apron in a Sophie Dahl-inspired industrial-chic kitchen?

Nowhere is the illusion of choice more prevalent and pernicious than in the 'question' of whether mothers should work. The 'Mommy Wars' – the American (and British) media's ongoing obsession – are presented as a two-sided debate. But a debate isn't a debate, and a choice isn't free, when one side is regularly sanctified and the other pilloried. Educated women across the developed world are applauded for leaving challenging careers in order to wipe their babies' bottoms full time. And if they stay working, they're not allowed to regard their jobs as important: the highlight of Sarah Jessica Parker's day, she assured a British TV chat show audience in 2009, is picking her kids up from school. Readers of the *Daily Mail* and the *New York Sun* are used to this kind of thing, but it's even worse coming from the *Observer* and the *New York Times*, because it lends the world of *Mad Men* a patina of liberal respectability. Contemporary culture has taken the boring old story of female oppression and repackaged it as a new form of feminist liberation.

'Respect'

The language of respect has become ubiquitous in relation to class, race and gender, because respect is a substitute for genuine equality. That's also the case with religion, but with hushed awe and solemn handshakes replacing the high-fives and overuse of the word 'sister'. Religious groups are now 'faith communities', a phrase that conjures up worthy consultation exercises and ecumenical coffee mornings. Bill Clinton announced in 1995 that 'the United States has great respect for Islam'; and in Barack Obama's keynote address to the Muslim world in Cairo in 2009, he said, 'There must be a sustained effort to listen to each other; to learn from each other; to respect one another.' These flattering gestures suggest that religious minorities have a special, privileged position; but this is simply a polite form of whitewash. The language of respect conveniently removes the material aspect of the grievance. And that is why offence, the modern flipside of respect, has no teeth. Because if you say you are offended, that is not the same as saying you are disadvantaged. The relationship between minority religions and the state is intensely fraught. But since religion thrives on symbolism, the semblance of inclusion is easy to confect: a London council can pay lip service to its Jewish community by erecting a giant menorah in Golders Green. But I really don't see why the whole country has to shut down for two weeks over Christmas. And from burkinis on Sydney's beaches to the eruv in London's Stamford Hill, religious distinctiveness is expressed through symbolic markers which serve only to mirror the empty gestures of the establishment. All sides want to deny the relationship between religion and power. Some religions dominate others, and religious affiliation correlates with social and economic imbalance. Despite the oft-cited wealth of the 9/11 bombers, Islam is the poorest religion in the world. It's these issues that need addressing, but they get lost in all the posturing and pandering. It is as meaningless for religious minorities to complain about being offended as it is for members of the establishment to claim that respect confers anything substantial. But in a culture that celebrates equality of opportunity, nobody wants to admit to being lower down the pecking order.

Respect is rather like tolerance, that other weasel word which Victorian patriots made into a national virtue at a time of anxiety about mass immigration. Now, in the wake of the supposed failure of multiculturalism, British political leaders are returning to this nineteenth-century idea as a rallying call in the midst of religious disintegration. Tony Blair, Gordon Brown and David Cameron have all claimed tolerance as a 'core' British value. In a speech in Downing Street in 2006, Blair made the following not very tolerant statement: 'Our tolerance is part of what makes Britain, Britain. So conform to it; or don't come here. We don't want the hate-mongers, whatever their race, religion or creed.' In the same year, Brown hailed the union flag as a 'British symbol of unity, tolerance and inclusion'. This is a benign form of coercion, but it's coercion nonetheless, because rather than being neutral, tolerance is freighted with patriotism and concealed power dynamics: the powerful tolerate the powerless. In Britain, as long as Christianity remains the official religion, non-Christians are 'included' via superficial cultural and institutional displays of diversity. Local authorities organise festivals, the school curriculum finds more time for religious studies, and public officials hold consultations with 'faith leaders'. But most of it is window dressing. Religions are not equal, now as in previous centuries. What is new is the lip service paid to respect and tolerance that obscures this enduring fact. Genuine religious equality will not be achieved in the UK until the Church of England renounces its dominance. It will not be achieved in the US until the creeping Christian influence on politics is reversed. And it will not be achieved in France until what appears on the face of it to be an impartial *laïcité* is revealed for what it really is: a tradition which finds Christianity far less objectionable than Islam.

Inequalities in wealth, class, race, gender and religion have become a taboo which not only the powerful but also the powerless would prefer to gloss over. I'm not saying there hasn't been progress. But we're becoming less and less willing to look unfairness and prejudice in the face. We've developed instead a back-to-front world view which appears to address discrimination but actually lends it an alibi. Role models, our faith in self-determination, the illusion of choice, and the language of respect exist in an alternative world of symbolic solutions. They create the impression that we are all on an equal footing, or at least have the ability to make ourselves so. They provide us with the next tool in our ideological kit: namely, that if things look fair, they are fair. This ideology is coming down from the top, to be sure: from traditional vested interests using modern PR. But it's rising upwards, too: from a working class that no longer believes in class as a determining factor; from ethnic minorities who buy into the rhetoric of role models; from women whose belief in their free choices is as illusory as the glass ceiling is transparent; and from Muslims who believe that gestures of respect will truly elevate their status. The good intentions of political correctness have inadvertently joined forces with traditional hierarchies, creating an inverted world where language stands in for reality, and box-ticking and iconography replace structural change. If we want a fairer society, we need to divert our gaze from politicians to policies, look at the role played by role models, and resist being fobbed off by figureheads. We need to sort the symbolic from the real.

FOUR

Electric Dreams

I like my holidays natural and outdoorsy, with no mobile phones, no internet, and no TV. Holidays like the ones my parents took me on when I was a child, in other words. Except with more sunshine and alcohol. But when I get home, I am gripped with technophile excitement. I cannot wait to switch on my phone and open my laptop. There's an addictive itch in my throat that resembles the urge for dark chocolate, for the first drag on a cigarette, for a nice glass of red. That itch is about checking my email. The excitement builds as the egg timer on my screen performs its unhurried rotations. So what do I get? A request from the gas company to provide a meter reading. Several notices from eBay about items I didn't win. Some emails from friends that are nice but need to be answered. And a couple of inconsequential messages to do with work. I even check my junk folder to see if the spam filter has let a tasty little fish slip through the net. But no, they're all about fake lottery wins or Viagra. I close the laptop and look around the living room. It's lovely to be home, but I feel a slight twinge of existential panic. I think: What now?

That let-down encapsulates for me the frustrations of new technology. The internet and mobile phones do not satisfy desires, they channel them. They send them swooshing down an infinitely long pipe, and there's no real payoff at the end. There's only the ability to check our emails – again. It's tempting to buy into the hype of new technology, because the experience of surfing the net feels so much like exploring unlimited possibilities. But these desires are unlimited because they remain ungratified. New technology didn't used to be about desire; it used to be about getting things done. It used to be about weaving looms and steam engines and factories that produced furniture. But although the promises of new technology are far more seductive, I think we are being led on. I think we are being encouraged to buy into devices and gadgets that promise much more than they deliver. In the process, we're concealing problems that exist in the real world and diverting our energies away from solving them. And the version of new technology that we're buying into is actually destroying aspects of that real world that provide genuine satisfaction. So what are these delusions of digital destiny? And are we compelled to believe in them?

Bullshit 2.0

In the summer of 1994, a group calling itself the Progress and Freedom Foundation released a manifesto entitled 'Cyberspace and the American Dream: A Magna Carta for the Knowledge Age'. 'Cyberspace is the latest American frontier,' it announced. 'The proposition that ownership of this frontier resides first with the people is central to achieving its true potential ... as it emerges, it shapes new codes of behavior that move each organism and institution – family, neighborhood, church group, company, government, nation.' Jump to November 2009, and the Italian edition of *Wired* magazine launches a campaign to have the internet nominated for the Nobel Peace Prize. 'Men and women from every corner of the globe are connecting to one another,' its writers declare, 'thanks to the biggest social interface ever known to humanity. Digital culture has laid the foundations for a new kind of society. And this society is advancing dialogue, debate and consensus through communication ... that's why the Internet is a tool for peace.'

These two proclamations sound pretty similar. But something happened between the first and the second: the bursting of the dot com bubble. In his book *Zombie Economics*, the Australian economist John Quiggin describes how the financial crisis of 2008–09 killed off many of the fallacies of free-market economics, for example that the

Efficient Market Hypothesis would always ensure the safety of speculative investments. But these dead ideas still live on in the minds of
politicians, economists and members of the public. Likewise, the
NASDAQ crash of 2001 seems not to have dented the enthusiasm of
cyber-utopians today. It's there in the countless books on the digital
revolution and interactivity. It's there in Twitter's founders hailing
their invention as 'a triumph of humanity'. It's there in freedom-of-
information campaigner Heather Brooke's claim that 'Technology is
breaking down traditional social barriers of status, class, power,
wealth and geography – replacing them with an ethos of collabora-
tion and transparency.' And in the writer and political adviser Charles
Leadbeater's belief in the internet's power to liberate us from 'the
hierarchy of top-down organisations', its 'huge potential to create new
stores of knowledge to the benefit of all, innovate more effectively,
strengthen democracy and give more people the opportunity to make
the most of their creativity'.

But there is a crucial difference between Web 1.0, as it's retrospec-
tively known, and Web 2.0 (I'm ignoring 3.0, because no one seems to
agree on what it means). There's now a real business model behind
the language of people power. If the rhetoric now has a more solid
foundation, though, it's also more deceptive. The idealism has become
a delusion. Back in the 1990s, as the first wave of techno-euphoria
broke over the ecstatic venture capitalists' heads, dot com pioneers
were young, edgy, and went to genuinely outrageous parties. In New
York, there was pseudo.com, an internet TV station founded in 1993
by the extraordinary performance artist Josh Harris, which made a
deranged stab at recreating Andy Warhol's Factory. Harris went on to
'curate' *Quiet: We Live in Public*, a post-Orwellian experiment where
a hundred artists lived in an underground bunker under total mutual
surveillance, with hedonistic results that make *Big Brother* look like
The Waltons. In LA, there was DEN.net, where a group of teenagers
were recruited to the Bacchanalian project of making properly
depraved online videos. The philosopher Sadie Plant founded the
Cybernetic Culture Research Unit at Warwick University in 1995, an
extraordinary semi-virtual institution whose 'members' covered the

office walls with intricate kabbalistic diagrams and sometimes spoke only in numbers. The Unit's remit was to explore the connections between animate and inanimate worlds, between human beings and digital machines. One year in, it organised an event called 'Virtual Futures 96: Datableed', featuring DJ sessions, science fiction talks and hardcore cybernetic theory; a year later Plant published her cyber-feminist manifesto, *Zeros + Ones: Digital Women + The New Technoculture*; a year after that they organised a conference on something called 'Virotechnics'. The CCRU was a kind of futuristic attempt to break down the barriers between humans and computers, philosophy and mathematics, and left and right politics. It was rather cultish and unlikely, not to mention incomprehensible, but like a lot of 1990s cyber-utopianism it was also radical, creative and visionary.

Today's internet gurus – Larry Page, Sergey Brin, Mark Zuckerberg and the late Steve Jobs – speak the language of liberation and wear faded jeans and zipped-up hoodies. But Web 2.0 is a reformed, cleaned-up version of cyber-utopia: yet another counter-example to the prevailing myth that behaviour gets more liberated with the passing of time. Web 2.0 is led by clean-cut, business-friendly, family-values-upholding men: men like Eric Schmidt, the former CEO of Google, who commented on the subject of internet privacy: 'If you have something you don't want people to know, maybe you shouldn't be doing it in the first place.' Facebook has the informal feel of a Harvard dorm not because it is either studenty or liberal, but because its aggressive corporatism is extending advertising tentacles into the most intimate corners of our private lives. Technology corporations pretend to be on our side, trumpeting the voice of the little guy. Silicon Valley executives brand themselves as hippy, beatnik philanthropists, wearing Crocs, brainstorming on beanbags in break-out time and drinking Fair Trade lattes. But this is not the humanisation of corporations. It's the corporatisation of humans. Cyber-utopian people-power rhetoric is now deployed by corporate elites.

'Windows 7 Was My Idea', according to a series of members of the public featuring in a 2009 Microsoft ad campaign; and Apple makes much of the 'ordinary people' who invent its apps (glossing over the

fact that 90 per cent of apps don't make their inventors any profits).
'The Internet is under new management: Yours', announced Yahoo's
2009 $100 million ad campaign, and Vodafone's brand identity now
carries the slogan 'Power to You'. 'It is not the big power', explained
Vittorio Colao, the global corporation's multi-millionaire chief executive. 'It is not the power of top-down. It is bottom-up power. It really
means that Vodafone puts the customer at the centre of what we do.'
But the real power is surely in figures like guru-magician Steve Jobs,
unveiling the latest closely-guarded secret creation to have emerged
from the laboratory of a cabal of highly educated, highly paid white
males. I wouldn't fancy my chances turning up at Google campus or
Microsoft village with a humble software suggestion. The idealistic
language of the digital future is infused with MBA business-speak. It
combines mystical credulity with in-crowd knowingness, optimism
with get-with-the-programme realism. It's misty-eyed but hard-
nosed; Paul McKenna crossed with Alan Sugar. It makes me long for
both valley girl irony and David Hume's critique of the confusion
between ought and is.

Along with corporate executives, it's also political elites that are
now talking the language of online liberation. The internet is central
to what US Secretary of State Hillary Clinton calls 'twenty-first-
century statecraft'. She's been using social networking to present a
softer, less overtly imperialist version of American power abroad. 'We
need to build new partnerships from the bottom up', Clinton said,
'and use every tool at our disposal. That is the heart of smart power.'
For 'smart power', therefore, read soft power, power that is disguised
as interactivity, as 'free conversation'. In 2008, James Glassman, US
Undersecretary of State for Public Diplomacy and Public Affairs, gave
a speech at the New America Foundation in which he launched
'Public Diplomacy 2.0'. 'We have arrived at the view that the best way
to achieve our goals in public diplomacy is through a new approach
to communicating, an approach that is made easier because of the
emergence of Web 2.0, or social networking technologies', he said. In
a beautifully slippery speech, he claimed that the internet is essentially
hostile to 'old ideologies' and 'extremism': 'This new virtual world is

democratic. It is an agora ... the new world is a marketplace of ideas, and it is no coincidence that Al Qaeda blows up marketplaces.' In a seamless move, freedom of ideas becomes the free market. As so often with cyber-utopianism, the apparently open-minded discourse of the internet – free-flowing information, the exchange of ideas – mirrors the vocabulary of capitalism. Glassman has been working with Jared Cohen, a former adviser to both Condoleezza Rice and Hillary Clinton and now head of Google's new geopolitical think tank, Google Ideas (Cohen has called Facebook 'one of the most organic tools for democracy promotion'). They've been getting groups of young 'anti-extremist' activists together with big technology corporations such as Google and AT&T. Such initiatives appear to be post-ideological, but they often incorporate an underlying ideology of pro-Western free-market economics. Clinton's condemnation of WikiLeaks' release of diplomatic cables in 2010 demonstrated that internet 'freedom' is OK as long as it's supporting established power.

In the biopic of Facebook's early days *The Social Network*, much is made of the fact that the old bastions of power and privilege, embodied in the wasp-jock Winklevoss twins, are finally breaking down. But just as the geek-chic films of Seth Rogen are extraordinarily patriarchal, this film downplays the power of its protagonists by portraying them as weedy nerds. I don't have any problem with geeks, being one myself, but this is not the school of geekery that wears corduroy and hides behind books. This is anti-intellectual geekery which sneers at girls and has sweaty dreams of taking over the world. And it's not just that the nerds now rule. It's that they rule through disavowal, through the invocation of the popular will. I find it ironic that the writer and consultant Clay Shirky disseminated his thoughts on social media in that most outmoded, elitist of forms – a book – yet he called it *Here Comes Everybody*. This is power disguised as deferral to the masses. We are all meant to be tapping into the wisdom of crowds and tuning in to the lingua franca of 'digital natives', the multi-tasking, zero-attention-span chattering of the young that is apparently the sound of the future. You adult dinosaurs, with your outdated principles and standards, get ready to be overrun by the infantile horde.

Such is the influence of the hollowed-out language of techno-revolution that the assortment of underdogs earmarked for certain world domination includes not only nerds and children, but also political dissidents in the developing world. In 1989, Ronald Reagan predicted that 'The Goliath of totalitarianism will be brought down by the David of the microchip.' In a speech in 2000, Bill Clinton said that China's attempts to control the internet were 'like trying to nail Jell-O to the wall'. And in 2009, Gordon Brown proclaimed that 'You cannot have Rwanda again because information would come out far more quickly about what is actually going on and the public opinion would grow to the point where action would need to be taken.' In June 2009, as Iranian protesters took to the streets, *Wired* editor-in-chief Chris Anderson posted a Q&A with Clay Shirky on the TED blog, about how 'cellphones, the web, Facebook and Twitter had changed the rules of the game, allowing ordinary citizens extraordinary new powers to impact real-world events'. Clay's excitement was palpable: 'It seems pretty clear that ... this is it. The big one.' And after Google's decision in March 2010 to pull out of China in protest at internet censorship, an editorial in the *New Republic* compared the corporation to the Soviet dissident activist Andrei Sakharov. Powerful people are selling virtual reality as people power. But the clue is in the word 'virtual'.

Reality bytes

Like Marx's camera obscura, the internet is a looking-glass world in which appearance is the opposite of reality. For a start, the notion that the internet drives democracy is optimistic, to say the least. As Evgeny Morozov points out in *The Net Delusion*, in post-modern mix-n-match China, Communist dictatorship rubs along very nicely with YouTube videos of teenage boys lip-synching along to the Backstreet Boys. If you can access Western consumer culture anyway via the internet, you are even less likely to bother pressing for political reform. It's what Morozov calls 'accommodating authoritarianism': the kind that holds up its hands and points out that it's not stopping its citizens doing what they want. As far as Google's 'heroic decision' to pull out of China is concerned, the company only held about 30 per cent of the Chinese market, so sacrificing its operations there was a small price to pay for appearing to stay true to its slogan: 'Don't Be Evil'. And while new technology played a role in the protests in Iran in 2009–10 and across the Arab world in 2011, it was frequently over-stated. Despite the Western euphoria surrounding Iran's 'Twitter revolution', only 0.027 per cent of Iranians are on Twitter, so it was never going to be a very effective coordination device. In fact, social media actually hindered Iranian protests in some ways: it provided a short cut for the authorities to track down dissenters, provided a plat-form for the government to mount a propaganda counter-offensive, and splintered the 'Green revolution' itself into competing groups. Social media facilitated the protests in Egypt, and helped the outside world to know what was going on – one baby was named 'Facebook' in honour of the site's role – but the web mainly functioned as an organising tool, not an engine of change. The online world of symbols and appearances is perfectly suited to those weird new pseudo-demo-cratic states like Russia (and also the increasingly hollow democracies of the US and the UK) that are free and fair in name but not nature. Communications revolutions and information revolutions come and go, leaving power structures intact.

And just as my long-suffering mother would confirm that tech-nologies like texting and emailing can be used for evasion as well as for connection, there's no reason why the internet can't be used for oppressive as well as progressive ends. Online activism is a great way to create the superficial impression of meaningful change without actually achieving it. Social networking sites like Facebook are hosts for what's become known as 'slacktivism'. With a few clicks and ticks, you can join a campaign group or sign a petition. Job done. Except nothing really comes of it in the real world, except that you've adver-tised your 'efforts' to your 'friends'. According to a study by the Pew Research Center, an American think tank, internet users aged eighteen to twenty-four were the least likely of all age groups to contact a public official or donate to a political party. They are too busy scratching their slacktivist itch. So what about WikiLeaks' infamous release of US diplomatic cables in 2010, an event that, according to Christian Caryl in the *New York Review of Books*, 'changes everything'? It's true that the leaked cables and the revealingly draconian response by Western elites did, for a moment, show power with its pants down. But the whole affair had very traditional coordinates. The cables were released under strict embargo to a handful of old-fashioned newspapers. WikiLeaks itself is not very 'wiki': it's a tightly-controlled hierarchical organisation headed by a charismatic leader, Julian Assange. And most significantly, the affair left us with the dangerous illusion of a new across-the-board transparency. If diplomats and politicians learned anything, it was to keep information more tightly under wraps. In 2011, after one of those old-fashioned newspapers, the *Guardian*, pioneered the exposure of corrupt relations between News Corporation, government and police, the *New York Times* reported breathlessly that 'in truth, a kind of British Spring is under way … social media has roamed wild and free across the story, punching a hole in the tiny clubhouse that had been running the country. Democracy, aided by sunlight, has broken out in Britain.' Never mind the fact that a series of interminable public inquiries looks set to kick the issue into the long grass, leaving the 'tiny clubhouse' to quietly regain control.

Outside politics, too, there's a lot of virtual Kool-Aid going around. Take Wikipedia, for example, the most prominent grassroots poster boy. Daniel Pink, the business guru and author of books like *Drive: The Surprising Truth About What Motivates Us*, praises Wikipedia's 'radical decentralisation and self-organisation', the way it represents 'open source in its purest form'. *Wired*'s Chris Anderson revels in the fact that 'each Wikipedia entry simply arrives, conjured from the vacuum by the miracle of the "Edit This Page" button'. But the Wikiworld is carefully policed by editors, who exercise scrupulous control over entries' validity, impartiality and quality of citation. If claims are not referenced to real-world sources, the Wikipolice turn up to threaten deletion. The other day I read an article accompanied by an exclamation mark icon. 'This article may contain original research,' an editor warned. I saw another article accompanied by an icon of a broom. 'This article is written like a personal reflection or essay and may require cleanup,' it scolded. 'Please help improve it by rewriting it in an encyclopaedic style.' It's no wonder spontaneous contributions are actually declining. Rather than showcasing the sparkling diversity of the crowd, Wikipedia displays all the stylistic hallmarks of control by pernickety committee. The good news is that – contrary to the stereotype – it's pretty accurate. But its prose is about as lively as my dishwasher instruction manual.

Real-world hierarchies prevail in cyberspace: they're just much harder to spot. When an internet academic called Mark Graham collated Wikipedia articles by country he found a huge geographical disparity: there are almost 100,000 devoted to the US, and less than ten about Tonga. Eighty-five per cent of Wikipedia's entries are written by men. The social media researcher Danah Boyd has shown how Myspace and Facebook are starkly divided by race and class, with migration to Facebook resembling urban 'white flight'. And while it's often claimed that the online world empowers individuals to choose exactly what suits them, what we ultimately end up with is not variety but mass uniformity. What looks like freedom leads millions of people to 'choose' to do the exact same thing at the exact same time: buy the latest iPhone, and watch 'Star Wars Kid' on YouTube. The internet has the aura of spontaneity, a breaking of the moulds of convention and genre. But what could be more conformist than the willingness to stick to a 140-character limit? If the categories and inequalities of the real world extend into cyberspace, our fixation with new technology also distracts precious attention from trying to make the real world fairer. Over the last few years I've heard endless talk of access to broadband, as if online consumption will solve all the problems of an impoverished and isolated pensioner living on the outskirts of Halifax. And online mechanisms for voting and complaint, and constant requests for comment and feedback, are PR for persistent disparities in political and cultural influence.

Socio-economic inequality requires political action. But what the new technology hype is doing is shifting the battleground to the cultural sphere of knowledge, media, arts and music. It is replacing the achievement of real, material equality with the levelling-down of journalism and cultural production. Chris Anderson seeks unlikely support from Karl Marx for his claim that the internet is revolutionising both work and creativity. In a discussion of what he calls 'Pro-Ams', people who pursue amateur activities to professional standards, Anderson writes that 'Marx was perhaps the original prophet of the Pro-Am economy ... it is when the tools of production are transparent that we are inspired to create.' He seems to be forgetting that small aspect of Marx's work concerning wages. And programs like Garage Band (for writing songs) and machinima (for making animated films) are not in any case 'transparent'. They are not like recording a song with your mates on old acoustic guitars. They contain pre-programmed formulas which users can only assemble. They are like those new cars which, as the academic-turned-motorcycle-mechanic Matthew Crawford notes in his book *The Case for Working with Your Hands*, you can't fix yourself because they are operated by computers. If you open the bonnet, what you see is not the mechanical innards of the car but a smooth surface, basically another bonnet. Any real connotations of work – creative or otherwise – attached to the word 'garage' have all but disappeared.

In 1936, the cultural critic Walter Benjamin published an influential essay entitled 'The Work of Art in the Age of Mechanical Production'. It described what happens to a work of art, such as a painting by Leonardo da Vinci, when it becomes an image which can be distributed: as an illustration in a book, for example, or a poster on a living-room wall. As a painting, it has an 'aura', a connection to the way in which it was produced by the painter. Visitors to an art gallery can see this aura in the texture of the paint on canvas, produced by Leonardo's very own brush. Prior to the nineteenth century, people didn't think great painters were geniuses, necessarily – they thought they were very good at painting. But now, in the modern age, despite the fact that we presume ourselves to be very democratic and egalitarian, we have a strong investment in the notion of artistic genius. So when a painting is reproduced as an image, the vacuum left by the original painting's aura is filled with another kind of aura, and one that is harder to spot: this mystical idea of the artist as a genius. As John Berger put it in 1972 in his seminal TV series and book, *Ways of Seeing*, 'Very few people are aware of what has happened because the means of reproduction are used nearly all the time to promote the illusion that nothing has changed except that the masses, thanks to reproductions, can now begin to appreciate art as the cultural minority once did.' In other words, beware the fanfare about the technological democratisation of cultural production and consumption, because it contains a potent and invisible form of elitism. What's missing from both the genius model and the instant internet fame model is time, money, and old-fashioned hard graft.

In the summer of 2010 I read about the launch of an online virtual 'studio' equipped with free music-making software. A spokesman praised its 'democratising' potential: 'Whether you are a fifteen-year-old kid or an established producer, this puts you on a level playing field … this is putting the ability to make music into the hands of people who couldn't afford it. It's giving them a voice and that has to be applauded.' How interesting that this spokesman's company, Graphite Media, promotes itself as providing 'a stamp of authority and quality in the music, brand and lifestyle world'. Authority, quality *and* a level playing field: that is having one's cake and eating it. Oh, and the software, 'Burn Studios', sponsored by Burn energy drink, made by Coca-Cola. This is absolutely archetypal: an attack on professional excellence dressed up as an attack on elitism, advertising a multinational corporation. Even the wide-eyed techno-prophet Alvin Toffler has observed that 'prosumers', those who 'produce as well as consume', provide the money economy with 'an enormous free lunch'. And frankly, I don't want a world where expertise is flattened. I'd like my utopia to be ruled by democracy and excellence, please, but not by the crowd. The most listened-to band on the social network music site Last FM is, after all, Coldplay. As Jaron Lanier in *You are Not a Gadget* and Andrew Keen in *The Cult of the Amateur* have eloquently warned us, we are heading for the collapse of entire cultural, intellectual and journalistic industries. It'll be a cultural revolution all right, but of the Chinese variety.

Now I know we're all trying to become less materialistic, but I find all this talk of virtuous decluttering misses the point. We are speeding towards a post-materialistic age, and that will be even worse. I like physical objects like books, magazines and records. I would rather have my family photos in an album than languishing unprinted in the 'cloud'. And the thing about physical objects like newspapers and books is that you can charge for them. Chris Anderson uses the pious language of anti-materialism to argue that creative production isn't all about making money, y'know, and culture isn't just about owning things. It's about creativity 'for the love of it', and the generosity of sharing. But, as Lanier notes, the end result will be no funding for the pursuit of truth or beauty, and plenty of funding for the makers of mobile phones and e-readers. These are objects too, of course, it's just that the companies that profit from them don't produce any content. It's journalists and artists who will in the future be expected to provide content for free. I find it all very maddening. How can we let this happen? Well, take a 2010 *Guardian* article entitled 'Twitter Power: How Social Networking is Revolutionising the Music Business', the kind of article I seem to be reading all the time. Dave Haynes, the founder of a social network site where artists can share music for free, invoked the familiar model of the old world of elitism and traditional power structures: 'In the past, there were just a few gatekeepers to music, and you had a powerful network of labels, A&R men, radio and TV executives and magazines who decided what you should be listening to.' The article went on to describe how those 'barriers' are coming tumbling down, thanks to the 'magic' of the internet and of Twitter. We are letting this happen because we are swallowing the revolutionary, egalitarian delusion. I keep hearing that the internet breaks down walls and hierarchies and creates networks and connections. But that's because it's a corrosive acid, dissolving the boundaries that give us meaning: of time and place, importance and context.

Amongst the many radical transformations that took place on 11 September 2001 was an apparent revolution in journalistic reportage.

'Something profound was happening,' writes Dan Gillmor in *We the Media: Grassroots Journalism by the People, for the People.* 'News was being produced by regular people who had something to say and show, and not solely by the "official" news organizations that had traditionally decided how the first draft of history would look.' For Jeff Chester, author of *Digital Destiny: New Media and the Future of Democracy*, however, the reality was rather different. The much-hailed paradigm shifts of 9/11 – which included the foregrounding of 'user generated content' – provided an excellent cover for a massive colonisation of cyberspace. Two days after the attacks, the US Federal Communications Commission announced that it would review key policies which new media companies had been lobbying against for years, because they restricted their voracious appetites for monopolistic expansion. While new media companies were trumpeting their public-interest, bottom-up coverage of the terrorist attacks, they were at the same time pursuing private-interest, top-down commercial goals. And the public had little sense of what was going on. Because although a slogan like 'Power to You' can appeal to anyone, the language of the virtual corporate takeover is detailed and specialised.

Concepts like 'the cross-ownership rule' and 'network neutrality' are not very sexy. So coverage of these issues is invariably confined to techy websites and industry media, which is a problem, because they are utterly vital to us all. In 2010, astroturf lobby groups including Americans for Prosperity and the National Taxpayers Union clubbed together to fund a $1.4 million TV advertising campaign claiming that 'Washington wants to spend billions to take over the internet.' The campaign was a response to the FCC trying to prevent telecoms companies from slowing down the internet connections of people who accessed their competitors' websites. In an extraordinary inversion of reality, a spokesman for the lobby groups complained about the prospect of state regulation by telling BBC News, 'This is a naked power grab.' The level playing fields of the digital future look set to be landscaped by two or three telecoms giants. The principle of a one-speed internet for all will be abolished. Our emails, photos, recordings and videos will increasingly reside not on our personal computers, but in the commercially owned 'cloud'. The internet will indeed be interactive and tailored to each individual user, but only so that personalised advertising can reach its target audience.

Because of the decline in the consumption of traditional media, advertisers now portray themselves as ailing underdogs. But they are creating a new system of interactive e-commerce that makes *Minority Report* look like *Blue Peter*. This online advertising conquest passes under the radar because it's expressed in liberal, anti-corporate terms. Steve Rubel, 'Director of Insights' for Edelman Digital, part of the world's largest PR firm, is something of a guru in a field which he calls 'micro persuasion'. 'The war is over,' he writes on his blog about 'how emerging technologies are revolutionizing marketing communications'. 'The people have defeated the corporation.' He lists '10 Commandments for the Era of Participatory Public Relations', which include 'Thou shall listen,' 'Thou shall tell the truth,' and 'Thou shall be open and engaging.' 'Involve your customers in the PR process,' he elaborates. 'Invite them to help you develop winning ideas and become your spokespeople.' In other words, encourage them to do your advertising voluntarily, and for free: post flattering comments on messageboards and circulate your apparently home-made YouTube videos. Even my local hippy health-food shop promises a free coffee to any customer who 'likes' the store on Facebook. Marketing magazines and corporate marketing reports are chock full of toxic guff about how getting people to do your marketing for you is really a new form of 'people power'. The business of selling stuff online not only inverts the real power dynamic, it is packaged in the fluffy language of interpersonal relationships. The most famous formula of online business is 'CTPM': Content > Traffic > Presell > Monetise. This approach is all about 'treating visitors [to websites] like human beings instead of like sales targets'. The goal is 'monetisation', but it's dressed up as something nicer. In the age of Web 2.0, people are not valued as individuals. They are valued en masse as foot-soldiers for corporate advertising, and their habits and interests are valued in aggregate as market-research data. In the age of 'open culture' and 'the creative commons', identity is being eroded and personhood privatised.

A 2005 article in *Business Week* headlined 'The Power of Us' references emergent (organic, self-organising) behaviour and swarm theory to describe this brave new egalitarian world: 'New research indicates that cooperation, often organized from the bottom up, plays a much greater role than we thought in everything from natural phenomena like ant colonies to human institutions such as markets and cities' (there's that old bottom-up chestnut again). The article quotes the late management guru C.K. Prahalad as saying, 'We are seeing the emergence of an economy of the people, by the people, for the people.' It also quotes Howard Rheingold, whose 2002 book *Smart Mobs: The Next Social Revolution* is typical in the way it elides the motivations of new, tech-savvy businesses with those of the masses. Other culprits are Cass Sunstein's *Infotopia: How Many Minds Produce Knowledge*, and James Surowiecki's much-quoted *The Wisdom of Crowds: Why the Many are Smarter than the Few and how Collective Wisdom Shapes Business, Economies, Societies and Nations*. At some point in the future, when we realise the full implications of the virtual take-over, the rhetoric is going to come unstuck. Because we'll realise who's got the power now. And when it comes down to it, people don't want to be aggregated. They don't want to be a speck in a swarm. They want to be respected individuals. They want to be paid for their work. They want their blog to get them on TV, or be published as a book. Real people want real power. We might find internet popularity novel and exciting, but the validation of success is still provided by the old media that we are so enthusiastically destroying.

If new technology promises to 'solve life's little problems, one app at a time', why is it that, in a single week, I log on to pay London's congestion charge only to find the website is closed for maintenance. I upload some photos to Bonusprint and the system crashes. I try to find out which Windows 7 laptop to buy, but Microsoft has apparently banned shops from releasing any information. I go to Channel 4 On Demand to watch a TV show, only to find that episode unavailable. Yahoo tells me that 'The Internet is under new management: Yours.' But I do not feel like the internet's new manager. I feel like the internet's sucker. And I feel that the internet, itself, sucks. Of course it would be ridiculous to argue that the web is entirely useless or evil. But there is a close affinity between the web itself, its airy, insubstantial nature, its intangible ungroundedness, and the rhetorical claims that are made for its potential. Cyber-utopianism is rhetoric taking over the world.

Because if those claims are overblown in relation to political liberation, social equality and the future of culture, that's also the case with practical problem-solving. No matter how many times we use phrases like 'paperless office', new technology won't be a revolution until it proves capable of sorting out basic, unglamorous problems. Like getting trains to run on time, or making it easier to deal with a call centre. The washing machine was arguably more revolutionary than the internet. And it will never be possible to Google one's car keys. Some websites are hugely useful, but they rely on human micromanagement. My favourite site is that of the consumer watchdog Which?, which has scrupulously-maintained expert reviews of everything from mortgages to electric toothbrushes. 'The wisdom of crowds' is not a phrase that springs to mind when I am using Tripadvisor or Toptable, the 'user review' sites for hotels and restaurants. Neil Postman, the late author of *Technopoly: The Surrender of Culture to Technology*, argues that after successive dethronements from our privileged position at the centre of the universe, humans have turned to technology for evidence of progress and control. But he argues that there's been a shift from technocracy, the worship of technology as a tool to improve our lives, to technopoly, the worship of technology in and of itself. That sounds about right to me. The app, for example, seems to be a kind of symbolic after-image of technology being actually useful. Technology is currently in the business of creating new needs, without meeting existing ones. I'm not aware of an app for working out why your microwave has stopped working, applying for childcare vouchers, or finding out how much interest your bank is currently paying you (although you don't need an app for that. The answer is zero).

Cyber-utopian rhetoric creates the impression that the material stuff of life, the grease and sweat and rubbish and excrement, will in future be replaced by nice clean information. In their 'Magna Carta for the Knowledge Age' (1994), techno-futurologists Esther Dyson, George Gilder, George Keyworth and Alvin Toffler predicted that 'Putting advanced computing power in the hands of entire populations will alleviate pressure on highways, reduce air pollution, allow people to live further away from crowded or dangerous urban areas, and expand family time.' In an age of week-long traffic jams, rising CO_2 emissions, urbanisation and long-hours work culture, this vision does not seem to be coming to pass. In fact, new technology sometimes makes everyday life harder, because problems aren't lo-tech enough for us to be able to solve any more. And you cannot build a house out of information, burn information as fuel or cook it up into a nice tasty stew. In any case, all this emphasis on information is a bit rich at a time when the activities of those who actually produce information, namely journalists, writers and academics, are under assault from Web 2.0. We are enthralled by devices, platforms and software packages. Literally the packaging, rather than what's inside. It is more than ironic that in an age when information is everything, content is getting screwed.

Esc

The term 'Luddite' did not start off as an insult. In 1811, groups of textile workers began meeting at night on the moors around industrial towns in the north of England, planning their attacks on factories which were introducing mechanical looms. Perhaps taking their name from a fictional character, Ned Ludd, who was thought to have heroically destroyed two large looms in a Leicestershire village in 1779, the Luddites enjoyed high-profile support from, among others, the poet Lord Byron. The historian E.P. Thompson, author of *The Making of the English Working Class*, has argued that the Luddites were not opposed to innovation as such, but were protecting their livelihoods against the imposition of price cuts for their products. In other words, they were against capitalism rather than new technology. To prove it, they would selectively attack the looms of factory owners who were trying to cut prices, leaving the other ones intact. In their own time, the Luddites were opposed by many – there were frequent clashes with the British army – but they were not dismissed out of hand as quaint and backward-looking. But if you confess to being a Luddite today, you can only do so in a tone of mirthful self-mockery. It sounds very off-key now to dispute that the particular form of digital innovation we are adopting is a necessary and unstoppable force.

I'm not really a Luddite, even in the modern sense of the word. I use a lot of new technology. But we seem to have forgotten that technology is a set of tools that we have invented ourselves, and that we can use to improve our world in a manner of our choosing. Instead, new technology is talked about as if it were something we have no control over. Like the inexorable tide of the free market, it's simply pulling us along in its wake. There's a lot of techno-talk of natural evolution, as well as revolution (see for example technology reporter Steve Lohr's essays in the *New York Times*). That's handy: if it's evolution not choice that's driving this forward, then we don't have to examine our motivations. We can just gaze in wonder at these strange young creatures with their phones that play songs, and acknowledge our destiny. But this is regression, not evolution. Gadgets bring out our inner child, and not always in a good way: smartphones turn grown adults into impatient, distracted children. And just as evolutionary psychologists seem to want to drag everything back to hunter-gatherer days, when men got on with being men, and women got on with making the dinner, Web 2.0 evangelism risks erasing centuries of human civilisation and returning us to the dark ages, whereupon we will begin to reinvent our systems of talent-spotting, filtering and evaluation all over again.

'Everyone, from journalists to the people we cover, to our sources and the former audience, must change their ways,' Chris Anderson writes on the subject of new media in *The Long Tail*. Stewart Brand, co-founder of the Global Business Network, told readers of Anderson's *Wired* magazine: 'Technology is rapidly accelerating and you have to keep up.' Oh, right. Is that why the sound quality on MP3 players is worse than vinyl? And why we are reduced to watching films on lo-res

YouTube? Is it why the HD-DVD/Blu-ray format war has replicated the equally redundant choice, in the 1970s, between Betamax and VHS? And why Britain has adopted a different kind of radio transmission to continental Europe, so there won't be compatibility? Those last two are market and government issues, you might argue. But that is precisely the point. We drive technology, not the other way round. There are ethics committees carefully considering the implications of stem-cell research and other biomedical innovations, but not for digital developments. Where those are concerned, we wash our hands of any motivation. Technology is not about agendas, we tell ourselves; technological change is driven by scientific progress and consumer demand. That is a form of determinism which is supremely ideological: a delusion of pure, transparent function. There is no time to pause, reflect or ask for more influence in shaping our future. 'The world is changing fast,' we are constantly told, so we might as well give up trying to change the world. Take the launch of the Apple iPad, for example. This gadget is the result neither of technological revolution nor consumer demand. It is the result of a company, Apple, wanting to sell us, the consumer, an expensive piece of kit. According to one journalist, Steve Jobs has 'anticipated technological desires you didn't even know you had'. Actually, those desires did not exist until Steve Jobs claimed to have satisfied them. Meanwhile, our very real desire for books and newspapers is under threat. Is this really as inevitable as it's claimed to be?

Despite the apparent idealism of cyber-utopianism, it claims to be neutral and unmotivated: simply a force of nature. Covert ideology doesn't make a case for something; it doesn't set out its stall. It claims instead that it's simply meant to be. And here we have the next costume in ideology's dressing-up box: to claim that we don't have a choice. That's why I always smell a rat when some Web 2.0 advocate says, on the one hand, this is all great, and on the other hand, it's happening whether you like it or not. If new technology is so great, why is it being sold so hard? And why make a case for something that's going to happen anyway? Using the rhetoric of freedom and choice, and invoking the will of the people, corporate nerds are fashioning the kind of world that they themselves would like to live in. A world in which tech executives are free to make multi-billion-dollar fortunes, and intellectual and artistic standard-bearers become proletarians. A world in which people don't need to talk to each other face to face or even hear the sound of each other's voices; they can just sit in darkened rooms all day playing hyper-real computer games. A world in which the 'elitist' clutter of books, magazines and journals can finally be replaced by a sterile metal-and-plastic box.

It is the result of topsy-turvy thinking to accept this particular vision of the future as something that everyone wants. There is no intrinsic reason why the nerds should be leading the way: it's just that they're persuading the rest of us that this is our destiny. A clear illustration of this is the deliberate effort that's currently going into marketing computer games at an ever-broadening demographic. Ads for the elegantly titled 'Rooms: The Main Building' by Nintendo are aimed at middle-aged middle-class women, providing the cosy impression that this is more Agatha Christie than Arnold Schwarzenegger. 'Brain teasers' such as 'Professor Layton and the Curious Village' target 'senior surfers' by convincing them they need to make every electronic effort to keep their faculties sharp. Wii provides 'fun' for all the family. Even the aesthetic, avant-garde games praised by intellectual gaming fans serve an ideological function by legitimising the notion that gaming, an aggressively expansionist industry, is indeed for everyone. Instead of using technology as a means to an end, as a vehicle for whatever it is we democratically decide to do, we've started to believe that we must take our orders from technology itself. But it's not technology that's issuing the orders: it's a particular group of cyber-enthusiasts who are pushing an undisclosed agenda. Their anti-intellectual commercialism is masquerading as popular liberation.

And the cyber-gurus are not only deluding us, they're deluding themselves as well. Techno-utopianism is really a response to the fact that technology is not actually delivering universal improvements. Disease and famine are still widespread. Our most sophisticated ambitions are stymied by floods, droughts and hurricanes. Trains break down. Rates of depression are high. Medicines are not miracles. The world is frustratingly imperfect. But instead of looking for modest, realistic improvements, techno-oracles in Silicon Valley have developed the idea – following futurologists like Alvin Toffler – that a magic combination of cloud and crowd will eventually supersede the human mind; that at some point in the not-too-distant future we will be able to upload our brains onto the internet and achieve a kind of cyber-immortality. They believe, in other words, in a ridiculous religion. We don't have to believe in it too.

FIVE

Smokescreens

Time for a confession: I love reality TV. *Come Dine With Me, Country House Rescue, Phil Down Under*; I lap them up at the end of a working day, avoiding history documentaries with a shudder. I thought I'd weaned myself off *Come Dine With Me* when I watched five episodes in a row while in the early stages of labour, and the subsequent birth trauma meant I couldn't watch it again for a few weeks. But I was soon back on the sofa warming to Steve from Reading and his take on the traditional trifle. My husband and I tried switching to art-house films by Bergman and Tarkovsky, to make edifying use of our evenings in, but we found ourselves dozing off within minutes. There is something utterly reassuring and relaxing about these reality shows, but it's got nothing to do with reality. They are variations on the same theme, week in, week out. The rhythms of their near-identical scripts and plotlines greet you like an old friend.

Despite all the new-media hype, reports of TV's demise are somewhat overstated. In the UK and America, viewing is at an all-time high. New media is on the rise, but it's accompanying TV rather than replacing it – at least for now. We surf the internet with the TV on in the background, and we watch TV dramas and films online. According to a process known as 'convergence', TV, films, the internet and computer games are all coming together to form one big on-screen empire. The upshot is that our lives are increasingly lived through screens: whether it's the huge flat-screen TVs mounted on our living-room walls; the inescapable advertising screens on Tube platforms, on buses and in the backs of cabs; or the addictive, jewel-like screens on our phones, tablets and e-readers. And that means the texture of our lives is being tampered with more and more: it's becoming second-hand, constructed, abstracted from the immediacy of experience. In 1967, the Marxist writer and film-maker Guy Debord published his book *The Society of Spectacle*, in which he described how authentic social life has been replaced with images. 'All that was once directly lived has become mere representation,' he wrote. Modern social life can be understood as 'the decline of being into having, and having into merely appearing'. Debord's inspiration Friedrich Engels defined ideology as 'the deduction of reality not from itself but from a concept', and those ubiquitous siren screens are that concept. The version of the world that we see on our screens is nipped and tucked, tweaked and touched up by vested interests which are cultural, political and commercial. It's a Wizard of Oz world in which ideology is the man behind the curtain. Except that, of course, there is no man behind the curtain. He is inside all of us. We are complicit in absorbing the media's mendacious messages, and getting back to reality calls for critique.

It's not that life in the olden days was totally unfiltered and unmediated, and straightforwardly real. We've had books and newspapers and politicians for a very long time. But reality is currently falling victim to an unprecedented and sustained attack. In an influential article in the *New York Times*, published just before the 2004 presidential election, the veteran reporter Ron Suskind recounted an extraordinary encounter with a senior adviser to George W. Bush, widely thought to be Karl Rove. The adviser was telling him how much he disliked an article Suskind had written for *Esquire* magazine about the enormous influence exerted on the president by his former communications director, Karen Hughes. 'The aide said that guys like me were "in what we call the reality-based community",' Suskind wrote, 'which he defined as people who "believe that solutions emerge from your judicious study of discernible reality". I nodded and murmured something about enlightenment principles and empiricism. He cut me off. "That's not the way the world really works anymore," he continued. "We're an empire now, and when we act, we create our own reality."' This is what we're up against now: not just spin, not just Machiavellian realpolitik, but the creation of powerful new fictional realities. And the problem is even worse post-Bush, I'd argue, because at least Dubya's regime was widely regarded as playing fast and loose with the facts. Now we have the apparent authenticity of Barack 'Honest Tea' Obama.

The reality effect

It's ironic, therefore, but not that surprising, that as a culture we are obsessed with verisimilitude. Our saturation with film and media images has produced a surreal culture which has dispensed with ordinary reality but finds itself drawn to hyper-reality. Since the nineties, films have fixated on the boundary between fact and fiction, producing a heightened sense of the real: from *The Blair Witch Project* to *The Ring*, from *Catfish* to Joaquin Phoenix's *I'm Still Here*. The hi-tech yet juvenile bells and whistles of HD, CGI and 3D are styling TV and cinema's future. I was struck by this phenomenon while watching *The Matrix* in 1999, a film that is self-consciously – if somewhat incoherently – preoccupied with the theme of reality. Two scenes particularly grabbed me: one, a helicopter crashing into a glass building at full tilt, with concentric waves of yawning energy rippling out through the windows before they explode; the other, an ultra-close-up shot of bullet shells tinkling on a stone floor. These scenes evoke the look, the sound, almost the feel of the real. As David Boyle's book *Authenticity: Brands, Fakes, Spin and the Lust for Real Life* argues, the rise of fakery and spin has spawned a thirst for the real. But what we often get is not the real real; it's a *sense* of reality. During the spin-tastic 2010 general election, ads for Sky TV News's coverage promised 'Britain's first high-definition election-night programme'. Slogan: 'Nothing gets you closer'. And then there was that widely-circulated 2011 shot of Obama and his team watching real-time footage of Navy Seals commandos killing Osama bin Laden. Except that later it turned out that there wasn't any footage of the raid at all, and bin Laden's death was shrouded in confusion and conflicting reports. There it was again:

that craving for the real producing not reality itself but the reality effect: the impression that reality is not being spun.

And then there's the shift from 'virtual reality' to 'augmented reality'. Augmented reality seems even more immediate than virtual reality, because it modifies the way we see the actual world rather than taking us off into a parallel universe. It's there in football games on TV – the visuals analysing positions and shots. And it's there on an app called 'Acrossair', where you hold up your phone and a real view of the street in front of you appears, with icons superimposed onto it giving you info about nearby Tube stations and restaurants. A few weeks after I bought the flat in which I currently live, I found myself looking up its particulars on the estate agent's website. Clicking on the enticing pictures, I almost wanted the flat that I saw online more than the real one I now inhabited. How messed up is that? But it shows the value that is conferred by seeing something on a screen. The internet is supposed to be an unmediated realm of authentic realness, but that is an illusion: the internet is all about representation. Our endless desire to film things on our phones and post them online is a sign of how much we have made reality into a fetish: only by holding events at arm's length or framing them in technological inverted commas can they take on the sense of really existing. The world, it seems, is not enough.

But then again, nor is technology either. In Japan, it is against the law to produce a camera that does not make the clicking sound of an old-fashioned shutter when it takes a picture. Admittedly, this is apparently because some Japanese men were taking advantage of the silent operation of the first digital cameras to take pictures up women's skirts on the subway. But that retro click symbolises an irony of digital technology: like e-reading devices that try to evoke the look of old-fashioned paper in natural daylight, there's an odd reinventing-the-wheel quality to the technological revolution. Just think of all the gadgets that contain a visual echo of their manual ancestor; from the typewriter in the computer to the wireless in the digital radio. It's a bit like how, in about fifty years' time, there will be journalism academies set up to train bloggers in the basic skills of reporting. We shuttle between escapism and fake authenticity, but reality has gone.

The theorist Roland Barthes noticed a similar thing going on in nineteenth-century novels. In a 1968 essay entitled 'The Reality Effect', he described how novels produce the feel of the real through the use of the rhetorical figure *ekphrasis*, the creation of images in words. The reality effect is there in little incidental details that don't add anything to character or plot, but create an atmosphere of visceral immediacy. Barthes picks out a barometer on a wall in a story by Gustave Flaubert, and a knock on a 'little door' in Jules Michelet's *Histoire de France*, and writes that 'Flaubert's barometer, Michelet's little door finally say nothing but this: we are the real.' Similarly, *Star Wars* director George Lucas has talked about his attempts to evoke what he calls 'the immaculate reality'; using elaborate filigree ornaments to make the filmic illusion cohere. Rather than manufacturing artificial or electronic sound effects, *Star Wars*'s sound designer Ben Burtt used noises from an old 35mm projector to produce the hum of the light sabre, recordings of walruses for Chewbacca's bark, and water pipes and whistles for R2-D2. In the reality effect, fiction and reality are not opposed: they become the same thing.

When it was announced in 2009 that the epic reality franchise *Big Brother* was being dropped by Channel 4, pundits predicted the end of reality TV. After all, it seemed that with shows like *Who's Your Daddy?* in the US (where adults who were adopted as children try to identify their biological father in a room of twenty-five men) and Australian film-maker Justin Sisley's televised virgin auction, there was not much left in the bottom of the barrel to scrape. But the genre is weirdly resilient, and our appetite for it remains undiminished. This isn't because we can't get enough of reality: after all, reality is where we live. It's because the reality effect uses the trappings of authenticity to make fiction seem more real than the real world itself. We don't really want reality; we want escapism. But we want our escapism to be credible. Home-buying or renovation shows are daydreams with the reality effect of domestic banality: they may seem down-to-earth because they concern themselves with wall insulation or the dilemmas of choosing the right shower unit, but they are as fairy-tale as Jane Austen. As with her wedding-day endings, we leave the happy couple at the point at which they acquire their new property. I find it hilarious when there's a coda tacked on the end in which it's casually revealed that the couple never bought any of the houses on offer after all. But this coda always seems oddly irrelevant, even though it's more important than the entire preceding programme, because it's the search for the fantasy that counts.

In an apparent paradox, alongside the new emphasis on techno-wizardry and gritty realism, an old-fashioned cult of storytelling has come to dominate what we see on our big and small screens. Documentaries, once concerned with information and analysis, are now about telling 'compelling' stories. Robert Drew, the award-winning film-maker known as the father of *cinéma vérité*, or 'film truth', puts it thus: 'Why are documentaries so dull? What would it take for them to become gripping and exciting? Looking for answers, several … mentors steered me towards an exploration of basic story-telling … viewers become invested in the characters, and they watch as things happen and characters react and develop. As the power of the drama builds, viewers respond emotionally as well as intellectu-ally.' Robert Drew is a great film-maker. But the case he makes here sums up a regressive trend which dominates today's journalism, TV and film production. Screenwriting and documentary gurus proselyt-ise the Aristotelian narrative 'arc': 1. Get protagonist. 2. Give protago-nist obstacle. 3. Make protagonist surmount obstacle. It is all about drama, all about heart over head. But Robert, dull is so underrated. At least with dull you learn something, or you're given enough context to see that a particular agenda is partial. And the dominance of story-telling – especially the emphasis on 'personal stories' – doesn't bring with it an awareness that these shows are a fiction; it brings a sense of verity.

It is ironic that the pioneer of *cinéma vérité* should stress the virtue of telling stories. But the 'reality' of most TV shows is a fiction. From *Airport* to *The Family*, footage is stitched together so that viewers are taken on a 'journey'. The 'characters' are encouraged or edited to interact in dramatic ways. What started as fly-on-the-wall has turned into carefully staged formats and genres. If you compared the script of relocation shows side by side, you'd see a hundred slightly different versions of the same story: a couple with kids on the way swapping wine bars for wellies. What's interesting to me is the status of that fact in the producers' and consumers' consciousness. It exists as a kind of open secret: so obvious as to be almost banal, and yet somehow still taboo. In a 2004 column for the *Los Angeles Times*, the comic writer and journalist Joel Stein wrote that 'Through sources I cannot reveal but would definitely not go to jail to protect, I got hold of a nineteen-page, single-spaced outline of an upcoming episode of *Queer Eye for the Straight Guy*. Every moment is planned in advance, including a few specific lines for the straight guy to deliver, which [cable TV station] Bravo says is not unusual for any reality show. It's something that people in Hollywood know and think is no big deal.' There's the ambiguity: Stein gets his info from 'sources [he] cannot reveal', but what they 'reveal' appears to be industry common knowledge. Much as I love the comforting repetitions of shows like *Come Dine With Me*, they make me long for Michael Apted's *Up* series, which interviews the same real people at seven-year intervals throughout their lives. One of the many things I admire about *Up* is the way the interviewees are asked to reflect on what it's like being part of the series. You can't get rid of artifice completely, but at least you can face it head on.

That is also what studio-based shows such as *The Big Breakfast*, *Noel's House Party* and *TFI Friday* used to do when they put the cameramen in shot or featured production staff as characters. Such self-reflexive games now seem to belong to a different era, and the process of making the programme has become as invisible as it is in *The Truman Show*. TV has for the most part become pathologically averse to actual reality. Participants, bystanders and audiences of reality shows have all learned to discreetly ignore the visible apparatus of production: those microphone packs tucked down the back of the trousers. And they've learned to ignore the massive effect of being on TV on apparently 'real' experiments: Gordon Ramsay's efforts to turn around a failing restaurant on *Ramsay's Kitchen Nightmares*, or Hugh

Fearnley-Whittingstall's forays into market-stall entrepreneurship. It promotes the illusion that anyone can do it, when actually national TV publicity kinda helps. You can only just see the unwitting cracks on later series of shows like *The Secret Millionaire*, when the eponymous hero reveals his or her true identity to the manager of a canteen for the homeless or whatever, who then dutifully makes the effort to look surprised, despite the fact that they have been followed around for days by a camera crew. Whether it's through the lo-fi shaky camera, the authenticity of 'mumblecore' or the trappings of reportage on the one hand, or through ultra-hi-res HD, 3D and spectacular special effects on the other, our media touts its realness and denies its status as an artificial construction. There is endless lip service paid to the audience, but a terror of the real viewers sitting in their living rooms. Contrast this with the genuinely outrageous moments on *Noel's House Party* when secret cameras hidden in viewers' TV sets would suddenly reveal them, sprawled indecorously on the sofa, to the nation. That stunt would look weirdly retro now. The buzzword of the TV, film, computer game and 'enhanced e-book' industry is 'immersiveness'. Audiences are to be submerged in what they are watching, to feel as if they're part of the action. We are encouraged to celebrate Britain's architecture by feeling Jonathan Dimbleby's awe as he abseils down St Paul's Cathedral. Immersiveness is supposedly all about participation and engagement: it's part of the blurring between the media, the internet and 'gaming'. I do love ghost trains, Disneyland and art installations that you can climb around in. But I also think immersiveness is a con. It produces an illusion of non-contrivance, it reduces critical distance, it underestimates viewers' rationality, and it helps screens take over our lives.

What do Shakespearean soliloquies have in common with Bugs Bunny cartoons? Answer: they both break the fourth wall, that imaginary barrier that separates the actors on stage or on TV from the audience. The sweet prince turns to the audience to ask, 'To be or not to be?'; similarly, after being pushed to the brink by Elmer Fudd, Bugs looks directly at the screen and pronounces the catchphrase, 'Of course you realise this means *war*' – itself borrowed from the Marx

Brothers' 1933 film *Duck Soup*. The fourth wall originally referred to the invisible 'wall' at the front of the stage in a traditional proscenium theatre. It was Denis Diderot, the philosopher and one of the authors of the *Encyclopédie*, who coined the phrase in 1758, although he personally was in favour of keeping it intact. 'When you write or act,' he wrote, 'think no more of the audience than if it had never existed. Imagine a huge wall across the front of the stage, separating you from the audience, and behave exactly as if the curtain had never risen.' From Michael Caine as Alfie to Eugene O'Neill's play *Strange Interlude* to the 1980s sitcom *It's Garry Shandling's Show*, actors used to break the fourth wall for comedy value, or to reflect on the constructed status of the show in which they were appearing. But there isn't much of an opportunity for breaking the fourth wall in an IMAX cinema. And my impression is that such self-reflexive tactics are considered gauche and outmoded in contemporary theatre. If audiences are involved, it's usually in a worthy attempt at 'participation'. TV producers and audiences alike collude in a coy disavowal of the fourth wall's existence. In doing so, both sides tacitly agree to a very traditional suspension of disbelief. Underlying the outrage about 'fakery' that rocked British broadcasting in 2007 – when footage of the Queen was shown out of sequence suggesting she had stormed out of a photoshoot, production staff posed as phone-in competition winners, and even *Blue Peter* rigged a viewers' vote to name its cat – was not only the fact that 'real' events on TV were revealed as fiction, that audiences had been conned. It was also that those revelations disrupted the audience's ability to believe in those fictions. The problem was not one of too little reality, but of too much. Today's media creates an illusion of immediacy and transparency that disguises the extent to which it is telling stories. And that's a problem, as I'm about to argue, because those stories have dubious morals. If breaking the fourth wall used to disrupt the illusion that those stories were true, the reality effect and immersiveness work to reinforce that illusion. Contemporary TV might pretend to be super-modern, hyper-real, and all about the audience, but it's basically with Diderot.

Malice in wonderland

To Roland Barthes, the reality effect in literature may have been about illusions, but it performed a real purpose. It produced the impression that there was no case being made, no spin being put on things. That facts is facts. Like the back-to-basics 'transparency' of contemporary politics and capitalism, the reality effect consolidates delusions: it enables us to believe that our view of the world is not increasingly mediated; that our imaginations are not being moulded according to the agendas of Rupert Murdoch or Simon Cowell. The reality effect illustrates the next in our roster of ideological gambits: to distort reality with realism. The problem with these techniques is that they allow TV and films to take a particular line, to shape the debate, while creating the impression that they are simply reflecting the world as it is; that they are value-free. The new emphasis on unmediated realism, on democratic participation and engagement, on telling compelling, authentic stories seems to be empowering, but it's not. What's empowering is for what we watch on our screens to present an argument, to display its self-aware, vulnerable status as a fiction or a point of view. Because there is a point of view if you look hard enough; and it's generally neither egalitarian nor life-affirming.

We may be aware of the ways in which lifestyle, home-makeover and parenting shows create a seductive arena shaped by the narrative of wish-fulfilment, in which we play out our fantasies of escaping the urban rat-race or becoming a domestic goddess. But it's easy to underestimate just how much today's TV uses the reality effect to conjure a complete inversion of ordinary life. *Dallas* and *Dynasty* never pretended their worlds were within reach. But *Windfall* and *Britain's Got Talent* present as fact the fiction of instant fame and the transformation from rags to riches. Take those money shots on *The Secret Millionaire*, for example, when the charity worker acts dumbstruck and delighted to receive a cheque from the recently unmasked millionaire. I myself have been known to shed a tear. But I pull myself together with the thought that such moments uphold the illusion that the problems of poverty and a cash-strapped voluntary sector are being solved through a few very visible acts of philanthropy.

These programmes include a crucial element of gritty realism to conjure their authenticity: there's *Tower Block of Commons*, where 'politicians swap their comfortable homes and move into council estates across the country, encountering first-hand the reality of residents' lives', and *Peckham Finishing School for Girls*, in which 'four privileged young ladies ... move onto a council estate and immerse themselves in the alien and unfamiliar world of Peckham's vibrant, multi-ethnic community'. Billed as category-busting reality checks, these programmes actually reinforce stereotypes of class, gender and race. In today's media world, Oxbridge-educated TV producers stage trashy parables of aspiration in the name of giving mass audiences what they want. The redistribution of wealth is accomplished through a week-long life-swap, and our education system is revolutionised by parachuting in a bunch of celebrity 'teachers'. The message is that anyone can make it if they want it enough. Yet according to a 2011 study by researchers at Teesside University, 82 per cent of British youngsters found the 'unachievable role models' created, ironically, by 'reality' shows like *Big Brother* and *The Apprentice* damaging to their self-esteem, particularly in an age when it has actually become harder to achieve even modest career ambitions.

Above all, we are sold the lie that we, the viewers, are now in charge. In news programmes, the apparently direct immediacy of 'citizen journalism' and 'user-generated content' camouflage the increasing dominance – as documented in Nick Davies' book *Flat Earth News* – of the political or corporate press release. And multi-millionaire mogul Simon Cowell found himself able to say of *Afghan Star*, the Kabul-based imitation of *American Idol*: 'The fact we're allowing the public to make the decisions most of the time is a really good thing ... the great thing is when you start seeing it in places like China and Afghanistan. It's democracy. We've kinda given democracy back to the world.'

To some extent, we've become wise to Cowell's megalomaniacal fantasies, and watch these shows with our tongues planted firmly in our cheeks. But look again at those TV 'fakery' scandals. In the brave new world of realism and media-savvy irony, we weren't supposed to be duped any more. Yet thousands of TV viewers suddenly realised they were simply not aware that clips are sometimes reordered, and guests on quiz shows sometimes see questions in advance. The outrage they directed at broadcasters corresponded to the horror they felt at being taken in by it all. As one example of 'fakery' appeared after another, a kind of McCarthyite hysteria broke out which regarded even narrative convention or scriptwriting shorthand as a crime. The climate of 'zero tolerance' that ensued created a kind of exceptionalism in which 'offences' came to be regarded as bad apples in an otherwise pure barrel. This ensured that a much more powerful form of dupery remained safely hidden from TV audiences' now supposedly vigilant view. Have you ever seen an *X Factor* contestant with both a tragic backstory and a crap voice? No. Because the lowly must be seen to triumph, and the true implications of adversity be airbrushed out. TV today is piously mendacious in a way that passes under the radar. Audiences may feel empowered through the mechanism of voting, but the terms of the show are set.

Not only are crucial issues of equality and opportunity being distorted through the filter of TV, computer and film screens, but those screens even change the texture of our lives as we live them for real. That's because they change the way we see ourselves as well as the world; and – like fairground attraction mirrors – in weird and contradictory ways. Let's take the first fairground mirror: the one that makes you look really skinny. We've seen this flattering effect at work in the myth of the user-generated technological utopia where everyone is equal and shares all the world's information. But there's also the mirror that makes you look fat. It's a truism of our culture that many films, TV shows and computer games are incredibly violent. But I only really noticed this properly after I had a baby, and found I couldn't even watch reruns of *Inspector Morse* any more. There's a reason for that, I'm sure: maybe I was super tuned in to my son's vulnerability. But it enabled me to see, as if I was an alien arriving from outer space, how utterly bizarre the prevalence of violence on screen really is. Nearly every male lead actor you can think of has been portrayed at some point or other shooting someone dead with a gun. How weird is that? There are lots of theories about why on-screen violence is so popular: some believe that it provides us with a safe way of experiencing fear; others aggression. But what is clear is that unless you live in downtown Detroit or a *favela* in Rio de Janeiro, this violence portrays the world as being far worse than it actually is. You might argue that this has the effect of restricting violence to a demarcated sphere, but I think it bleeds into our sense of the world around us. Perhaps it's why so many people overestimate levels of violent crime in their societies. It's a rare instance of covert ideology working in the opposite way to the rose-tinted fashion it normally does; but it's pernicious nonetheless. On-screen violence carries with it what the writer and theorist Mark Fisher calls in his book *Capitalist Realism* a kind of 'machismo of demythologization' – you can see this in the fictional world of James Ellroy, in *The Wire* (itself a throwback to nineteenth-century realism) and also, more gratingly, in Quentin Tarantino films like *Reservoir Dogs* and *Pulp Fiction*. These dramas use violence to claim that they are realer than thou, and this stops us from noticing that they are representing the world in a particular way. For instance, isn't it a little weird that for all the trappings of liberal diversity, there's invariably a white male lead?

It's not only spectacles of violence, though, that make us feel worse about our lives. It's the supposedly 'feel-good' success stories too: Susan Boyle wowing the *BGT* judges, milkman's son Lee McQueen becoming the then Sir Alan's apprentice, the impossibly slick choreographed numbers on *Glee*. They present a virtually impossible life and pretend it's open to everybody. If playing *Grand Theft Auto* makes us feel kind of paranoid, leafing through weekend broadsheet magazines looking at gorgeous photo spreads of shabby-chic kitchens or at unrealistic recipes for pinenut muffins is even worse. We hear a lot about the evils of consumerism, but what we have now is a kind of pseudo-anti-consumerist emphasis on knit-your-own and bake-your-own which evokes a nirvana of 1970s craftivism but is way harder to fulfil than nipping out to Marks and Spencer.

And when I'm standing on a Tube platform waiting for a train, I can't help noticing how many poster adverts feature smiling people. The imagery of advertising – especially advertising for mobile phones or broadband – is all summer street parties and thousands of balloons released into the air. Barbara Ehrenreich in *Smile or Die* and Pascal Bruckner in *Perpetual Euphoria: On the Duty to be Happy* put their finger on a really insidious contemporary predicament. Seeing feel-good imagery everywhere doesn't actually make us feel good; it just raises the stakes of expectation and gives us an unsettling suspicion that we're in denial about life's inevitable downsides. It makes us feel as if something is very wrong when we encounter very ordinary problems. When we experience something really bad, like grief or serious illness, we find ourselves out of kilter with the prevailing creed of happiness and success; we're left to deal with it on our own. I don't think it's a coincidence that Woody Allen's early films, the ones that were still funny, are obsessed with death. I don't want young comedian Russell Howard and his upbeat 'Good News' show featuring the 'little things that make him smile'. I want Woody Allen's Boris Grushenko dancing a mazurka with the Grim Reaper in a bleak Russian forest. In the end, the ideological effect of the media on our imaginations is mind-bendingly complex, because it makes us feel that things are both better and worse than they really are. It's a fairground mirror that makes you look fat and skinny at the same time.

In the modern developed world, when people basically have everything they need, films and TV help to manufacture demand. The media not only keeps us entertained, it makes the grass look greener on the other side of the screen. But it's a complex form of envy. Take the example of *Sex and the City*. The TV series and the two films make much of their feminist credentials: these are four go-getting women enjoying their men, social lives and careers. But although these 'sisters' are supposed to be having fun fun fun, they spend most of their energy fretting about finding The One. The shots that stick in my mind are of Sarah Jessica Parker's face falling as she is let down for the zillionth time by Mr Big. Even Anthony Lane, a film critic I would not class in the same hardcore feminist league as Andrea Dworkin, wrote of the first *SATC* film: 'I walked into the theatre hoping for a nice evening and came out as a hardline Marxist, my head a whirl of closets, delusions, and blunt-clawed cattiness.' *SATC* appears to portray women as happy and successful, but do they really look happy to you? It's the happiness equivalent of the kind of Emperor's-new-clothes syndrome that frames Tina Fey in *30 Rock*, Lea Michele in *Glee*, and America Ferrera in *Ugly Betty* as – well – ugly. As one blogger put it, 'If Tina Fey is ugly, I'm doomed.'

The pesky point about women and equality and media representation is this: if they are shown as equal to men on screen, that's denying the reality, which is that they should of course be equal to men, but are not in fact treated that way. But if they are shown pandering to men's whims, and given metaphorical slaps on the face, that is more realistic, but also more discouraging. It creates the kind of world view in which it's normal for women to have a tough time. If enough films show men going out with women half their age – *à la* Richard Gere and Winona Ryder in *Autumn in New York* (2000) – then that becomes the done thing. Most of the time, film portrayals of women and ethnic minorities are so formulaic and negative that there's not even an attempt to provide role models. When challenged, film-makers respond that audiences are conservative, and they are giving them as much as they can handle. But I think they belittle audience expectations. In a way, the media can't win. But in another way, they are playing a very shifty game. They're the guys who make the culture, after all.

The movies have always seduced us, spinning their webs of desire and escapism around our enthralled imaginations. We are well aware that Hollywood tells lies. But what I'm most interested in are those supposedly liberal, indie films that cloak their retrograde messages in a progressive style. Films like *Dances with Wolves* (1990) and *Schindler's List* (1993) eulogise equality while lionising – once again – a white male hero and consigning the 'minority' characters (Native Americans and Jews respectively) to supporting roles and background crowd scenes. Or there are the supposedly right-on films that deliver old-fashioned ideals in countercultural packages: from straight-down-the-line family values wrapped in surrealist humour in *The Royal Tenenbaums* (2001), to guy-worship wrapped in guy-satire in *Superbad* (2007), to chain-store corporatism wrapped in romantic fatalism in *You've Got Mail* (1998).

Who is ultimately to blame for the production of screen-based confections that make us feel worse about our lives, give us a false sense of progress, and offer illusory solutions to real-world problems? Is it the fault of the producers or the consumers? What is clear is that there is a collusion going on; that we are bound together in a feedback mechanism. The announcement that there would be a bank holiday to celebrate the wedding of Prince William and Kate Middleton was greeted with eye-rolling cynicism; but somehow, as the day approached, the bandwagon of media publicity became a juggernaut. Over 8,000 journalists descended on Westminster Abbey, and two billion people (yes, I found myself sucked in too) were reported to have watched the ceremony. It was difficult to distinguish supply from demand, but what was clear was that the world had gone wedding-mad. As we lurch from one media sensation to the next, there's a general avoidance of the ups and downs of life, the power imbalances between different types of people, the effects of poverty or war. The very immediacy of the footage from the war in Iraq, the on-the-ground embedded reporters bringing Operation Desert Storm right into our living rooms, was an ideological cover for the airbrushing out of civilian casualties. It's as if everyone wants to pretend that real-world problems are not there; or that we can solve them by imagining a fantasy world in which they are simply magicked away. It's that unhealthy alliance of public relations and political correctness again. It's true that media images can help to set the tone of a culture, to shape its norms and its possibilities. But replacing idealism with illusions doesn't get us anywhere.

Back to life, back to reality

Now I realise that representing reality is not a simple matter. Philosophers all the way from the Ancient Greeks to twenty-first-century post-modernists have grappled with what reality is, and whether or not it even exists. There was Plato's Allegory of the Cave, which suggested that we live like shackled prisoners, never seeing the world outside, just shadows projected on the cave wall. Zoom up to the eighteenth century and you find Bishop Berkeley, who argued that the world didn't exist as such; it just seems to exist because we perceive it. Samuel Johnson famously responded to Berkeley's theory by kicking a stone and declaring, 'I refute it *thus*.' The German philosopher Immanuel Kant didn't go as far as Berkeley, but he did argue that although the world does exist for real, we can only ever encounter it via our perceptions: what he called the 'phenomenon' ('that which appears to be'). That means that the only version of reality that means anything is the one that is coloured and distorted by our minds. Two later philosophers, Edmund Husserl and Martin Heidegger, developed Kant's ideas into phenomenology, which tried to reconcile perception and reality once and for all. Phenomenology breaks the problem down by focusing on the everyday experience of living in the world: what it's really like to think, I'm going to lift my coffee cup off the table, and then see your arm going to lift the cup, and then feel the cup in your hand.

Some late-twentieth-century thinkers, especially literary critics like Jacques Derrida, argued (in part following Kant) that the real world was not accessible to human apprehension except via language. And language wasn't a very good way of depicting reality, because words are not directly related to things. We might think that 'woof woof' refers to a dog barking because it sounds like the sound a dog makes. But Chinese people don't say 'woof woof'. They say 'wang wang'. Albanians say 'hum hum'. And Indonesians say 'guk guk'. Then take words like 'tooth', or 'house'. You can point at a house and say 'House.' But we only know what words like 'mystery' or 'regulate' mean because we define them using other words. More than once I have gone to the dictionary to look up word A, and been directed to word B, and then to word C, which is itself defined by word A. It's a circular system. Post-modernism gets a really bad press, but it does have a point.

So getting real is, I acknowledge, a tricky thing. Isn't our approach to reality always mediated by some kind of filter of perception? And whose reality are we talking about? In which place or time? These are all valid questions. But in a way, today the problem has become less philosophical and more urgent, more political. The thinkers I've just been talking about were questioning the concept of reality before delusions really took over the world. One thinker who tried to get to grips with what's happening to reality today was the French critic Jean Baudrillard. In 1996 he published a book called *The Perfect Crime*, in which he turned detective in order to investigate a dastardly deed: the 'murder' of reality. In pre-industrial societies, he argued, there was reality and there were images of reality. The two were easily distinguishable – like the Suffolk landscape and a painting by Constable. Then came the age of mechanical reproduction: the age of photography and mass publication, of copies and fakes. You might see a replica Egyptian relic on someone's mantelpiece, but at least if you got up close enough you could tell it wasn't real. It's the phase that came after that which is the problem: when reality got stabbed in the back. Because in the contemporary world, Baudrillard argued, image and reality have become totally confused. It's not even just that our world is artificial. It's that we now live in the Ronseal world of gritty 'footage' from Iraq and Afghanistan, hyper-real computer games and 'authentic', down-to-earth PR-men-turned-politicians. It's hard to get real when that seems to be what the arch illusion-mongers are telling us to do. Even if you attempt to escape the multiplying 'outdoor' advertising screens or the siren calls of TV and internet by driving out into the country, you are greeted by signs that inform you that you are now entering a nature reserve. If realism is now a con trick, reality has been put in a frame, in quotation marks. The more you try to grasp at it, the more it slips away.

The good news is that there's hope in the sheer audacious extent of modern deception and spin. It means that while these philosophical questions are still worth asking, we've really got our work cut out just moving things in a more realistic direction. 'In this era of exploding media technologies,' the president of the world's biggest PR firm Richard Edelman told *Esquire* magazine, 'there is no truth except the truth you create for yourself.' It's a sign of the times that this relativist nightmare is portrayed as individual empowerment. There are such things as evidence, analysis and agreed standards of accuracy. It's just that they no longer command the respect they deserve. It wasn't good enough for Tony Blair to say of the Iraq war, 'Hand on heart, I did what I thought was right,' but not because he was lying: conviction and lying are two sides of the same red herring. It didn't matter what he thought; what mattered was his action in the face of the evidence. In a world which has spawned a replica twin made of capital, and then another one online; a world in which books, music, letters, greetings cards, money, information, Christmas presents, sex and corporations are all becoming virtual, insubstantial and fictional, our recourse to empiricism is being silently corroded. We inhabit a political and institutional culture where a neurotic emphasis on audit and measuring outcomes is disguising the fact that facts and evidence have ceased to matter. Power is trying to do away with the irritating obstacle that is the real. We still need to think about reality in a nuanced way. But we can try to get a bit closer to it.

And getting real is not just about reality; it's about saying candidly what you mean, and what you want. If the media can help us change the world by revealing its flaws (and don't get me wrong, good news reporting is a vital reality check), it can also help us to imagine what a better world would look like. That's the good thing about all those screens and images and all that virtual reality. But despite the popularity of escapist life-swap shows and feel-good chick flicks, it seems that shows that promote realistic idealism – taking the lead, setting out a point of view and an achievable agenda for change from whatever standpoint – have fallen out of style. We just get pseudo-real fantasies that are hardly a blueprint for action.

And today's media renounces initiative and idealism in relation to cultural excellence as well as social change. Terrified of being branded 'elitist' or lecturing to the audience, TV executives claim that they are simply supplying demand. The race to the bottom is carried out in the audience's name, although I'm sure the public's appetite for quality is underrated. Out go the lecterns, the talking heads and the long speeches to camera; in comes the amateur presenter getting involved in the action and not presuming to be an expert. But there's a disguised elitism in this amateurism, an assumption that you don't need to work hard or become a specialist, you can just dabble in a casual, aristocratic sort of way. A lot of so-called amateur presenters these days are middle-aged, middle-class white men who are already famous for something else. Just as respecting audiences means exposing them to demanding programmes, having presenters with an angle, an expertise, an explicit point of view is more up-front, more honest, more empowering for audiences. Otherwise, what we get is a weird combination of second-guessed lowest common denominator and camouflaged snobbery. Instead of candid polemics like John Berger's *Ways of Seeing*, we get dilettante Kenneth Clarks, enthusing about high culture.

When media strategists focus-group audiences, they say, 'Just keep doing what you're doing.' They want programme-makers to take the lead. But just as in modern politics, taking the lead is now considered authoritarian. So, not content with this answer, the executives attempt to 'read between the lines'. They place the audience on the couch and try to divine what it is they really want. What are their hopes, their dreams, their fears? Depressingly, the result of these consultation exercises is invariably yet more home-renovation shows and programmes about parenting. At no point is it ever considered that people are not necessarily spontaneous originators, in-control free agents; that our desires and anxieties could be the product of a circularity of supply and demand, of self-perpetuating consumer culture and stoked-up tabloid concerns. In contrast to the official ideology of Orwell's *Nineteen Eighty-Four*, 'Ingsoc', today's media is quite capable of getting right inside us. Not only because it beams at us through an ever-greater number of screens, but also because it speaks to us in what seems like our own words. And what it says is a series of paralysing contradictions. It portrays the world as being fairer than it actually is, but it makes us feel as if our lives are less satisfactory than they actually are. It pretends that life-swap and relocation fantasies are a hop, skip and a jump away, leaving us to fall back down to earth with an incapacitating bump.

And there's a more purposeful intent underlying modern media in all its converging forms. It's the intent of a monopoly of global media corporations, advancing under the rhetoric of the popular will. The persuasive power of programmes is now accompanied by covert advertising in the form of product placement, PR, and interactive 'participation'. In fact the one is blurring into the other. In his book *The Art of Immersion, Wired* journalist Frank Rose quotes a Madison Avenue ad exec who says: 'Advertising used to interrupt life's programming. Now advertising is the programming. And if you're actually being marketed to successfully, you have no idea.' We may be media savvy, but we're also under media's influence, and that influence is getting harder to spot now that it's sold as realism and audience engagement. We've got numerous remote controls on the sofa and unlimited channels of internet TV; but how much of that power and choice is real?

SIX

An Office Romance

The Bangles released their cheesy yet catchy single 'Manic Monday' in 1986. 'Just another manic Monday,' it went. 'I wish it was Sunday. Cause that's my fun day.' The song seemed to chime with the working week very well: the commute on the Tube. The men in suits. The start of the nine to five. Lunch run. Coffee break. The after-work drink. Short Friday afternoon, the approaching weekend. Two days of rest, Saturday night out. Then Sunday-night blues, and it all began again. Things have changed quite a lot since then. I often work at home, tapping away on the laptop while propped up in bed with a nice cup of tea. It's not uncommon for me to look forward to Monday mornings. And if you work in the 'creative industries' or for a whacky, dynamic company or do something involving the internet, your routine may be very relaxed indeed. You may be lucky enough to start your days with a brunch meeting. Follow that with a brainstorm in the breakout area. A quick game of table football, and a chinwag on the beanbags. How about a free mid-afternoon muffin? Then after work, an industry get-together with canapés and networking opportunities. Although you may have to keep on top of things at the weekend via the ever-present BlackBerry. But then sometimes, when I'm listening to the radio on my crappy old Walkman, 'Manic Monday' comes on, and it still strikes a chord. So how much has modern work culture changed?

In this chapter I'll be arguing that as work gives us less and less, we're encouraged to want it more and more. As blue-collar work becomes harder to find, the demand for a job gets louder, eroding working conditions even further. And for white-collar and 'no-collar' employees (those in creative, dot com or freelance roles), a new ideology of work has transformed it from an externally imposed demand to an internally driven desire. For those people, a job is no longer just something they need, but also something they crave. Their work seems more relaxed, but its concealed demands are greater. I'll be exploring how work has seduced those people like a form of Stockholm syndrome, and how success at work unwittingly inhibits them from perceiving the hold it has over their lives. I'll be looking at how qualities that used to be associated with non-work – self-expression, creativity, play – have made their work into so much more than just earning money; and why this can be the very opposite of liberating. Work no longer offers a candid *quid pro quo* or clearly articulates its requirements: it dresses them up as entertainment, virtue and the true meaning of life. In this chapter and the next, I'll be arguing that without properly realising it, we've developed ways of thinking about both work and freedom which prevent us either from achieving our full potential or ever being truly off the hook. And all with our apparently free consent.

Kissing the rod

Advertising 'creatives' kick footballs around the office and media strategists spar at ping pong, all in the name of work. Google's offices sport a yellow brick road and Twitter's employees wear cowboy hats. The *Economist* reports that Acclaris, an American IT company, has a 'chief fun officer', and TD Bank has a 'Wow!' department that sends costume-clad teams to 'surprise and delight' high performers. A lot of white-collar jobs are now meant to be a source of stimulation, identity and pleasure. Even call centres spend a lot of time encouraging their workers to adopt the company values as their own. Employers at all levels have cottoned on to the economic benefits of encouraging employees to fall in love with their jobs. We all know that work is necessary, but since when was it attractive?

In the first half of the twentieth century, America and Europe became excited by the idea that new technology would liberate people from the burden of work. The Marxist writer Herbert Marcuse, along with the socialist libertarian Murray Bookchin, looked forward to a utopian era of 'post-scarcity economics' when a surplus of food would enable people to relax and enjoy the good things in life. In his 1931 essay 'Economic Possibilities for our Grandchildren', John Maynard Keynes predicted that within a hundred years, standards of living in the developed world would be so high that the working week could be cut to just fifteen hours. For others, however, this vision of the future was rather alarming: it raised the prospect of the 'problem of leisure'. There were fears that people would use their free time to get up to trouble. America, the country that feared the 'problem of leisure' most acutely, went on to develop the most onerous work culture in the industrialised world. The 1950s suburban dream and the demands of consumerism created a conformist culture of nine to five, six and seven.

Even after the sixties hippy rejection of the rat race, Americans still didn't throw off their shackles. They now work, on average, between two hundred and five hundred more hours per year than their European counterparts; and 35 per cent don't even use up their meagre holiday entitlement. In Britain, the number of people working more than forty-eight hours per week has more than doubled since 1998. To put this in a broader context, David Boyle and Andrew Simms of the New Economics Foundation have reminded us that the average medieval peasant in Europe would have needed to work for only fifteen weeks of the year. Centuries of 'development' have converted a means into an end. Twenty per cent of American undergraduates study business. University careers advisers encourage students to spend their holidays doing internships at law firms or investment banks. The introduction of massive tuition fees in Britain in 2010 was justified on the grounds of increased future earnings. Higher education is turning into lower employment.

In contrast to the overt eighties rat race, the ideology of work that emerged in the nineties was a covert, new age 'vision'. As Madeleine Bunting notes in her book *Willing Slaves: How the Overwork Culture is Ruling Our Lives*, HR managers in big corporations enlisted their marketing departments to sell the company brand to employees, the 'internal customer'. Work was no longer cast as a strict, traditional routine: employees were supposed to actively embrace their company's mission. Jobs for life were no longer guaranteed, but what did that matter when you now lived for work? Charismatic management gurus sold work as the ultimate form of self-expression. It was through your career, rather than through travelling the world, that you could now 'find yourself'.

A lot of this new ideology of work is subtly coercive. The 'dress-down Fridays' of the nineties had an unwritten code: jeans were a step too far, but chinos were just right. And they exacted a penalty somewhere else: if you came to work in your mufti, you felt you had to be doubly conscientious. Away days are the same: they may involve a trip to Alton Towers or Chelsea Football Club, but they are basically an eight-hour-long meeting.

I have to admit at this point that I'm one of those suckers who loves what they do. I regard my work as a kind of vocation or paid hobby. But I'm also unhealthily conscientious and driven, and find it hard to switch off at the end of the day. I know what it's like to be totally into your work, but to feel as if work has taken over your life. It's hard to tell sometimes if my urge to get to my desk is the result of genuine enthusiasm, or just my pocket superego flexing his fascist little muscles. And I suspect that a lot of the men who complain that they don't see enough of their young kids are actually quite glad to 'have' to stay in the office till seven or eight in the evening. That might be because compared to looking after children, work feels like a holiday. But all this complicates our sense of our own freedom and choice. As we'll see in the next chapter, freedom is a tricky business. But my own weakness for work shouldn't be something that enables a greedy economic system to get me to do more for less.

That system benefits from the fact that our complicated devotion to work is largely hidden in popular culture. In Hollywood films, for example, it's the escape from work that is represented, not our attraction to work itself. In *Pretty Woman*, released in 1990, Richard Gere snatches much-needed moments from his business trip to frolic in a hotel room with happy hooker Julia Roberts. In *Falling Down* (1993), Michael Douglas cracks under the strain of his Wall Street slavery and goes on an all-out bender. If escape for men means busting out of the structure, for women it means embracing marriage and children. Whenever a film opens with a career woman merrily going about her working day, you know that egregious state of affairs cannot last. From *Bridget Jones's Diary* (2001) to *Knocked Up* (2007), the heroine's attentions are soon occupied by romantic and domestic destiny. *The Devil Wears Prada* (2006) is a particularly pernicious example. Granted, the end of the film shows Anne Hathaway as the young aspiring journalist on her way to a new job on a newspaper. But the entire film dramatises her journey towards leaving the job 'a million girls would kill for': personal assistant to fashion-magazine editor Meryl Streep/Anna Wintour, a character who personifies the stereotype that being a proper career woman turns you into a bitch. From *American Beauty* (1999) to *Revolutionary Road* (2008) to *A Serious Man* (2009), our culture is still captivated by the clear boundaries of the nine-to-five suburban routine. That's partly because we are nostalgic for a time when work was work and escape was possible, and partly because we don't want to face our open-ended dedication.

If an atmosphere of voluntarism and the seductive informality of contemporary work have blurred the distinction between work and non-work, this has been given a powerful boost by the rise of new technology. With the home computer, email, the BlackBerry and the iPhone, employees can now keep in touch at any time of the day or night. Hotmail's ad campaign, 'The New Busy', is a perfect example of this cultural change. 'The New Busy' is 'not like the old busy', the ads read. One of them depicts a bucolic scene of two young lovelies lying in a rowing boat, one holding a smartphone. 'The New Busy navigates the worlds of work, leisure, friends and family like a Pacific salmon. The New Busy would rather spend an afternoon in the park than discussing ballpark figures. Thinks 9 to 5 is a good night out. Looks for interesting ways to be bored. Likes to play "fill the diary".' That last one hits the nail on the head: 'Fill the diary' is the new fun. It is truly hideous, but this campaign is on to something: people routinely complain about how busy they are, but it's being at a loose end that we find really scary. I keep seeing magazine features about how new technology is turning life into a continuous feat of multi-tasking. But it's harder to acknowledge our own desire for distraction. As Alain de Botton has noted in *The Pleasures and Sorrows of Work*, perhaps the real reason we keep ourselves so busy is to avoid facing our mortality. You only have to look at medieval *memento mori* paintings, with their symbolic skulls and dwindling egg-timers, or visit a Victorian cemetery, with its spectacularly ornate monuments, to get a sense of just how in denial we've become. Staring at a monitor all day in silence may be deadening, but hey! It stops us thinking about death.

Rank deceit

Those are some clues as to how the ideology of work became so bottom-up. But I'll admit that I've been concentrating not on the bottom but on the middle ranges of the pay scale. That's partly because it's the sector I know best, and partly because it's in that sector that the co-optive ideology of work is at its most powerful. Marx and Engels argued that proletarians were not only oppressed because they were forced to work for poor pay and conditions, but also because they bought into their own subjection. They came to believe in the legitimacy of the working arrangement, and that prompted them to provide the surplus labour that produced capitalism's profit. The fact that so many white-collar and no-collar workers are now positively attracted to their jobs means that, in a sense, those people are becoming an army of new proletarians. They are willing to go that extra mile for free. Because the Marxist analytical spotlight was trained almost exclusively on labour rather than capital, white-collar managers were not thought of as workers themselves. That created a blind spot that is even bigger today. Of course, the more people buy into the ideology of work, the more satisfaction it provides. But there's something about being successful or having an interesting job that means it's especially hard to acknowledge both sides of the coin: to think about what it really feels like to live in this way.

The professions are being pounded by privatisation, digitisation, global outsourcing, falling wages, and audit mania. And those who work in the 'creative industries' are being turned into unlanded peasants. When Arianna Huffington sold The Huffington Post to AOL for $315 million, her argument that the voluntary bloggers who wrote for it were not exploited because they were provided with a platform to do what they enjoyed seemed more outrageous than ever. But that's the way things are going in the world of creative work. 'We're hosting people who express their ideas and if they want to write, fine, and if they don't, fine,' she said. 'We get thousands of submissions, so it's not like anyone is pursuing people to write for free.' The chance to commodify ourselves online is supposed to make up for the fact that we're all becoming unpaid interns. That pseudo-democratic voluntarism is threatening entire industries. Employees' advances are being spurned by their beloved masters. According to the super-utilitarian capitalist logic currently taking over the world, if you get satisfaction from your job, that doesn't mean that you can therefore be paid less: it means that you can be paid nothing. Large swathes of the new proletariat are finding that there's only one thing worse than being exploited, and that's not being needed at all. Is it too much to ask to enjoy our work and to get properly paid for it too?

The ideology that papers over the gap between expectation and reward is most prevalent in the middle-income bracket, but there's ideology working at all levels of income. And there are shared forms of ideology in our culture which sustain widening inequalities in income. A few stats, if I may. In 1960, the average American CEO made twice the $100,000 salary paid to President Kennedy. By 2001, the average CEO made thirty times President Bush's salary, even after he'd doubled it to $400,000. CEO pay jumped over 500 per cent in the 1990s. In Britain in 2009, the average FTSE 100 CEO was paid £4.9 million, a figure that rose more than 50 per cent that year. In the US in the same year, the CEO of a Standard & Poor's 500 index company was paid on average $9.25 million. CEOs today earn about four hundred times as much as the average worker, compared to about forty times as much in 1980. They are the new oligarchs.

Such gross inequalities are sustained not only by the force of financial clout, but also by mythical justifications that circulate endlessly in the mainstream media, despite talk of 'banker-bashing'. 'If CEOs or bankers are taxed more, there will be a mass exodus to more favourable regimes,' goes one popular theory. Well, there's no evidence of such hissy fits resulting in any large-scale migrations. American CEOs rake in a lot more than their European counterparts (despite the lack of evidence of better performance), but the last I heard there were still CEOs living in Europe. Incidentally, globalisation means very different things for the super-rich and for everyone else. The 'skills' of the super-rich are supposed to be totally transferable: they can run any company anywhere in the world, no matter whether that company makes soft drinks or cars. Whereas for everyone else, it's not their skills that are transferable: they themselves are interchangeable for the best market price. 'CEO pay reflects the market value of their extraordinary talents, just as with star footballers,' goes another theory. Actually, it's really expensive hiring and firing CEOs, so it's not a fluid market; companies are risk-averse, and only like hiring people they know; and anyway, if it was a real market, executive pay would fluctuate, whereas it's just gone up and up. 'Highly paid CEOs increase the productivity of their companies.' Not proven. 'Bankers may earn huge sums, but they also pay huge taxes.' Well, to take just one example, in 2009 Barclays Bank made £11.6 billion in profits but paid just 1 per cent of that in tax. The question of private wealth used to be scrutinised and regulated by the state. But with shrinking state power, more and more of our common wealth is outside democratic decision-making and control. National governments have entered into abusive relationships with banks and big corporations, who string them along and persuade them that they really need them, when they should just be told to sod off.

Instead, private profit is enjoying really positive public PR. Ironically, since the financial meltdown there's a renewed sense that business is plucky and productive – the Protestant work ethic has made a comeback. What is not examined is the material impact of private 'compensation' on everyone else. There's a widespread assumption that the money these suits make simply comes out of a separate pot. We've lost the ideological language we need to debate the connection between the private and the public realms. That's why complaints about excessive 'compensation' and bonuses are articulated in moral terms. There's a lot of talk of 'remorse and apology' and calls for bankers to 'show restraint'. Moral appeals are a sure sign that we've lost any sense that this is a matter of political choice. It's about overt ideology.

Bankers and business leaders still have an X factor, a secret ingredient, a *je ne sais quoi* that keeps their mystical status unchallenged. You only have to watch a single episode of *The Apprentice* to see the reverence with which the aspiring entrepreneurs pay court to Lord Sugar. In his entertaining critique *The Management Myth: Debunking Modern Business Philosophy*, the former consultant Matthew Stewart pulls back the curtain on an entire commercial and academic industry devoted to the 'philosophy' of management, business and leadership. This is taught on MBA courses across the US, it's the subject of innumerable mass-market books, and it filters through companies around the world via the work of highly-paid consultants. It's a school of thought that purports to be a rigorous science, but is more like a religious cult. It engenders a deep respect for legendary business leaders and the sages who know the secret of their success. And yet it likes to talk about hierarchy-busting and 'breaking all the rules' (see Tom Peters' 1992 classic *Liberation Management: Necessary Disorganisation for the Nanosecond Nineties*). It claims that business leadership is open to anyone via a step by step guide; but at the same time it presents leadership qualities as products of a mysterious alchemy. And although it ostensibly addresses a select audience of CEOs, its main readership is actually lower down the food chain, particularly middle managers, those new white-collar proletarians. It promotes 'I made it' narratives of aspiration, but these serve to mask entrenched continuities of class and rank. It claims to 'put people first' and is closely related to the self-help literature which tells its readers they 'have the power'. But it ends up reinforcing hierarchy by concentrating risk at the bottom and reward at the top. While material inequalities of money and status increase, the management rhetoric keeps them from view.

I'm not saying that high earners are always having a great time, that they don't suffer from fatigue or status anxiety, that the statement by Stuart Fraser, head of the Corporation of London's policy committee, that a second tax on bankers' bonuses after the financial crash 'will kill us' was entirely disingenuous. In America in the 1890s the poorest worked longer hours than the rich, but by the 1990s the richest 10 per cent were working longer hours than the poorest. But although they are affected by the same attraction to work as the middle earners, their astronomical salaries mean that for them it's less of an ideological con. And not only do these people earn massively more than their fair share, they are also sustained by the new shared illusion of value.

Meanwhile, on the other side of the tracks, blue-collar work is mainly subject to simple exploitation, rather than ideological mind-games. But even here it's not entirely straightforward. The trade unions were not just hammered into submission by Margaret Thatcher, they've also suffered from a more insidious form of erosion as a result of the working-class turn to the Tories, a corrosive discourse of aspiration and the leaching away of public support for strikes. Politicians on all sides can now easily undermine a strike by British Airways cabin crew by making a pious case for the interests of the 'travelling public'. Nowadays, to reject the demands of the capitalist, consumerist economy doesn't mark you out as a free spirit, it marks you out as a nutter. And to demand better pay and conditions doesn't mark you out as strong, it marks you out as a victim. Adversity these days is so passé. So while false consciousness seems to be a factor in the decline of workers' resistance, there's also the problem that at a time when arguments for fairness are needed the most, they've become harder than ever to make. As the low-wage sector mush-rooms, everyone is supposed to have what it takes to become an executive – or at least an entrepreneur. As workplace hierarchies widen and harden, management and human-resources rhetoric spins an illusion of empowerment and equality. As more and more people become proletarians, it's rare even to hear the phrase 'working class' any more. With the decline of the unions, no one knows the reality of how their own pay compares with other people's. At all levels there's a denial of exploitation, oppression, imbalance of any kind. It's a new taboo that doesn't help anyone; apart from employers and high earners, of course.

Out of the box

In 2010 a coalition of British unions organised a campaign under the banner 'The Right to Work'. It was an understandable response to massive public-sector job cuts, but as the philosopher Nina Power observed, it illustrated the extent to which everyone, even those on the lowest incomes, is chasing the world of work as it's currently set up, rather than lobbying for its terms to be changed. But jump back to a Parisian prison cell in 1883, and the Cuban-born French revolutionary Paul Lafargue, son-in-law to Karl Marx, is working on an essay entitled 'The Right to be Lazy'. He is criticising his contemporaries for idealising work, and reminding them that their ancestors took a different view. 'The philosophers of antiquity taught contempt for work, that degradation of the free man, the poets sang of idleness, that gift from the gods,' he writes, before exhorting the workers to 'Listen to the voice of these philosophers, which has been concealed from you with jealous care.' Nowadays, it seems less and less possible for us to think in such blue-sky terms. It's true that people need to eat. But we seem to have forgotten that, as a society, there are different ways of organising the making of a living.

As Lafargue was arguing, a bit of history shows us that the role of work has changed beyond all recognition. In the fourth century BC, Aristotle believed that only slaves and animals should have to work. Fulfilment – through philosophy, art or politics – required a life of leisure. The elevation of work into a worthy and satisfying activity was a gradual and deliberate process. Early Christianity shifted the meaning of work in a virtuous direction by arguing that it was necessary for the expiation of sin, although making money was sinful. In the nineteenth century, Max Weber's Protestant work ethic took care of that, reconciling the accumulation of wealth with godliness. He'd been helped along by the publication, in the mid-eighteenth century, of Denis Diderot and Jean le Rond d'Alembert's twenty-eight-volume *Encyclopédie*, a 'systematic dictionary of the sciences, arts, and crafts'. As well as being a compendium of Enlightenment thought, the *Encyclopédie* extolled the nobility of manual craftsmanship (a similar case has been made in our digitised information age by Richard Sennett in *The Craftsman* and Matthew Crawford in *The Case for Working with Your Hands*). Gradually, work became a Good Thing.

After I went on maternity leave, I found myself in a curious twilight world of confinement but also incredible liberation. Some days I was stuck at home on an endless treadmill of feeding and changing; other days I felt I had the run of the city and could pop the baby in the sling and go anywhere I liked. My image of work became equally contradictory: in some ways I relished being free of the desk-zombie drill; in other ways I missed work the way I missed going to parties. It was as if the categories with which I used to think about work and leisure had suddenly lost their meaning. My year opened another window onto the weird, unexamined way in which working patterns are utterly subjective, yet imbued with the quality of inevitable necessity. With the cost of childcare now comparable to a salary, many women decide that it's not financially worthwhile to go back to work. But many still do so because of the sense of identity it provides: those women will literally – like interns – work for nothing. And yet some mothers leave their careers to look after their children full time. Now it's the connotations of work as labour and constraint that come into view: how lovely to be able to stay at home all day. But hang on, isn't the home the site of domestic imprisonment and the limitations of the private sphere?

Well, before the nineteenth century, the home was actually a place of work. Work, the earning of daily bread, was done in private: whether through serf subsistence or aristocratic estate-management. One of the effects of the Industrial Revolution was to swap private and public around: the home became 'a haven in a harsh world', providing the respite and regeneration necessary to face the working day. In the 1960s, of course, women's confinement to the domestic sphere became a *cause célèbre* for feminists who campaigned for them to be able to go out into the public world of work. So what is the home today? A place of captivity, or freedom? A place to change nappies, or write novels? Any sense of history is absent from those endless media debates about whether mothers should go out to work; but history shows us that our categories are contingent and up for grabs for both women and men. We have subconsciously chosen to invest a certain set of arrangements with a sense of what is both necessary and desirable, but the long view reveals a much wider choice. Players of ideology's game obey a cardinal rule: they don't let on that things haven't always been this way.

It's ironic that at a time when work is becoming so abstracted from subsistence, and all the solid guarantees of our working lives are melting into air, that we're not taking the opportunity for a rethink. With the decline of manufacturing, with the rise of the service industries, the information age and the ballooning of bureaucracy, more and more energy is taken up with producing things we do not need. Work has become a surreal, groundless activity, unmoored from the tangible specifics of sustaining life. The ratio of IT consultants and account managers to engineers and cabbage farmers is yawning. How can a culture place so much emphasis on work when so much of that work is essentially pointless? That's where the contemporary ideology of work comes in particularly handy: it encourages us to keep our heads down. A visiting Martian would find it peculiar to observe a brand manager at his desk, spending a significant proportion of his time surfing the internet, setting family photos as his desktop background and talking to his colleagues in the staff kitchen; turning up at a particular time every day to a strange institution that creates a product no one really needs; and worrying at the end of each day about whether his boss likes him less than his colleague at the next desk. We need to step back from the daily routines of work and look at all the little ways in which people domesticate their work environment; all the time that is spent not really producing anything real: because those things raise the issue of what the whole overdeveloped structure is for. The ways in which work has seduced us into investing ourselves in it, body and soul, have stopped us wondering how much work, in its current arrangement, really benefits us. There is a very basic question, one that Marx and Keynes asked repeatedly but which seems to have been mislaid amongst the papers on our desks: what is the point of work?

Work used to be a stick, but now it's a stick disguised as a carrot. It poses in the guise of a charismatic guru, offering us friendship, community, identity and fulfilment, so that we voluntarily fall in love with its concealed demands. At the same time it retains the sense of being fixed and immovable, obscuring the liberating lessons of history and the possibility of different choices. Employers certainly benefit; and we do too, to some extent: it's more rewarding to believe in your work than not to believe in it. There's nothing wrong with loving your job, just as long as it's a respectful and reciprocal relationship. But it's important for us to do our own audit to see where the payoffs lie; to ask whose interests are ultimately served by combining obligation with attraction. Because it's not clear whether this sea-change makes our everyday lives more or less fulfilling. The modern 'opportunity' to imagine our working selves as individuals – as standing out from the pack, as entrepreneurial free spirits, as our own special brand – stops us seeing the big picture. Some workers are doing a lot better than others. And if this is about power and covert ideology, it's about overt ideology too. The way we organise work is about making political decisions. But that ideology has been driven underground: by a false sense that certain arrangements are immovable; by an embarrassment at every level about admitting exploitation; and by our own sense of duty and voluntarism. Let's get it all out on the table. Employers: don't lead us on; make your demands explicit. And employees: don't be coy; make your own demands in return. Office romance is so overrated.

SEVEN

The Age of Consent

Since the supposed death of ideology at the end of the Cold War, happiness has been the one thing we can all believe in. In the liberal democracies of the developed West there's a belief that people are generally free, and free to have fun. The smiley-face symbol of the ecstasy-fuelled nineties rave scene morphed into the upbeat digital emoticons of the post-millennial SMS craze. If the nineties was the decade of dance music and slacker chic, the fireworks parties of the millennium ushered in the excitingly-named 'noughties', a decade that celebrated man-child mayhem and cyber-liberation. George W. Bush used the word 'freedom' twenty-eight times and 'liberty' fifteen times in his second inaugural speech in 2005. And the British government appointed a 'happiness tsar' in 2007. The traditional assumption that as time goes on, rules are relaxed and behaviour is increasingly liberated, had never felt more true.

As Thomas Frank notes in *The Conquest of Cool*, the hedonistic culture that evolved in the nineties presented itself as a reaction to work. Just as the swinging sixties had rejected the drab fifties stereotype encapsulated in Sloan Wilson's 1955 novel *The Man in the Gray Flannel Suit*, the nineties shunned the rigid, workaholic world of Tom Wolfe's *Bonfire of the Vanities* (1987). If the eighties subjected us to manic Mondays, the nineties supplied much-needed release, using the hippy sixties for inspiration. Or at least, that's what our culture was telling us. The intro to Primal Scream's 1990 breakthrough single 'Loaded' sampled the *Easy Rider* forerunner *The Wild Angels* (1966): 'We wanna be free/We wanna be free to do what we wanna do/And we wanna get loaded/And we wanna have a good time'. And the Rolling Stones' song 'I'm Free', from their 1965 *Out of Our Heads* album, was covered in a jangly Madchester style in 1990 by a Scottish band called the Soup Dragons: 'I'm free/To do what I want/Any old time'. Tellingly, the song had a further incarnation in 2007 in an ad for the Chase Freedom Card: 'Feel free to choose cashback, and then change to points, and then change again … That's freedom.' If you say so, Chase.

There'll be more about corporate co-option in a moment. But for now, suffice to say that the attraction to work that I described in the previous chapter has become obscured by a prevailing belief that we've entered an era of satisfying escape from work, of unprecedented freedom and pleasure. This hedonistic atmosphere sits uneasily alongside the playful ideology of work, because it depends on a sense of liberation from work in its traditional, structured form. Hence all the films about work which portray it as the old-fashioned nine to five. The freedom illusion keeps the seductive logic of the workplace hidden away. It obscures the fact that people are so attracted to their work that they can't resist taking it home. It creates a fictional feeling of respite that prompts us to embrace our jobs with enthusiasm. And, as I'll argue in this chapter, it also prevents us from noticing that what we consider to be free time isn't really free at all. In a culture that celebrates its own liberty, norms silently replace laws and soft power and self-control rule the day.

Now I'll admit that I find relaxing at weekends and on holidays a bit of a challenge. Lying on a beach, my head buzzes with anxiety about sunburn. If I visit a new city I'm immediately a slave to the guidebook's list of Top Ten Attractions. I have to visit every church, every gallery, every landmark of historical importance. Florence is a nightmare. And if I go to the country, every mountain in sight has to be climbed to the very top. So this is a subject close to my heart. But I don't think I'm entirely alone. If a pervasive sense of hedonism and liberty creates the perverse desire to be busy, it also conceals the expectations and social codes that shape our apparently free lives; not always with our conscious awareness, and not always to the good.

Freedom incorporated

If it's in employers' interests to make us fall in love with our jobs, it's in corporations' interests to make sure they still have our full attention when we're not at work: specifically, that we spend our free time shopping. A consuming passion for retail has sprung up in explicit opposition to the demands of the nine to five. But that opposition is an illusion. As Naomi Klein in *No Logo* and Andrew Potter and Joseph Heath in *The Rebel Sell* have shown, brands from Nike to Sony relentlessly recruit images of freedom and counterculture to sell symbolic forms of escape from structure and authority. Although amusingly, in the wake of the English riots in the summer of 2011, Levi's hastily withdrew an ad featuring a young man defiantly confronting a line of police: corporations disown this edgy imagery as soon as there's a whiff of controversy. I keep seeing three billboard ads: one for the Vauxhall Corsa, slogan: 'Fun unlimited'; one for an HTC Smartphone, slogan: 'Go wild'; and one for Three Mobile with the slogan 'Set free' inside an image of breaking chains. Campaigns like these blur the traditional lefty language of liberation with the celebration of individualist consumerism. This apparent critique of capitalism and work and 'the system' enables us to feel that there is a part of our lives that remains sacred and untouched. It's not just that shopping has become a form of voluntary labour, as anyone who has tried to maintain an even vaguely respectable wardrobe will know. It's that despite being presented as mutually opposed, earning money and spending it are two sides of the same coin. Our time is ostensibly our own, but terms and conditions apply. And while we are constantly told that consumers are faced with a bewildering choice of products to buy, when the choice is between Adidas and Reebok, it's not even a choice at all.

Similarly, the anti-capitalist tactic of 'culture-jamming', devising spoofs and parodies of ads and brands, has been energetically absorbed by the corporate and political establishment, who've produced 'ironic' ads and viral marketing campaigns of their own. 'Al Gore's Penguin Army', an animated spoof of the environmental film *An Inconvenient Truth*, appeared to be a maverick YouTube posting but was later revealed to have been made by a PR company called the DCI group, whose clients include General Motors and ExxonMobil. While the Obama campaign denied any links to the viral 'Obama girl' videos, which featured a scantily clad young woman confessing her devotion to the then presidential candidate, the advertising executives who produced the videos subsequently announced a partnership with VoterVision, a multimedia political marketing group. Subversive activists are fond these days of employing playful techniques. The anti-corporate protest group Billionaires for Bush dress up in tuxedos and top hats. The Harry Potter Alliance motivates young campaigners by adopting characters and themes from the eponymous saga. But two can play that game: Sony's ads for its LCD TV screens depicted a drab council estate being showered in an explosion of multicoloured paint bombs triggered by an orange-haired clown, 250,000 balls bouncing down the streets of San Francisco, and animated Play-Doh rabbits cavorting to the Rolling Stones. Ads for Barclays Bank turned one man's commute to work into a 'liberating' rollercoaster ride and another man's journey home into a waterslide run (with a spin-off app game that was downloaded two million times in one week), and had a woman turning somersaults on a huge white bouncy castle (a vision of modern desexualised fun if ever there was one). YouTube is brimming with brand-driven viral videos, such as the 'compare the meerkat' ad campaign. The ads direct the viewer to two separate websites: on one, comparethemarket.com, you can find quotes for car insurance; on the other, comparethemeerkat.com, you can compare meerkats according to size, location and hobbies. The meerkat site is a perfect example of ideology in action. It is more pernicious than a straightforward insurance-comparison site, because it's providing recreation, not cynically selling. It doesn't just try to make finding car insurance fun. It encourages us to spend our free time watching ads.

So does all fun and all resistance become co-opted and 'sewn up' by the branding svengalis of adland? I like to remain optimistic that the game is still up for grabs. But we still need to acknowledge that the dominant mainstream and the counterculture that opposes it are engaged in a symbiotic, dialectical relationship. Subversive 'freedom' is styled in opposition to the commercial mainstream. And the market thrives on this 'critique' because it spurs on the constant reinvention of new products. Everything is always so *over*.

Just as business has insinuated itself into territory we like to think of as free, play is now being used for serious ends. Since 'gaming' is, apparently, the future, everyone from educational consultants to the military wants a piece of the action. The US Army uses a computer game called America's Army to attract new recruits (EMPOWER YOURSELF. DEFEND FREEDOM). Interactive games are becoming so popular in museums that children soon won't tolerate learning anything unless it involves touch-screen technology. Computer games are being developed for the worthy aim of 'informal pedagogy'. On its website, an organisation called Games Based Learning makes the case for the educational benefits of computer games in terms that are unintentionally fabulous: 'Knowledge acquisition in games that use more factually accurate content such as Medieval Total War, Full Spectrum Warrior and possibly Assassin's Creed ... sit quite harmoniously within proposed twenty-first-century skills frameworks.' In her manifesto for computer games to improve the real world, *Reality is Broken*, Jane McGonigal describes how games are being used to engage the elderly in care homes, to combat depression and obesity and even, via games like the World Bank-commissioned 'Evoke', to address poverty and climate change. It's not only the critique of the establishment that's employing ludic techniques; mainstream institutions are loosening their ties and learning the same tricks.

I'll offer one last example that encapsulates the curious mingling of consumerism, work, leisure and street cred in contemporary culture. It's Coca-Cola's 'Open Happiness Global Platform', a massive advertising campaign launched in 2009 on *American Idol*, and featuring a single performed by Cee Lo Green from Gnarls Barkley and P. Diddy's protégée Janelle Monáe. Coke has flirted with the entertainment industry for decades, once owning Columbia Pictures, but in recent years the business of selling soft drinks has become indistinguishable from the business of entertainment. But the really weird thing about this campaign is that it's all about work. The ads feature something called the 'Happiness Factory', a fantasy world that lives inside a Coca-Cola vending machine where hundreds of miniature workers operate a vast system of ingenious pulleys and levers to manufacture the customers' drinks. Admirers in the industry eulogised about how the ads were a 'true work of art' and that, tellingly, they 'made you forget you were watching an ad'. And the ads are indeed spectacular. But it is their rackety, Heath Robinson authenticity that is so maddeningly ideological. Just as the ripped and frayed and asymmetrical imperfections of modern animation are perfectly rendered by the digital technology that puts real cartoonists out of a job, the conjuring of an old-fashioned factory is a figleaf not only for the patchy working conditions of real Coke employees, but also for the very modern phenomenon of virtual, marketing-driven, half-work-half-play. There's an 'immersive' Happiness Factory gaming website, where 'users choose the role of one of the Happiness Factory workers, punch their timecard and then get to work completing a list of tasks'. Fun! And there is *Happiness Factory: The Movie*, launched at an 'online red carpet premiere event' in Second Life. The premise of one of the ads is set out thus: 'In today's busy world, everyone has become dependent on technology. While iPhones, BlackBerrys, texting and computers keep people virtually linked, they create a lack of real connection between people, causing them to morph into avatars. The unexpected sharing of a Coca-Cola between two people in a diner breaks down digital walls and creates a human connection through a moment of happiness.' This, again, is dazzlingly ideological: the invocation of real-world human pleasures as part of an online marketing campaign, masquerading as a critique of a world in which simple human pleasures have been taken over by work and internet technology. Brilliant.

Any flavour you like, as long as it's vanilla

'It is news to no one, not even me, that eroticism in popular culture is a twenty-four-hour, all-you-can-eat buffet,' wrote Lawrence Downes in a 2006 *New York Times* op-ed piece. This view is broadly echoed by

Ariel Levy in *Female Chauvinist Pigs*, Pamela Paul in *Pornified* and Natasha Walter in *Living Dolls*. The feminist critique in these books is spot on: waiting in Venice airport recently I caught sight of not one but two enormous bra adverts, one on either side of the departures board. 'Raunch culture' is everywhere, from Britney Spears to art-house burlesque; and ever-younger girls are being recruited into the act. Primark has been caught marketing knickers to seven-year-olds that bear the slogan 'You've scored', and Tesco has tried to flog a toy pole-dancing kit (slogan: 'Unleash the sex kitten inside'). Except that if you subtract the industrial-scale objectification of women and girls, how much hedonism do you get? Not a lot.

James Bond used to enjoy not just one conquest but two: typically, first the double agent, then the triple agent. But as the prodigious philosopher and psychoanalyst Slavoj Žižek has noted, *Quantum of Solace*, released in 2008, was the first film out of twenty-two in which the Bond girl only gets kissed. Remember *9½ Weeks*? That steamy 1986 tale of an affair between Mickey Rourke and Kim Basinger may have been naughty, but it was also mainstream. Contrast that with today's coyly scrubbed-up cinematic fare. Or weigh up the relative amounts of nudity in *Porky's* (1982) and *American Pie* (1999). The rules governing the display of erect penises are neurotically strict (like God, the great phallus cannot be shown; its power can only be implied). The famous nanosecond crotch shot in *Basic Instinct* (1992) was hardly a viable source of erotic stimulation, even for those who were quick with their pause buttons. But it was one of the last real glimpses of rudeness before Hollywood's legs were slammed shut. Janet Jackson's breast, exposed by Justin Timberlake for half a second during the 2004 Super Bowl half-time show, was suspiciously pre-fitted with a 'nipple shield'. Even so, it prompted national outrage, an immediate crackdown on indecency in broadcasting, and a record fine for CBS of $550,000. Our world is full of what psychologists call reaction formations: where anxiety-producing impulses are managed through the exaggeration of the directly opposing tendency. All kinds of topsy-turvy phenomena result, from the sexualisation of young girls and the simultaneous panic about paedophilia, to the rise of obesity in the West combined with an obsessional dieting culture. There has got to be something weird going on when a half-second shot of part of one breast produces such a conniption. It seems that in the twenty-first century, having genuine freedom in our sights makes us come over all Victorian.

In contrast to the reputedly colourful private lives of Cary Grant, Judy Garland and Marlene Dietrich, today's pop stars and film icons emphasise their traditional morality and domestic ideals. I'm not saying there's a complete lack of freedom or fun; it's just that there's so little variety compared to what you'd expect, given the lack of constraints. *NME* 'Cool List' topper Laura Marling says she hates being around people doing drugs, boy band the Jonas Brothers proudly sport their chastity rings, and British rapper Tinie Tempah says he prays 'as much as possible'. The actors Emma Thompson and Maggie Gyllenhaal have urged the US readers of *Good Housekeeping* to take their example and discover the joys of housework. 'If you give it the time, it's profoundly enjoyable,' Thompson explained. And Gyllenhaal finds 'so much pleasure' in going to where her husband (actor Peter Sarsgaard) is working and 'tidying up his trailer'. We are, in theory, liberated enough to live out any number of sexual scenarios and arrangements, but our social mores are in practice much more conservative than the ménages of Weimar Germany or the Bloomsbury set. Perversity is allowed by law, but laughed out of court. S&M, leather and gimpery are ridiculed as freakish nerdism. Sex shops used to be appropriately seedy hovels of semi-legal intrigue; now they are coy temples to burlesque 'girl-power'. 'Harmony' chain stores set the tone: they are bright, clean and professional. The porn industry has expanded and diversified in recent years, but for all the niche markets it caters for it is also curiously uniform. Porn stars look identical, with their 'whatever' eyes, fake tans and obligatory Brazilians; and they mime through a series of moves as strictly routine as the positions of classical ballet.

Slavoj Žižek correctly observes how society, like some passive-aggressive grandmother, is forever telling us to 'Enjoy!' The injunction to be hedonistic is something of a turn-off. But if sex is everywhere, it's also nowhere. When did you last see a genuinely hot evocation of real passion in a film, or on TV? Sex has been co-opted for the marketing of products, but in the last few years even that is on the wane: the classic Flake advert which draws a not very subtle analogy between eating a chocolate bar and performing fellatio now looks almost charmingly retro. *Carry On* films appear to the modern eye to be bafflingly preoccupied with innuendo. It seems that Freud's account of the sex drive underlying all aspects of our lives is finally being superseded by a rampantly mutating corporate culture that's realised that even better than using sex to sell us products is to make products themselves the Thing. Prostitution notwithstanding, sex used to be one area of life that was sacrosanct; not in the sense of being holy, obviously, but in the sense of being out of reach of the demands of capitalism: because you can get it for free. That's why the corporate world had to divert our attention towards something that actually makes some money. I keep thinking about Saatchi's 'make.believe' ad campaign for Sony Ericsson, in which twentysomething lovelies bounce down the street on multicoloured space hoppers with faces drawn on them, filming each other on their phones. 'What if dreams could become reality?' the campaign asks. 'We're here to make it happen.' Forget idealism: the real dream is to convince us that commercially packaged childlike fun is better than sex – and its realisation doesn't seem that far off. The apparent abundance of sex in our culture is an ideological cover for this commercial incursion into the most secret corners of our private lives, a campaign to put us off this precious source of independent pleasure. It creates the impression that we're all having a crazy time, when what we're actually doing is working too hard and spending our free time on eBay.

What about the interweb, you might ask. Isn't that opening up a whole new world of naughty possibilities? The rise of new technology in the nineties was indeed accompanied by some fevered speculation. In 1992, Mike Saenz, a creator of early cybersex CD ROMs (I do like the oxymoron of a sexy CD ROM), made a series of predictions in *Future Sex* magazine. First Generation Cybersex (1992) involves 'simple interaction in a pornographic video game'. Second Generation

Cybersex (1995) would involve a '3D display' and a '3D input device (glove)'. By 2000 we'd be donning 'multiple 3D tactile feedback/input devices (gloves, shorts, helmet)', and 2020 would see the invention of the 'orgasmatron', 'an all-in-one helmet system with direct brain feed'. Had he been watching Woody Allen's 1973 film *Sleeper*, I wonder. Even now there is endless media hype about social networking sites enabling young people to hook up for after-school orgies. Because some teenagers post news of their sexual conquests on Facebook, it's assumed that they have no boundaries, either sexual or digital. The founder of Facebook, Mark Zuckerberg, has argued that privacy is no longer a social norm. But that's because he's overlooking the Byzantine privacy codes that govern young people's lives online. As the internet researcher and ex-anthropologist Danah Boyd has shown, young people maintain strictly regulated tabs on who sees their profiles. It is big corporations that are trying to break down those privacy codes, not teenagers, in order to sell them tailored products. The internet fosters conservatism as well as sexual possibility. Content filters proliferate, and the potential for revelation becomes a prompt for prudery. You might think twice about misbehaving if there's a chance it'll turn up on Twitter.

So much of our attention is focused on the internet becoming a conduit for sex that we are failing to take account of how new technology – the ultimate consumer fetish – is becoming an object of desire in itself. 'YouTube' now outstrips 'sex' in internet search popularity. Anyone who has watched with gadget lust as Steve Jobs unveiled his latest creation on a dimly lit stage, anyone who is susceptible to the charms of a 'superphone' called the 'HTC Desire', anyone who has turned around in an IMAX cinema to face row upon row of captivated spectators wearing outsize 3D glasses, has witnessed at first hand technology's weird sublimations. Some aspects of technology are like crude substitutes for the real thing – the suggestive joystick or the portal as a kind of virtual vagina – but there's something about the magic of new technology which distracts us from sex altogether. It's a combination of the toy you never owned as a child, a religious relic, and *The Hitchhiker's Guide to the Galaxy*. None of which is especially hot. Perhaps the most telling proof of this unsex-appeal is that the Wii has not come up with what is surely its most obvious application. Instead of indulging in raciness, we play Nintendo's 'Mario Kart' till three o'clock in the morning.

Technology is not only taking over from sex; it's becoming a lot like work. As the writer Steven Poole has acutely observed, computer games – once the escapist fantasy of many a teenage boy – are now structured like the day job, with players slogging through a labyrinthine series of preordained tasks. Even apparently open and creative games such as The Sims contain buried rules: Sims don't go off and found communes – they live in the suburbs, commute to work, and like shopping. Poole reminds us of the prescient insights of the critical theorists Theodor Adorno and Max Horkheimer, who as early as 1947 wrote that 'amusement under late capitalism is the prolongation of work ... mechanisation has such power over a man's leisure and happiness, and so profoundly determines the manufacture of amusement goods, that his experiences are inevitably after-images of the work process itself ... what happens at work, in the factory, or in the office can only be escaped from by approximation to it in one's leisure time'. Technology has not created a 'problem of leisure'; it has made leisure into work. We can't even sit back and watch TV these days: we're expected to get busy with our red buttons. And the fact that computers are the portal for both work and leisure has compromised people's ability to switch off at the end of the day. If you've been checking emails or surfing the net at the office, why stop when you get home?

The emphasis in our gadgety age may be on fun, but it's a weird, new kind of fun. Like the Eloi, the feeble future race in H.G. Wells's 1895 novel *The Time Machine*, who are childlike, have a short attention span and sit around all day gently playing, our fun is structured and stupefied. It's watching a zany viral video while you eat a sandwich at your desk. Or taking part in T-Mobile's 'flashmob dance-a-thon' as you film it on your smartphone. The psychoanalyst Adam Phillips has pointed to a great taboo of our times: that it's not how much people want to have sex, but how little. In the very best sense, sex is hard work. After a long day in the office, or looking after children, or after you've been with the same person for twenty-five years, you don't always feel like it. Rather than putting the hours in, and reaping the rich rewards of intimacy, it's easier to fiddle with your iPhone.

Artistic licence

The illusion of freedom not only influences our attitudes towards sex, but also towards that other supposedly non-utilitarian realm: culture. When Salman Rushdie's novel *The Satanic Verses* was denounced as blasphemous against Islam in 1989, culminating in a *fatwa* demanding the author's death, even the Conservative government of the time stood up for the principle of freedom of speech, and paid for Rushdie's police protection. Yet when Rushdie received a knighthood in 2007, members of the liberal elite as well as Tory MPs expressed their concerns about the 'Muslim reaction' around the world. Cultural risk-taking is fine, as long as nobody takes offence. In the past, cultural censorship came from the conservative Right. Nowadays, as the critic Mark Lawson pointed out after images of young naked girls by Nan Goldin and Richard Prince were removed by the Baltic and Tate Modern galleries on police advice, there is bleeding-heart censorship in the name of protecting women or children. In 1977, visitors to the Galleria d'Arte Moderna in Bologna had to squeeze between the naked bodies of performance artist Marina Abramović and her boyfriend Ulay, standing facing each other in the doorway. But when the installation was repeated at New York's MOMA in 2010, this time with actors, Abramović had to attend daily security meetings. 'In 1977 there was no problem, and it looks like now there is a problem,' she said in an interview. 'Why is there a problem with nudity?'

Another prime example of this stealthy trend towards cultural containment is what's happened to buskers on the London Underground over the last ten years. In 2001, busking was defined as an 'illegal and unregulated activity', and a new law was passed to permit it under licence. Together with Viacom Outdoor (now CBS Outdoor, the international advertising conglomerate currently filling public transport with advertising TV screens), LU created the Carling Live Underground Music scheme. Buskers now had to perform on weird demarcated pitches, stickers on the floor in the shape of a stage, adorned with Carling advertising. They were 'chosen on talent, with emphasis strongly placed on meeting the wide-ranging musical tastes of Tube passengers'. 'We at Carling are committed to supporting new emerging Underground talents,' a press officer announced, and stories were released to the press about artists being 'discovered' by big record companies and being invited to play for the Queen (although they weren't allowed to sell their own CDs). This is a familiar story of corporatisation and regulatory control, but it's the legitimating language that is really maddening. The phrase 'legalised licensed busking' implies a kind of liberation, but with gossamer strings attached – buskers have to meet the musical tastes of Tube passengers, albeit with that insidious disclaimer 'wide-ranging'; and the impression is created of fostering grassroots talent, with a double meaning extracted from the word 'Underground'. Banksy, the anonymous graffiti artist welcomed by the establishment with open arms, provides another illustration of our culture's self-consciously 'edgy' attitude towards cultural subversion. His iconoclastic murals have been shown in Tate Britain, the British Museum and four major New York galleries, and fetch handsome sums at auction: *Bomb Middle England*, a screen-printed canvas showing elderly lady bowlers rolling grenades across a lawn, fetched £102,000 at Sotheby's in 2007. The jury is out as to whether his anti-establishment positioning is ironic, and many people are wise to his bourgeois sanctification, but he is still emblematic of a broader cultural habit of co-option in denial.

Banksy and busking perform a useful function for the cultural establishment, because they serve as a kind of safety valve. I don't want to suggest that this is a problem across the board: I see brilliant and challenging exhibitions, plays and films all the time. But there's a creeping risk aversion in our cultural mainstream, and it's justified by reference to an imaginary (and conservative) popular will. Our current cultural landmarks are often unexpectedly retro and nostalgic, with *Gosford Park* and *The King's Speech* in the cinema and *Downton Abbey* and *Mad Men* on the TV. In contrast to the militant modernism of 1980s synthpop, there is no musical Sound of Now; as the music writer Simon Reynolds has noted in *Retromania: Pop Culture's Addiction to its Own Past*, we just have (albeit excellent) pastiches and harkings back to the late twentieth century *à la* Arcade Fire, the Wild Beasts and the xx. It seems that we still crave old structures, whether of work, lifestyle, social class, or musical genre. A whiff of the obscure or difficult brings on a quivering loss of nerve. Publicly funded art has to be seen to have a social or economic impact. Accessibility is mandatory, and popular culture is eulogised for appealing to all. Avant-garde culture, on the other hand, is routinely dismissed as elitist; but as the philosopher Nina Power observes, the avant garde does not necessarily shut people out: it opens a radical window on how society might be otherwise. It's for this reason that the most ostensibly depressing plays by Samuel Beckett are oddly uplifting.

But if many cultural institutions are suffering from a loss of nerve, restrictions on cultural free expression are also the result of audiences' self-imposed norms. Miroslaw Bałka's 2009 installation *How It Is* at Tate Modern was an open, free, user-orientated installation, allowing people to literally get inside an experiential work of art and engage with it however they chose. But the vast majority of those who entered the pitch darkness of Bałka's cavernous bunker did so in an attitude of respectful awe. John Cage intended his notoriously unscored 1952 composition *4′33″* to be an opportunity to hear whatever ambient sounds happened to be around: coughing, shoe-shuffling, a door being opened and shut. Cage was drawing attention to the impossibility of true silence. But modern audiences tend to receive the piece in a reverential and embarrassed hush.

The new era of 'democratic participation' in public art is often hailed as an opportunity to break down traditional bastions of deference, but in reality it often works in the opposite direction. Take for example those visitor-friendly exhibitions that feature one object per room which you're allowed to touch. Seems benign enough. But that object buys people's tacit consent not to touch any of the others. The Institute of Chicago may have created a new 'Touch Gallery', but it offers up an exception that proves the dominant silent rule. 'Please do not touch objects located elsewhere in the museum,' the signs politely remind us. 'With your cooperation, we can preserve the Art Institute's treasures for future generations.' Cooperation is key: many galleries have replaced ropes in front of pictures with a thin ridge on the floor that you feel with your feet. That ridge is our acquiescence in material form. I'd rather be governed by the kind of up-front attitude I saw in an ancient sign fading on the wall of London's Royal Academy: 'IT IS STRICTLY FORBIDDEN TO TOUCH ANY EXHIBIT.' At least you know where you are.

In 2009, Antony Gormley wrote that his *One & Other* installation, allowing 2,400 members of the public to spend an hour on the empty fourth plinth in Trafalgar Square, 'has provided an open space of possibility for many to test their sense of self and how they might communicate this to a wider world'. The comedian Frank Skinner echoed the enthusiasm of many when he commented that 'The fact that a corner of one of our most famous landmarks has been given over to a group of ordinary citizens, to do with it what they will, is a fabulous symbol of freedom and free speech.' Yet there was relatively little nudity, public defecation or other evidence of iconoclastic rebellion. Offered an 'open space of possibility', many participants spent their hour just kind of standing there, texting their friends. Under the permanent surveillance of a CCTV-like webcam, and hedged around with health and safety netting, *One & Other* didn't look like a 'fabulous symbol of freedom' to me; it was more like an unwitting symbol of our tentativeness, of our individual and collective fear of freedom.

The secret policeman

Self-control can be a necessary, even a good thing. But it's also an example of the next in our series of mendacious ideological methods:

external expectations passing as our own intentions. When twenty-four-hour licensing laws were introduced in the UK in November 2005, the authorities and the media feared that round-the-clock drinking would ensue, with revellers partying until the early hours, vandalising property and committing rampant street crime. A report by British judges warned of an 'inevitable explosion' in rape and other violent offences. Another report, by the Association of Chief Police Officers, warned that 'One only has to look to popular holiday destinations to see the effect of allowing British youth unrestricted access to alcohol.' In the fevered imagination of the *Daily Mail*, 'British town centres may come to resemble squalid foreign party destinations such as the notorious Greek resort of Faliraki.'

Yet a review three years later found that only 3 per cent of pubs or clubs had applied for twenty-four-hour licences, and there was negligible evidence that the change had resulted in a rise in crime. Alcohol-related illness and crime is still a problem in countries like the UK, but the change in licensing laws did not change the culture of drinking, with people still uncomplainingly finishing up their pints at eleven, even when they could now carry on till twelve. It's a similar situation with drugs: the classification system can be read as a kind of neurotic response to the visions of unbridled excess that drugs conjure up in the minds of lawmakers. But the Netherlands, where the use of cannabis is broadly tolerated by the law, has one of the lowest rates of adult use in Europe. Britain is seeing a new moderation in drug use which has surprised those experts who predicted that the rising late-twentieth-century trend would carry on up and up. In 1995, nearly 50 per cent of all young people in the UK said they had taken drugs. By 2010 the figure had dropped to 20 per cent. The pervasive yet 'soft' injunctions against casual sex, smoking and overeating are met with a new voluntary compliance. We choose low-fat yoghurt and go to the gym. A family-friendly Puritanism has disinfected Las Vegas and Times Square. Modern political watchwords are 'responsibility' and 'respect'. In a culture which is both infantile and over-responsible, adults spend their weekends reading Harry Potter books while their teenage children apply for internships; and knackered mortgage-slaves drink a bit too much wine in front of *Law and Order*, with every bottle carrying a reminder to 'drink responsibly'.

What these warnings about sexual licence, binge drinking and drug use illustrate is that we persist in imagining that we are essentially free agents, and that without constant legislation and guidance we would descend into hedonistic anarchy. But civility, politeness and social protocol order our lives. We observe a hundred unspoken rules a day, rules which are brilliantly illustrated in TV shows like *Seinfeld* and *Curb Your Enthusiasm*: the 10 p.m. cut-off for phone calls, or the law against double-dipping crudités. Larry David is unusual in making them explicit. For all the talk of an imminent switch to 'active' 'on-demand' TV-watching, research in both the UK and the US shows that we've never spent longer in front of the box (on average, nearly four hours a day in the UK and five in the US). And 80 per cent of this viewing is of the old-fashioned, linear variety. Human passivity is hugely underestimated, and being a couch potato is not the same as being free.

In 1939, before the age of post-modern 'liberty', the German sociologist Norbert Elias published *The Civilizing Process*, a two-volume work that traced the historical development in Europe of *habitus*, or 'second nature', the seemingly instinctive forms of behaviour that are in fact moulded by social codes. For Elias, the twentieth-century assumption that it is not the done thing to spit, vomit or urinate at the dinner table, to fornicate in public, or to commit acts of uncontrolled violence, did not evolve naturally. Those codes were developed in the sixteenth and seventeenth centuries, via the example set by Renaissance court culture. Modern civilised values came into being through the conformist social avoidance of shame. And Elias goes on to describe how communal etiquettes such as eating with cutlery in public were internalised into the self-regulating habit of eating with cutlery even when alone at home. A later articulation of this soft power would be Freud's superego, the personalised copy of the Highway Code inscribed on our hearts. Or our pants.

Norbert Elias's groundbreaking ideas were developed by two French scholars, Michel de Certeau and Pierre Bourdieu. De Certeau came up with two key concepts: the strategy and the tactic. The strategy was the dominant way of doing things, sanctioned by institutional norms and the powers that be. The tactic was the means by which individuals amended and shaped these strategies to fit their own particular needs or desires, for example altering a story while you read it to a child, or tweaking a recipe. While de Certeau stressed the power of individuals to improvise, to refashion the materials they were given, Bourdieu criticised the debilitating power of social and institutional codes: what he called 'the order of things'. As far as I know, Bourdieu is never name-checked by behavioural economists, but he was an early opponent of rational-choice theory as an account of how individuals operate. He argued that people do not consciously calculate their decisions according to explicit criteria. They operate according to Elias's concept of *habitus*, by internalising societal expectations. Bourdieu mounted a powerful critique of the way in which elites portray arbitrary social arrangements as natural and universal. Those slogans on London Mayor Boris Johnson's signs banning alcohol on the Tube – 'Making everyone's journey more pleasant' – appeal to an imaginary generalised will, but are basically just there so that Boris's ilk can enjoy a civilised commute home free from the beer-swilling rabble, before popping open the Prosecco in the privacy of their own dining rooms.

The ideology of hedonistic liberty is problematic because it stops us recognising the ways in which we are not free. I'm down with the liberal critique of 'the surveillance society', but it keeps our attention focused on external, rather than internalised constraints: on the CCTV camera on every street corner rather than on our reluctance to make a scene when the boss announces a pay freeze. What do we do with the ostensibly liberating possibilities of new technology? We create highly regulated systems and rubrics for organising our online lives, like the tick-box world of Facebook. The dialect of the text message may depart from the Queen's English, but its coded abbreviations are as finicky as the 'emo' dress code. Even nonconformists are to some extent caught in the net: if climate-change protesters pride themselves on their conformity-busting eccentricity, why do so many of them have dreadlocks? It's a trivial point, perhaps, not to mention a catty one: I like climate-change protesters. But there's an important principle at stake: namely, that a perceived self-exemption creates an even bigger blind spot. In the developed West, the legacy of the Enlightenment has left us with an overrated sense of our own free will. Cognitive scientists now seem to be questioning that assumption of freedom. But they focus on hard-wiring and neural pathways, and not on the social and political pressures that, although powerful and hidden, are within our grasp to change.

I'm not opposed to rituals and routines as such: they help us get up in the morning, and oil the wheels of social interaction. They provide a frame for profound events in our lives: the births, marriages and deaths. And they constrain self-interest in favour of the greater good. There's a complicated road intersection near the library where I like to work. Cyclists, distracted pedestrian students and central London traffic all jostle for space. I'm sure there have been accidents. Anyway, there were roadworks going on there for months, and when they finally finished, the results were unexpected. Instead of more restrictions, barriers and road markings, they'd all been taken away. The whole area had been turned into a paved piazza, and there were even wooden chairs scattered around at the edges. The road planners had followed the 'shared space' model of urban planning pioneered by the Dutch road-traffic engineer Hans Monderman. He showed that if you remove all the road furniture and traffic signs, you end up with fewer accidents. Cars, cyclists and pedestrians watch out for each other more. It's a nice example of how civil people are to each other. But I find other rituals – such as the hen party and the baby shower – coyly retrograde. Organised by a friend of the bride, trying to do the right thing, hen parties second-guess the convention *du jour*, from spa weekends to cupcake decorating to flower-arranging classes. It's post-feminist hell on an invisible three-line whip. The mushrooming of regulation and audit culture betrays a lack of belief on the part of lawmakers and politicians that left to our own devices we tend to keep ourselves in check. The hidden traffic cameras that snap us unawares driving down a one-way short cut are a money-spinning betrayal of the social contract, the unspoken understanding which keeps the majority of motorway drivers to a reasonable seventy-one miles per hour. For better or for worse, we can usually be trusted to behave.

It seems like a paradox of the modern world that despite our ostensibly free choices, despite an emphasis on individuality and creativity and personal reinvention, we all tend to choose the same things: to live in IKEA-furnished houses and get hooked on the same HBO box set. But this uniformity is not really paradoxical: it's a clue to the covert workings of ideology. The first few times my baby son looked at his reflection in the mirror, he smiled uncertainly, then looked at me as if to confirm that the image in the mirror was indeed him. I smiled back in what I hoped was an affirming manner, and he looked satisfied, as if he'd got it. In 1949, the French philosopher Jacques Lacan came up with a theory to account for precisely this moment. He called it the 'mirror stage', and argued that it was foundational to human identity. Identity, he explained, was defined by the relationship between the individual and society. And the mirror stage was the microcosm of this relationship, because in that moment, the infant looks to the authoritative adult to ratify his proper existence in the world. For Lacan, this moment lay behind all those little ways in which our society and culture help to define who we are.

Another French thinker, Louis Althusser, applied Lacan's idea of the mirror stage to the following situation. You are walking down the street, minding your own business, when a policeman calls out, 'Hey, you there!' Instinctively, obediently, you turn around to see what he wants. To Althusser, this response went beyond mere compliance. It was these kinds of interactions that gave us our social – and therefore our essential – existence. 'By this mere one-hundred-and-eighty-degree physical conversion', Althusser wrote, one 'becomes a *subject*'. For Althusser, the word 'subject' has a rather bleak double meaning: on the one hand it means a human subject, a conscious, active individual; on the other it implies 'subjection' to the social order. In other words, you only become a person in society by submitting to its definitions and demands. No wonder ideology is so seductive: it makes us feel real and whole. This doesn't just apply to being accosted by a policeman. It's there any time anyone says 'Hello,' 'Excuse me' or 'Thank you' – those little rituals of politeness and convention make us into credible members of society. It's why 'chuggers' (those eager clipboard-brandishing charity workers who collar you in the high street) and people who hand out free newspapers at the entrance to Tube stations are so irritating: because they exploit the bonds of civility that are really fundamental, and really hard to break.

I'm not saying we should all be striving for true freedom. Contrary to the fantasies peddled by those adverts for cars and mobile phones, true freedom is an impossible state of affairs to sustain. And I don't believe that most people really want it anyway – just think of all those city-dwellers who give up their jobs and move to some rural idyll in France or Italy, only to find themselves staring into an abyss of madness, whereupon they return to the urban groove with a sigh of relief. Freedom is terrifying because it entails looking squarely at what we really want, and whether or not it's achievable. And to paraphrase both Jacques Lacan and Oscar Wilde, there's only one thing worse than not getting what you want, and that is getting what you want. Because what do you do then? In his 1942 book *The Fear of Freedom*, the psychologist and social theorist Erich Fromm describes how the act of breaking away from authority or oppression is often accompanied by feelings of emptiness and anxiety. Those feelings only go away when the old order is replaced with a new one. I do believe that it's possible to make conscious choices to live in different ways. I'm certainly more optimistic about our ability to change the world than all those cognitive realists and evolutionary psychologists who downplay our free will to an illogical extent, who say our behaviour is determined by our brains and our genes. But we need to think harder about the ways we are and are not free in order to make better use of the capacities we have. The endless touting of liberty in our culture, and our blind spots about norms and routines, stop us recognising the contours of our choices – both conscious and subconscious. Not only do they put us under constant pressure to be happy and have fun all the time, they also allow the limiting influences of corporate marketing and regressive social convention to pass as our own desires.

Even if we can't completely remove the constraints that shape our lives, simply seeing them is the first step to changing them for the better.

EIGHT

Science Fiction

Faith in facts

'All the great religions have a place for awe, for ecstatic transport at the wonder and beauty of creation,' wrote Richard Dawkins in 1997. 'And it's exactly this feeling of spine-shivering, breath-catching awe – almost worship – this flooding of the chest with ecstatic wonder, that modern science can provide.' It's ironic that Dawkins, the arch secularist, would use such religious language. But those who speak up for science in our culture now capitalise on the appeal of wonder. 'I'm an atheist,' said maths professor Marcus du Sautoy when he took up the prestigious Charles Simonyi Chair for the Public Understanding of Science at Oxford University. 'But for me the important thing is the wonder of science.' There's pop-star physicist Brian Cox's hugely successful TV series and books on the *Wonders of the Universe*. There's a British government select committee report on 'Introducing Wonder' to the National Curriculum. There are scores of science-education books with titles like *A Head Start on Science: Encouraging a Sense of Wonder* and *Organizing Wonder: Making Inquiry Science Work in the Elementary Classroom*. The Science Museum's 'World Wonders Trail' asks visitors: 'What would you choose to be an eighth wonder of the scientific world?' There's the World of Wonders science museum in California, and the cultish Silicon Valley-orientated TED (Technology, Entertainment and Design) conference in 2011 was entitled 'The Rediscovery of Wonder'.

Of course, for Dawkins and his fellow scientists, there's a crucial difference between religion and science. Religion is about belief, and science is about evidence. I'm an atheist myself, and I'm a big fan of science. But I have a serious problem with wonder. Because despite all the talk of public engagement, it creates an inaccessible, anti-intellectual aura around science which has little to do with what actually goes on in labs. Scientific wonder carries with it a sense of humility, which is ostensibly about meekness in the face of extraordinary facts. But it blurs into deference towards scientists, with their privileged access to those facts. A small but revealing illustration of this is the brochure for a 2010 science festival that introduced a talk by Dawkins as follows: 'He will take us through how science is done, why we should have confidence in its findings, and why a little scientific understanding can greatly enhance our awe, wonder and enjoyment of the universe around us, and make us realise how lucky we are to be alive.' When Stephen Hawking's book *The Grand Design: New Answers to the Ultimate Questions of Life* came out in 2010, I was brought up short in the street by a priceless *Evening Standard* newsboard. 'God Does Not Exist – Hawking', it said. No shit, Sherlock, I thought. But it's because of the fact that we deify Hawking as utterly authoritative on life, the universe and everything that his word on the matter is considered news. In modern culture, scientism is the new religion. God knows what's happened to scepticism.

Scientism is a form of faith that is particularly hard to discern, furthermore, because it appears to be all about down-to-earth facts, about the way things really are. As I'll be arguing in this chapter, that makes it possible for popular science to make all sorts of speculative and frankly dodgy claims about human nature. Since the advent of secularism, having a religious identity is increasingly the result of a positive, deliberate choice. From evangelical Christianity to devout Islam, religion today declares itself as an overt belief system, with explicit creeds and doctrines. Modern scientism, by contrast, involves covert leaps of faith.

So it's interesting that talk of a 'new Enlightenment' is everywhere: in the indomitable polemicist Christopher Hitchens's *God is Not*

Great (2007), in the cognitive linguist George Lakoff's *The Political Mind* (2008), and in a *Guardian* article by the columnist Madeleine Bunting, announcing her Damascene conversion to a new field of enquiry which is 'radically challenging the most fundamental assumptions on which human beings operate ... This is such dramatic stuff that Matthew Taylor at the Royal Society of Arts ... argues that we are on the verge of a new Enlightenment.' Omnipotent man, we are often told, has been knocked off his pedestal by three great revolutions: the Copernican discovery that the universe does not revolve around planet Earth, the Darwinian discovery that humans are mere animals, and the Freudian discovery that the rational mind is undermined by the wayward unconscious. And we appear to be teetering on the edge again. In the preface to the 2003 edition of his book *The Blank Slate*, which argues that humans are born with a powerful set of genetic predispositions, the linguist Steven Pinker argues that 'the Blank Slate is ... a doctrine that is widely embraced as a rationale for meaning and morality and that is under assault from the sciences of the day. As in the century following Galileo, our moral sensibilities will adjust to the biological facts.' This 'new Enlightenment' is the neo-Darwinian and neuroscientific breaching of the ultimate scientific frontier: the comprehensive understanding of human nature.

1975 saw the publication of a book entitled *Sociobiology: The New Synthesis*. Written by a biologist called E.O. Wilson, it introduced neo-Darwinian theories to a general readership. Wilson argued that the social behaviour of humans, as well as that of ants and bees, is a product of evolutionary history. That all aspects of our lives – from warfare to fashion – are shaped by natural selection for reproductive success. That since we are never off 'the genetic leash', free will is an illusion. He came up with some remarkable statements. 'Even with identical education and equal access to all professions,' he wrote, 'men are likely to continue to play a disproportionate role in political life, business and science.' Wilson's thesis was incredibly influential. Steven Pinker and the philosopher Daniel Dennett developed it in bestsellers such as *The Language Instinct* (1994) and *Darwin's Dangerous Idea* (1995). 'We are survival machines,' wrote Richard Dawkins, 'robot vehicles blindly programmed to preserve the selfish molecules known as genes.' These arguments were popular far beyond academia. Books, articles and TV programmes brought them to a broad and enthusiastic audience.

The dissection of human behaviour by evolutionary psychology was joined by cognitive neuroscience in the nineties. In his 1994 book *The Astonishing Hypothesis: The Scientific Search for the Soul*, Francis Crick, the co-discoverer of the DNA helix who turned to the study of consciousness later in life, announced to his readers that 'You, your joys and sorrows, your memories and your ambitions, your sense of personal identity and free will are in fact ... nothing but a pack of neurons.' Since then, a flood of books have promised to impart revolutionary discoveries that will change the way we think, the way we think about thinking, the way we see the world, and the way we see our own place within it: from Jonah Lehrer's *The Decisive Moment: How the Brain Makes Up its Mind* to Lone Frank's *Mindfield: How Brain Science is Changing Our World* to V.S. Ramachandran's *The Tell-Tale Brain: Unlocking the Mystery of Human Nature*. 'Our world is about to be revolutionised,' reads the blurb for Frank's book. 'The way we see economics, health, and law enforcement will change. Our perception of happiness, advertising, and even morality will be turned upside down.' The evolutionary biologist Armand Leroi added his endorsement by predicting that 'The coming Neurorevolution will destroy your certainties – but maybe set you free.' Neuroscience gets the biggest research grants and attracts the brightest, ahem, brains. In the coming years, says Ramachandran, a neurologist, its findings will transform the way 'we view ourselves and our place in the cosmos'. We are 'poised for the greatest revolution of all – understanding the human brain. This will surely be a turning point in the history of the human species.'

As I'm about to argue, bombastic and highly questionable assertions about diverse aspects of human life are now couched in terms of hard fact. And these grand claims meet little resistance in a culture that regards science as above debate. In 2009, Barack Obama lifted the ban on federal funding for stem-cell research by announcing that 'The promise that stem cells hold does not come from any particular ideology; it is the judgement of science.' Obama's stance may be admirable, but it's an illustration of how science is assumed to transcend political decision-making. This reverence for science as a neutral and absolute arbiter in contentious issues presents us with the next spell in ideology's magic book: to present partisan arguments as natural and universal facts. Since science is regarded as value-free, it is invoked to lend legitimacy to positions that are distinctly value-laden. Particular agendas now appear in an authoritative guise as 'discoveries' imbued with the cachet of empirical truth. The key to scientism's persuasiveness, in other words, is in the way it purports to be above persuasion.

I'm not saying that science is always bound up with ideology, either overt or covert. It's possible, at least in principle, for science to be ideology-free. It has a methodology that strives to take context, influence and perception into account. That's not always the case in practice, as documented in doctor and columnist Ben Goldacre's book *Bad Science*, and in historian of science Steven Shapin's *Never Pure: Historical Studies of Science as if it was Produced by People with Bodies, Situated in Time, Space, Culture, and Society, and Struggling for Credibility and Authority*. Research is often swayed by funding and fashion. But proper science strives to be neutral.

In this chapter I'll be exploring scientism's covert ideologies where they are both pernicious and naturalised, in relation to gender difference, fertility, childbirth and parenthood. I'll be talking about how both genetics and neuroscience are recruited to the task of presenting a particular organisation of human affairs as objectively correct. And I'll be arguing that science should be a tool for overt ideologies, a way of enabling us to achieve democratically agreed ideals.

Because despite our implicit faith in science, we've become oddly reticent about channelling its capabilities. Instead, we've started to confuse science with nature, with a reductive sense of inevitability. At the same time as we believe scientists' grand claims to understand how we work, we limit the variety and potential of human experience to a narrow idea of what's natural. And at the very moment at which our scientific hubris is reaching an infotech and biotech peak, we're doing our best to convince ourselves that we don't really have much agency, much ability to improve the world or do things differently. We're diverting precious resources and attention up a blind alley labelled human nature; poring over the firing of neurons instead of making simple vital decisions that could save our race from extinction. As a society, we could be using science to test assumptions and deliver priorities. But instead, for all scientism's revolutionary language, we're using it not only to justify the status quo, but to drag us back to a primitive past.

Basic instincts

Because what do all these world-changing, certainty-wrecking new ideas reveal? That 'maternal instinct is wired into the brain', that men are generally good at 'systematising' and women at 'empathy', and that 'Blue is for boys but girls really do prefer pink.' The first bombshell is from a 2008 article in the *New York Times* about a Tokyo study in which a group of mothers had their brains scanned while they watched videos of their babies smiling and then crying. Not surprisingly, when the babies cried, the mothers' brains displayed agitation. The researchers concluded that this response was 'biologically meaningful in terms of adaptation to specific demands associated with successful infant care'. It did not conclude that the mothers' responses might have been honed through experience and social expectation. And the study didn't do dads.

The second is from a 2010 *Guardian* article headlined 'It's not sexist to accept that biology affects behaviour' by the psychopathologist Simon Baron-Cohen, who argues that because there are many more male mathematicians than female ones, men must be better at doing difficult abstract things with their brains than women. I'd like him to have witnessed the horrified incomprehension among my friends when I chose to do physics at A-Level. It certainly taught me the importance of social context.

And the third is from a *Times* article of 2007 that reported, along with the rest of the world's media, on the findings of a study by

Newcastle University scientists which suggested an evolutionary basis for why men like blue and women like pink. 'At last', the article announced, 'science discovers' that parents who dress their boys in blue and their girls in pink 'may not just be following tradition but some deep-seated evolutionary instinct'. While male hunter-gatherers needed to be able to detect blue skies propitious for hunting, the researchers speculated, females would have needed skills in gathering ripe, red fruits and identifying flushed, emotional faces in their roles as 'care-givers' and 'empathisers'. But prior to the mid-twentieth century it was actually boys, rather than girls, who were dressed in pink, because pink symbolised strength. In 1914, the *Sunday Sentinel*, an American newspaper, advised mothers on how to dress their children with the following formula: 'Use pink for the boy and blue for the girl, if you are a follower of convention.' As Ben Goldacre, Cordelia Fine and Natasha Walter have all observed in their great books on bad science and sexism, scientists' enthusiasm for pursuing this kind of research is more than matched by the media's delight in de-nuancing the results. In 2004, a *Sunday Telegraph* science journalist wrote that 'in recent years, various studies have concluded that sex differences are more than skin deep: the brains of men and women handle language and emotion in different ways, with differences in brain structure. This, in turn, may reflect our evolutionary past, and how men's brains were optimised to hunt and women's to gather.'

That *Sunday Telegraph* article reminds me of a time when those who claimed a scientific basis for gender difference were generally confined to the conservative end of the political spectrum. Now they're on the liberal left, too. Progressive broadsheets report scientific 'evidence' suggesting that it's men's competitive aptitudes that explain why they succeed in the top jobs, and women's nurturing empathies that explain why they are left holding the baby. Simon Baron-Cohen concluded his *Guardian* article on a feminism-friendly note, saying, 'There is plenty we can do to make public life both more attractive and more accessible to women, including making prime ministerial debates less like a boxing fight, general elections less like tribal warfare, and the House of Commons' working practices more family-friendly.'

This modern, politically correct talk of change masks a regressive and determinist view of women's capabilities. Whenever people talk piously about making politics less pugnacious, it sounds as if being pugnacious is a bad thing. But combative success in the workplace is what our society rewards: the clue is in the cash. The new Enlightenment that we're supposed to be on the verge of sells us hoary old myths dressed as fresh discoveries.

As the late Stephen Jay Gould observed, evolutionary psychology is prone to telling 'just so stories' which conjure a mythical origin to justify the current status quo. We actually know very little about the hunter-gatherer past, but evolutionary psychology projects particular prejudices back onto this 'foundational' era. Likewise, brain scans are regularly misconstrued as revealing causes rather than just showing symptoms; a phenomenon which researchers from the Stanford Center for Biomedical Ethics have called 'neuro-realism'. If, as a 1996 *Newsweek* cover story indicated, men's brains light up when they see women with a waist-to-hip ratio of 0.7, this is apparently not because the ratio corresponds to the bodies of models that appear in every magazine and advert in the Western world, but because their response is determined by a hard-wired 'mental module'. In actual fact, seeing part of someone's brain light up doesn't tell you anything about the origins of that response: it just tells you it is being felt. Brain-imaging technologies are not, as Lone Frank would have it in her book *Mindfield*, offering us 'a true mirror of the soul'.

It's true that our most sophisticated imaginative feats are performed by the lump of meat called our brain. But that doesn't lead to the conclusion that our minds are any less amazing, as the reductive language of these books suggests. And it doesn't get us anywhere in explaining the myriad psychological, social, cultural and political influences on the way we think and act. Jonah Lehrer opens his book with an anecdote about landing a plane in a flight simulator and the quick decisions he had to make to avoid a crash. 'For the first time in human history,' he writes, 'we can look inside the brain and see how humans think: the black box has been broken open.' But I was immediately reminded of a gripping section in Malcolm Gladwell's book

Outliers, where he posits 'the ethnic theory of plane crashes'. In the case of both the Colombian Avianca flight 52 in 1990 and Korean Air flight 801 in 1997, the co-pilot was so loath to break his country's cultural code against contradicting one's superiors that he preferred to let the plane crash than to raise safety concerns. Those decisions, like any others, were the result of firing neurons. But to explain them in neurological terms is to miss the main issue.

The new science of human nature appears to provide radically liberating insights that can empower us all to transform our lives. That is an illusion. What this new science does is to present human beings as humble, irrational, instinctive machines which require the operational assistance of scientific experts. We are essentially naked apes, say the neo-Darwinians. Our minds may seem to be instruments of lofty reason, but they are basically a bunch of nerve cells, say the cognitive realists. The human mind 'is really just a powerful biological machine', says Jonah Lehrer; 'complete with limitations and imperfections'. According to the Royal Society of Arts' Matthew Taylor, 'Most of our behaviour, including social interaction, is the result of our brain responding automatically to the world around us rather than the outcome of conscious decision-making.' As the author Marilynne Robinson has eloquently argued in her book *Absence of Mind*, along with the polymath Raymond Tallis in *Aping Mankind*, there is a curious desire to downplay the unique capabilities of the human mind. It's as if in order to get their heads around their own minds, neuroscientists have to make the mind itself seem more simple than it actually is. Verily, we are animals. But it's amazing how quickly we lose sight of the fact that unlike all other animals, we have the capacity for ideas, intentionality, literature, art, science and idealism. The new genetic and neuroscientific determinism drastically underestimates our ability to live in ways that are not determined by stereotypes.

Popular evolutionary psychology and cognitive neuroscience claim that our lives are largely spent following a script prescribed by our genes or neurons, and that this script is now being decoded by scientists. Only scientists, in other words, are capable of telling us how to live in this new science-determined world. 'We finally have tools that can pierce the mystery of the mind, revealing the intricate machinery that shapes our behaviour,' says Jonah Lehrer. 'Now we need to put this knowledge to work.' The title of *The Invisible Gorilla*, a 2010 popular-science book by two psychologists, Christopher Chabris and Daniel Simons, is taken from a famous experiment in which a group of volunteers were shown a video of a basketball game and told to count the number of passes. Half the group failed to notice a woman in a gorilla suit walking leisurely across the court. 'Reading this book will make you less sure of yourself – and that's a good thing,' say the authors. By the end, they say, you will have gained 'a sort of "x-ray vision" into your own minds, with the ultimate goal of helping you notice the invisible gorillas in your own life'. It's the same pattern time and time again: the new science-based humility, followed by the promise of a new science-based mastery. But the ease with which the word 'Enlightenment' is bandied around these days indicates the false modesty of this new scientific 'revolution', with its grandiose claims about all aspects of human nature. It's an attempt to impose a new form of mastery over how and why we think and act. For all the talk of irrationality, it reveals the fact that we are more attached to the myth of the conscious, rational individual than ever before. The cult of scientism is profoundly hostile to the notion that there are broader social and cultural forces at work in our world, which shape our decisions and the way we live our lives. Scientism depoliticises public debate. The real invisible gorilla, I would argue, is the covertly dominant scientism in our culture that promises the revolutionary empowerment of individuals while stealthily reinforcing the authority of scientists and those who are traditionally powerful in society. I don't think we need neuroscientific x-ray vision into our own minds to notice these illusions. We don't need to be told we're irrational, and then be rescued by scientific experts. We just need to cultivate our own ordinary scepticism.

But our scepticism, along with our idealism and our sense of having real choices, is being eroded by popular scientific authorities that purport to know us better than we know ourselves, and to be able to predict how we are going to behave. Contrary to the tabloid mysticism around Stephen Hawking, there is a limit to what scientists can know, now and in the future. But the everyday business of lab work, with all its limitations and complexities, is not the version of science that is popular in our culture. Instead, it's the wonder of science that is emphasised again and again as the best way to make it accessible to the public. It's hierarchical while it purports to be democratic, and it's anti-rational while it purports to defend rationalism against religious faith. It portrays scientists as powerful gatekeepers to the mystical beyond, and it's infantilising and incapacitating for everyone else. All we can say in response is Wow.

There's another concealed power dynamic at work. Scientism's dominance is obscured by the delusion that scientists are society's underdogs. The 'God Wars' evoke the romance of embattled scientists bravely resisting the irrational majority. And I often hear scientists criticising the dominance of the arts in the media and the public conversation. Why are there never any scientists on culture shows on TV, they ask, discussing recent scientific discoveries alongside the latest exhibition, book, or film? The same complaint was made by the physicist and novelist C.P. Snow in his famous 1959 lecture 'The Two Cultures'. 'A good many times,' he said, 'I have been present at gatherings of people who, by the standards of the traditional culture, are thought highly educated and who have with considerable gusto been expressing their incredulity at the illiteracy of scientists. Once or twice I have been provoked and have asked the company how many of them could describe the Second Law of Thermodynamics. The response was cold: it was also negative. Yet I was asking something which is the scientific equivalent of: Have you read a work of Shakespeare's?'

It's true that the general public is not very well informed about what scientists actually do. But what this grievance both ignores and reinforces is the quiet dominance of scientism in our culture, stronger now even than in Snow's time. There's a reverence for science that neither scientists nor culture buffs recognise. It's reflected in the prioritisation of science education funding and the ubiquitous and generously funded public-engagement-with-science initiatives. And it's there in the 'Sci-art' collaborations aestheticising magnetic-resonance imaging or fibre optics, and funded by science organisations which, for all their talk of a two-way relationship with the arts, are primarily in search of attractive vehicles for science education. Our new-found faith in science as the hard reality, the fundamental explanation for everything, is actually justifying a radical undermining of the arts and humanities. In his 1997 bestseller *Guns, Germs and Steel*, the geographer and physiologist Jared Diamond argued that science will ultimately render history redundant, as geography explains humanity's past as well as its future destiny. Speculation about mirror neurons is taking over literary criticism and film studies, and neuroscience is often referred to as 'the new philosophy'. We may feel more comfortable talking about *Hamlet* than heat exchange, but respect is a different matter.

There are a lot of scientists in my family. When I was applying to university, I chose to study English literature. Some of my relatives thought that was a waste of a degree. I could read books in my spare time, they said. And worse still, analysing literature would take all the fun out of it. But English is what I ended up doing, and I discovered that the humanities is not just about enjoying novels or appreciating the opera, but about reading the world and questioning its received wisdoms, including those about science. It's about regarding the world not as an arrangement of rigid facts, but as a place that's open to interpretation and therefore change. Of course, science can be about that too. Good science is the sceptic's friend, spiking stereotypes and deflating myths. But right now in our culture it plays the opposite role.

It's only natural

If you visit Kenilworth Castle in Warwickshire you can take a stroll round an authentically reconstructed Elizabethan garden. The formal style is not to everyone's taste, but there's a kind of honesty about the geometric boxed beds and carefully clipped hedges. The artifice is on display. Francis Bacon, the seventeenth-century father of scientific method, probably visited Kenilworth. He certainly had designs on

Mother Nature. He dreamed about 'putting [her] on the rack and extracting her secrets', of 'storming her strongholds and secrets'. 'The true sons of knowledge', he wrote, must 'penetrate further' and find the 'secrets still locked in Nature's bosom'. 'The mechanical inventions of recent years do not merely exert a gentle guidance over Nature's courses,' he continued, 'they have the power to conquer and subdue her, to shake her to her foundations.' If Bacon's metaphors were violent, his motives were benign: the improvement of human society. And indeed from Bacon's time onwards, science was regarded as a useful tool that humans could employ for the benefit of all. But something weird has happened recently. The idealism has been jettisoned and the ambition hidden. Bacon's words may sound hubristic to our ears, but we are now trying to dominate nature as never before, only without admitting it. It's no accident that in the twenty-first century, it's the wild, indigenous, meadow look that's currently in horticultural style: the wholesale modification of nature is kept carefully out of view. In an age of forest theme parks, nature trails and eco-lodge holidays, we put nature on a public pedestal and exploit her in private. It's ironic but not surprising that in an age of unprecedented environmental destruction, we're mesmerised by David Attenborough.

Instead of admitting our influence over nature, and trying to channel it positively, we disown our own agency by conflating science with nature. We pretend that science is simply a matter of following nature's logic. But our view of nature is often a very human projection, and the projection of particular motivations and prejudices. Good-quality state-sponsored childcare may not be natural, but neither is institutional sexism. Socialism may not be natural, but neither is free-market capitalism. Even technology, the most deliberate human application of science, speaks the language of primeval justification. The founder of Facebook, Mark Zuckerberg, talks about its success in neuroscientific terms, citing research showing that users navigate the site via the faces of their friends and family: 'A huge part of our brain is hard wired to process what is going on around us and how to stay connected to people.'

This faux-natural scientism is most busily at work in areas which seem immune to ideology: the most intimate and fundamental areas of private life. Let's take for starters the age at which women have children. Yes, the biological clock is real enough, but in the Western media it has a particularly loud tick. 'The modern career woman who delays starting a family into her thirties is defying nature and risking heartbreak,' one *Independent* article warned in 2005. 'Women who try to have it all may lose the one thing that matters most – the opportunity to have a family.' Well, getting pregnant in my thirties seemed a pretty natural business to me. These newspapers' version of the 'natural' age at which to have children seems to be between twenty and twenty-nine. Headlines such as 'Well Done, Young Mum' or 'Career Women Risk Late Motherhood Heartbreak' overlay the natural reality with a whole load of cultural pressure. By using words like 'heartbreak', and gleefully printing shots of red-carpet baby bumps, the media glorifies motherhood, further ramping up the anxiety of women trying to get their careers off the ground or find a man.

And then there's the business of childbirth itself. When I was first pregnant, I read about an array of different birth options: I could have the baby on a labour ward, in a 'home-from-home' birthing unit or in the privacy of my own living room; with an epidural, with gas-and-air or in an inflatable pool. But this apparently free choice was an illusion, because it turned out that one way of giving birth – in the 'natural' birthing unit, with no 'artificial' pain relief – was prized above the others. At my NCT antenatal classes, epidurals were implicitly frowned upon as the cop-out option for lily-livered middle-class women with a low pain threshold. I read stories of tribal women in Africa and working-class women in Ireland who could just squat down and pop the baby out like the proverbial bar of soap. While stressing that she had no agenda, and that every woman was free to choose, our instructor subtly drip-fed the message that 'giving in' to pain relief was selfish because it could be bad for the baby. This was all done in a softly-softly faux-non-judgemental tone, but with an underlying note of scientific fact. Epidurals would prolong the labour by X number of minutes, and epidurals lead to Y per cent more interventions. In fact the medical data on epidurals is subtle and contradictory. If they were really harmful to either mothers or babies, they wouldn't be offered at all.

In 2009, a senior British midwife, Denis Walsh, revealed in an interview with the *Observer* the real reason for the pressure on women to be stoical. 'More women should be prepared to withstand pain,' he said, describing pain as 'a useful thing', with a number of benefits, including 'preparing a mother for the responsibility for nurturing a newborn baby'. Belinda Phipps, the chief executive of the NCT, agreed. 'If we just dropped babies like eggs without noticing, what would that say about the responsibilities we're taking on for the next twenty years?' she said. 'Birth marks you out as a mother and a carer for a very long time.' Pain in childbirth as a fitting preparation for maternal martyrdom is a great example of moralising misogyny, and there's an unspoken class dynamic in play as well: a good dose of traumatic hazing brings those narcissistic career women back down to earth. But what I really object to is the way in which these judgemental pronouncements are increasingly clothed in scientific 'evidence'. Those who advocate 'natural' childbirth appeal more and more to scientific or pseudoscientific arguments: even Denis Walsh's book, which critiques 'scientifically managed birth' and endorses a more 'humane, midwifery-led model', is entitled *Evidence-Based Care for Normal Labour and Birth*. Lamaze International, an organisation that promotes 'natural' and 'normal' childbirth, emphasises the scientific rationale for intervention-free childbirth on its 'Science and Sensibility' blog and fills its publications with references to statistics and studies. In a culture that increasingly values science, it's not altogether surprising.

This science-sprinkled sexism appears innocuous because it's wrapped in a naturalistic Earth-Mother fake feminism. The annual Midwifery Today Conference in 2010 was entitled 'Birth is a Human Rights Issue'. 'Women and babies are suffering abuses at the hands of medical professionals,' it announced. 'Many of these abuses are similar to the travesties done to women in Africa and the Middle East. It is also similar to domestic violence. Women's voices are being squashed.' And according to an editorial in *Midwifery Today*, 'Birth today is a doctor dictatorship in many practices and in many hospitals … This is so unnecessary because women have within them the ability and the instinct to have a great childbearing experience.' As a pregnant woman, I found myself being implicitly marshalled to support the David of midwifery against the Goliath of the medical establishment; invited to 'choose' between a nasty, sterile, 'medicalised' birth on the one hand, and a 'mother-friendly', 'drug-free' birth with mood music and scented candles on the other. Personally, I wanted to be on a ward during labour, where I knew I would be safe. And in the event I was one of the small but significant minority of women who develop a dangerous complication requiring an emergency caesarean. Giving birth is not an illness, but for some it can be life-threatening. What is natural is for a proportion of women to die in childbirth, just as it's natural for a proportion of children to die before they're five. We don't really want what is natural, so why don't we go for what's good? NCT and midwifery literature creates the impression that women in labour have epidurals foisted upon them. But my own experience and that of nearly everyone I have spoken to was the exact opposite. When women ask for epidurals, they are coaxed and cajoled and told to 'See how you get on.' When later on they exercise their choice very decisively by screaming for an epidural, they are told it's too late. As a good friend put it, there is no bell for last orders. I for one didn't find it very empowering for my requests for pain relief to be quietly ignored. I wanted to benefit from real science, not be fobbed off with pseudoscientific nonsense about following my 'inner physiological wisdom'.

The NCT, the National Childbirth Trust, was founded in 1956 as the Natural Childbirth Trust. Its first president, an obstetrician called Grantly Dick-Read, argued in his book *Childbirth Without Fear* that women felt pain in childbirth because they were socially conditioned to do so. An anaesthetic was both undesirable and unnecessary, he argued, because if women could be trained to not fear childbirth, they would have a satisfying and even enjoyable experience. Labour pains seemed pretty real to me. But I can see that his protests against medical intervention had more traction in the 1950s, when women were shaved, given an enema and strapped into stirrups to give birth. Back in the mid-nineteenth century, however, Queen Victoria was a convert to chloroform, despite the clergy's protestations that women should suffer in childbirth to atone for Eve's sin. The Suffragettes promoted 'twilight sleep' – a mixture of morphine and an amnesiac. In the eighties, epidurals were commonplace, and the nineties saw a vogue for elective caesareans. Birthing styles have come and gone, but we're still labouring under the outdated myth of an all-powerful patriarchal medical establishment. It's the pseudoscientific natural birth movement that's the real dictatorship now – in New Age feminist disguise.

And then there's the business of bringing children up. There's a modern assumption that parenting advice was more authoritarian in the past, a matter of strict routine and feeding by the clock. But Dr Benjamin Spock, the 1950s childrearing guru, actually made a point of reassuring parents. His bestselling *Baby and Child Care*, first published in 1946, opens with the line: 'Trust yourself. You know more than you think you do.' As writers Zoe Williams and Jennie Bristow and academic Ellie Lee have pointed out, it's actually modern parenting advice – in the mountains of childcare manuals, in TV programmes like *Supernanny* and *Nanny 911*, and in government 'early years' programmes – that is more overbearing. This advice is famously contradictory, riven by debates between those who are pro Gina Ford, and those who are anti. But the well-worn complaints about a confusing cacophony of voices obscure the fact that one way of doing things, one school of thought, is valued and promoted above all others. Gina Ford is sneakily demonised as a childless monster who urges women to force their babies into military routines so they can enjoy their careers and cocktails in peace. Ford sued the online child and parenting website Mumsnet in 2007 for publishing comments about her that she said were defamatory; Mumsnet settled out of court. But one sleep-deprived first-time mother was still posting a tentative enquiry in 2011 titled 'Gina Ford – please don't flame me yet …'

The favoured school of thought doesn't promote itself as a 'school' at all, but as simply the natural way of doing things. It appears to transcend the parenting debate because it claims to have scientific evidence on its side. As with childbirth, it's the apparently 'soft' side that has the support of 'hard' science. It's the supposedly instinctual, nurturing approach that obeys implicit yet highly prescriptive rules. It's the approach that can be found in books such as *Why Love Matters: How Affection Shapes a Baby's Brain*, *The Baby Bond: The New Science Behind What's Really Important When Caring for Your Baby*, and *What Every Parent Needs to Know: The Incredible Effects of Love, Nurture and Play on Your Child's Development*. And it's the approach that lies behind a cross-party attempt in Britain to move away from a socio-economic explanation for social outcomes to one that is based on the effect of parenting style on brain development.

In *The Essential First Year: What Babies Need Parents to Know*, the parenting expert Penelope Leach writes that 'It is not an opinion but a fact that it's potentially damaging to leave babies to cry. Now we know that, why risk it?' Leach's work is increasingly informed by recent neurological research – in this case that high levels of the stress hormone cortisol can be toxic to the brain. But what does 'toxic' mean in this context? Such 'findings' are often highly contested scientifically, yet they take on the ring of truth in an area where it seems no risk is worth taking. Leach's point may apply in extreme cases of abuse and trauma, but the scientific lessons of those cases are popularly applied to mainstream parenting, so that ordinary parents start worrying that the smallest variables in the way they bring up their kids will have profound and lasting consequences. Often those who worry the most are middle-class parents who provide their children with such comfortable and attentive environments that this kind of thing is academic anyway. Most babies are indeed left to cry, at least for short periods of time, and it doesn't seem to do them any harm. But the invocation of hard science creates a kind of cognitive disconnect from everyday common sense. As the writer Nancy McDermott puts it: '"Science" in these discussions has nothing to do with the investigation of the world … It does not question or enlighten, so much as endorse a particular set of views about child-rearing … It's about trying to determine what's natural scientifically. If it was natural, why don't people just do it?'

Bonding, nurturing, attachment: the terms of this new scientific-natural style of parenting sound warm, progressive and liberal. The 'attachment parenting' approach promoted in bestselling books by William and Martha Sears warns parents to avoid advice and baby trainers. But attachment parenting is itself gently prescriptive. It encourages parents to fit their lives around those of their children: 'wearing' them constantly in slings, sleeping in the same bed, making their organic baby food, and attending immediately to their every whim. Attachment parenting is opposed to 'convenience parenting' and the 'cry-it-out crowd'. It piles pressure on parents – and generally that means women – to give up work and devote their lives to their children. In the 1950s, this was known as being a housewife. But now it's associated with both liberal empowerment and behavioural chemistry. Our new scientistic reverence for the primacy of the natural maternal bond undermines all those worthy claims that we should be aiming for equality in childcare. And what really gets my goat is the way no one actually comes out and says it's mothers, not fathers, who should be with their babies in the first few years – it's just darkly hinted at. These new-old ways of thinking – about fertility, childbirth and parenting – employ a scientifically-framed projection of nature as a justification for what conservative elements of our culture happen to think is right.

In 2010 the Royal Society of Arts in Britain launched a new initiative called 21st Century Enlightenment, based on 'research emerging from fields such as neuroscience and evolutionary psychology'. 'Might it be insights into human nature which help prompt a twenty-first-century enlightenment?' asked the RSA's chief executive, Matthew Taylor, in an accompanying essay. He called for 'a deeper sensitivity to our nature as a species. We can know ourselves better. Perhaps we need to.' But using scientific research as a way of divining true human nature seems to me to be barking up the wrong tree. If certain arrangements of human society are possible, like introducing deterrents to committing murder or making it possible for women to have jobs, then that means we have choice. Some societies have more gender equality than others. So why would we not try to increase it across the board? The only logical reason is that some people don't want that to happen. If certain other aspects of human behaviour are determinedly natural, they will happen anyway. We don't need to make a case for them. The point is that some people do want to make that case. These supposedly value-free 'discoveries' about natural hierarchies and divisions of labour are arguments made by certain people with a vested interest in maintaining them. Science-as-nature fundamentalism is a new cover for the prevailing norms of our society and the desires of its dominant groups. The original Enlightenment *philosophes* were frank about their ambitions: they believed in the exercise of human reason to achieve the best possible outcome for everyone. But we are channelling our much greater scientific capabilities into a pernicious and covertly hubristic exercise in navel-gazing.

Tomorrow's world

When my brothers and I were children, the endless fights with our parents over TV-watching would enjoy a happy truce when it came to *Tomorrow's World*. Because this show was about innovations in science and technology. It was improving for young minds. *Tomorrow's World* ran from 1965 to 2003, and during its 1970s heyday it had ten million viewers a week. It's intriguing to imagine what the show would be like today. For a start, it would be tricky to explain to viewers how the latest gadgets work: imagine the presenters trying to unpick the secretive workings of an iPhone, or even getting the case open. But there's something more fundamental about the incongruity. Watching the original *Tomorrow's World* is an exercise in retro nostalgia. Like *Star Trek*, it's endearingly comical to see how people in the past conjured up the future. There was a robotic secretary, and a fold-up car that fitted into a suitcase. Where has all that optimism, that idealistic excitement gone now? With all the modern scientific tools at our disposal, we have somehow disowned the sense that the world is our oyster, that we are free to shape it whichever way we choose. The world is changing faster than ever before, yet progress doesn't seem to be about harnessing human capability any more. It looks to me as if we're moving backwards as fast as we're moving forwards, and the atavistic past has somehow become our programmed future. On *Tomorrow's World*, science was about an unlimited horizon of improvement. But now, even with all the excited talk of a new Enlightenment, the possibilities of scientific progress seem curiously limited.

I think a big part of the problem is our culture's seemingly boundless enthusiasm for Charles Darwin. In 2009, on the two hundredth anniversary of Darwin's birth and the 150th anniversary of his *On the Origin of Species*, there were over 750 commemorative events in forty-five countries. As Steven Shapin noted in the *London Review of Books*, there were the 'Darwin-themed T-shirts, teddy bears, bobbleheads, tote bags, coffee mugs, fridge magnets, mouse mats, scatter cushions and pet bowls; the "Darwin Loves You" bumper-stickers, the "Darwin Is My Homeboy" badges, and the "I ♥ Darwinism" thongs.' Darwin-mania was everywhere.

It's interesting to speculate why Darwin's ideas are so enduringly popular. Perhaps it's because they offer a simple and reassuring rationale for apathy: things are as they are because that's the best way for them to be. But neo-Darwinianism, Darwin's ideas applied to contemporary human social life, is more than a justification for doing nothing: it also has a direction of travel. 'There is no denying,' Daniel Dennett writes in *Darwin's Dangerous Idea*, 'that Darwin's idea is a universal solvent, capable of cutting right to the heart of everything in sight.' Rather like the ruthless 'logic' of the internet or free-market capitalism, anything that's not about reproductive success, anything historic, aesthetic, meaningful or valuable in and of itself, is at risk of obsolescence. Neo-Darwinism is a fundamentalist covert ideology that downgrades human freedom and disguises particular choices as inevitable. It's that old confusion again between an 'is' and an 'ought'.

I go along with the geneticist Steve Jones, who argues that human beings – especially those living in the developed world – stopped evolving a long time ago. Since natural selection involves being in a life-or-death situation, its rules no longer apply in a protected, comfortable environment. We now have the luxury of choice. The evolutionary psychologist Geoffrey Miller argues in his book *Spent: Sex, Evolution and Consumer Behavior* that there is a 'universal sex difference in human mate choice criteria, with men favouring younger, fertile women, and women favouring older, higher-status, richer men'. When we read that it rings a Donald Trump-shaped bell, but we know from our own acquaintance that in reality, there's much more variety. It's the cultural authority of these scientific voices that makes us forget what we already know. Where stereotypes exist, we have the power to change them. It's telling that when it comes to the aspirational American dream or the Thatcherite get-on-your-bike doctrine, there are no limits to the obstacles we believe people can overcome. But we are apparently powerless in the face of pseudoscientific myths about genetic or cognitive 'predisposition'.

It's no accident that Darwinism is the orthodoxy of the moment, because it's a moment when free-market capitalism and a new strain of post-feminist patriarchy are doing really well. Although people talk about the market as if it were an unstoppable force, like gravity, it's neither natural nor scientific: it's a particular system we've chosen to adopt. The imposition of markets in areas where markets don't work – like rubbish collection or palliative care – is a costly illustration of that. And in contrast to the Enlightenment belief in using human judgement to tame a nature 'red in tooth and claw', to use Tennyson's phrase, we have replaced political idealism with obsessive quantification and 'scientific' measurement. I'm all for evidence-based policy to keep political folly in check, but we have totally lost our nerve. There's the drive towards measuring 'impact', and the infiltration of audit culture into every area of social policy. There's a creeping need to measure everything – from the impact of climate change to choosing the best school – in economic terms. It's not enough to make a moral case for reducing drug addiction: you have to produce statistics which show that addicts are a drain on the economy. The scientistic world view claims that since religion has been proved wrong, science provides the only moral compass. We've come to believe in an illusory scientific authority that will reveal authentic rules of human nature for us to follow, in our relationships, in our politics, in our workplaces, and in the raising of our children. But we just end up with influential people speaking through 'science' to promote their own agendas: gender hierarchy, economic self-interest and the 'invisible hand' of the market. If we were really running the world according to an evidence-based approach, we would be finding sources of alternative energy, developing new forms of antibiotics and legalising Class A drugs. At a time when science has progressed to such an extent that we can use 3D printers to 'print' objects, choose the eye colour of our test-tube babies, and reverse the ageing process in mice, there's no good reason why pseudoscientific fatalism and old-fashioned stereotypes should be winning the day.

According to Darwin's theory of natural selection, evolution is driven by accidents. Species become better suited to their environment because of the marginal success, on balance, of this or that entirely random genetic mutation. But as the philosopher John Gray has observed, Darwin's original idea has mutated into the optimistic conviction that the human race is on a trajectory of inevitable progress. We love Darwin because he appears to provide us with proof that everything is getting better all the time, without us having to make plans for the future. Where the environment is concerned, of course, that isn't exactly the case. We can use science to improve and even save the world, but that means acknowledging our unique human ability to make deliberate choices. Perhaps we are ignoring our most urgent priorities because if we can't eliminate the problems of the environment, serious illness or inevitable mortality, we'd prefer not to address them at all. We'd rather spend our time obsessively repeating experiments that prove what we already think we know about who we are, than go out on a limb using science to make ourselves a better – if not a perfect – world. Of course, some scientists are doing just that. But we don't tend to hear about them very much, because we are so busy listening to people using science to advance agendas that aren't about science at all.

NINE

Baloney

'I believe passionately that good food is for everybody,' says Old Etonian Hugh Fearnley-Whittingstall, balancing casually on one of his enormous pumpkins, in his extensive vegetable garden, with his handsome Devon country house in the background. I am watching an episode of *The River Cottage Treatment*, in which a number of 'fast-food addicts' and 'ready-meal junkies' are taught how to skin wild rabbits on the River Cottage estate. The blurb on the back of the recipe book *River Cottage Every Day* continues the theme: 'Putting food on the table for the family quickly and economically doesn't mean you have to compromise on quality. This book shows how Hugh's approach to food can be adapted to suit any growing, working family, or busy young singles and couples for that matter.' So what does Hugh's approach to food entail, exactly? One episode of *Beyond River Cottage* features a 'multibird roast', involving a woodcock, a pigeon, a partridge, a pheasant, a chicken, a guinea fowl, a mallard, something called an 'armed duck' and a turkey; all stuffed one inside the other. Another episode has Hugh shooting, butchering and cooking a whole deer, including preparing a canapé of venison pâté and preserving the meat for his venison jerky. In another, he brews pear cider, free dives for scallops and forages for wild mushrooms. How easy it is for any 'growing, working family' or 'busy young singles and couples' to 'Eat the River Cottage way every day'!

It's a truism that in the second half of the twentieth century, Western consumers were treated to an unprecedented array of high-quality, low-cost food. Monochrome national cuisines were spiced up by immigration, globalisation and holidays abroad. You were able, if you were so inclined, to purchase from your local supermarket such weird and wonderful products as Viennetta, Boursin and Primula prawn spread. Increased disposable income turned a restaurant pilgrimage into an everyday jaunt. You could have *pain au chocolat* for breakfast, a Mexican tortilla wrap for lunch, and a Thai green curry for dinner. Celebrity chefs began to take up residence in gastropubs. Farmers' markets popularised heritage tomatoes and chicken that tasted of chicken. And the trend for organics upgraded 1970s tofu and brown rice for the Google generation. Now I think it's great that in the last couple of decades we've woken up to the wonders of fresh, local, home-cooked food. But this new food culture is not quite as it seems. Here's a taste of what I mean.

I buy a tub of cottage cheese from Sainsbury's. The label says 'Be good to yourself. Less than 2 per cent fat.' I find the same bizarre combination of hedonism and virtue down the road at Marks and Spencer, where for a moment I flirt with 'Fairtrade rich chocolate truffle sauce. Equally gorgeous warmed or spooned straight from the jar!'. The day has come when you can treat yourself by going on a diet. Or salve your conscience about Third World poverty by gorging on chocolate sauce. Similarly contradictory is what's happened to fast-food joints. If you go into a McDonald's to scratch that rare yet potent Big Mac itch, you're greeted instead by their 'deli' range of bagels and 'garden salads' (which are surprisingly calorific). You can partake of this cosmopolitan fare seated on mock Arne Jacobsen chairs. A similarly odd reversal has occurred at the other end of the market. Upmarket restaurants aren't escapist emporiums of exotic choice any more – they serve simple food that you'd eat at home, if you still cooked: shepherd's pie, toad-in-the-hole, jam sponge with custard. Trendy gastropubs offer 'sharing' dishes for two, three or four in chipped enamel dishes, like family meals round the dining-room table. Sainsbury's ready meals are sold under an entertainingly para-doxical sign that reads: 'We make our Taste the Difference meals with the same ingredients you typically use at home.' Contemporary food culture obeys the topsy-turvy rules of the Mad Hatter's tea party. But it makes perfect sense in a world where everything means the opposite of what it says on the tin.

The contradictions are not just randomly surreal, however. The great food revolution has hidden within it hoary old power dynamics and pernicious new ones. The spectacle of a cheeky lad from Essex tearing basil leaves onto spaghetti was in some ways a step forward for equality, but in other ways it was a sneaky step back. Because it made it that much harder to notice the dodgy doublespeak that has come to dominate the way we talk about food. Like the homecraft stakes-raising of Martha Stewart and Kirstie Allsopp, the celebrity chef-endorsed culinary craze exerts invisible pressure on women (still usually the primary cooks) and those who are strapped for cash and time. Behind many an environmentally-friendly label lurks a polluting production process. Despite a ubiquitous rhetoric of consumer choice, food giants withhold the basic information consumers need to make the best purchases. And this impacts most on the poor and disadvantaged. So much, then, for revolution. But it's hard to discern this culinary politics, because there's something about food that seems so agenda-free, self-evident and real. It's homely and tangible: on our plates and in our stomachs. A piece of cake is a piece of cake. Cake is not political. And yet, as that famous phrase 'Let them eat cake' suggests, food used to be about poverty, and scarcity, and other very definitely political issues. The great thing about food getting cheaper in the twentieth century, as far as governments were concerned, was that they could claim that since everyone could afford to eat, food wasn't a political matter any more. But it was only certain products that became cheaper – unhealthy, processed foods and sweet, fizzy drinks. Prices for fresh produce have actually increased in real terms since the 1980s. And food prices in general are set to rocket.

Secret ingredients

I started this chapter with Hugh because although I'm sure he means well, to me he's such a champion of unrealistic 'real food', and such a figurehead for concealed class dynamics. But he's not alone. A lot of celebrity chefs claim to be just like you and me. 'I lead a normal life,' says Nigella in the introduction to *Nigella Express*, 'the sort we all share.' So that means living in a £12 million house in Chelsea, does it, and sharing an estimated fortune of over £100 million with her husband, the art collector Charles Saatchi? Or there's this, from *Jamie at Home*: 'Like most people these days, with a busy family life and a hectic working schedule, I began to struggle with finding a balance between the two. I seem to have evened things up a bit now, and it's all thanks to my veg garden, believe it or not.' That would be the veg garden that enjoys the attentions of a personal gardener, Brian Skilton. Watching Jamie plucking courgette flowers and assorted lettuce leaves for his supper is indeed a lovely sight; but as an answer to work-life balance it's the equivalent of teasing a marathon runner in the Gobi desert with an ice-cold pitcher of citron pressé. Jamie's book *Happy Days with the Naked Chef* is also all about 'reality': 'You know what I mean, simple, comforting, homely food is still what it's all about.' Reality, normality, hard-working families: this is the mantra of the multi-millionaire celebrity chef. But the recipes have trouble sticking to it, because despite the homely trappings, they are essentially restaurant food. Take *Nigella Express*, the book of the TV show promising 'fabulous fast food and incredible short cuts'. The recipes are quick to make, it's true, but look at the ingredients: mirin, poussin, pomegranate juice, quail, harissa, sake, garlic oil. It would take an afternoon to track them down. Gordon Ramsay's *Fast Food* keeps the stakes equally high with a starter of salmon ceviche and a salad containing frisée and tangerine juice. A 'carefree but realistic approach to cooking and eating' is offered by the mouth-watering *Ottolenghi: The Cookbook*. 'It mustn't be a chore or a bore, with lots of complicated ingredients to source and painstakingly prepare, but can be accessible, straightforward and frank. For us, cooking and eating are not hazy, far-off ideals but part of real life.' Sounds good to me, Yotam. But for the first four recipes in the book you need the following ingredients: endives, baby chard, speck, preserved lemon, green tahini sauce, orange blossom water, pomegranate, sumac and young Pecorino. What was that about not having to source complicated ingredients? Halfway through his recipe for shakshuka, a North African dish of eggs, tomatoes and onions, Ottolenghi instructs us to set four saucepans on the hob. That's a lot of washing up. To make his caponata, a Sicilian stew, you're meant to fry all the vegetables individually, before draining them on kitchen towels. I did it once, and it used up all the space on my worktops, all my kitchen towels, and all my sanity.

I have for many years wrestled with the matter of fresh herbs. They improve simple dishes no end: most of Jamie's *Quick Fixes* and *30 Minute Meals* rely on them. But I always seem to find myself rummaging impatiently through a supermarket's highly selective herb selection to find the one I need. A few years ago I decided, that's it, I'm going to grow my own. So I went on to Ehow, the website that tells you 'How to do just about everything', and this is what I found.

Step 1. Select plant pots or containers that complement the natural shape and size of the herbs you intend to grow. Choose pots with a height of one-third to one-half the height of the plant at maturity to provide balance and enhance the natural beauty of the plant.

Step 2. Fill the pot with a lightweight growing medium. Potting soil is dense and drains slowly and must be amended before using. Mix equal parts peat moss, potting soil and perlite for a lightweight soil that promotes drainage and aeration. Refer to the cultural requirements of the specific herb you wish to grow to determine whether sand is needed in your soil mixture (see resources).

Step 3. Choose a short, wide container (like a whisky barrel) to grow a selection of herbs in one pot. Place the pot in a sunny location that receives six to eight hours of direct sunlight a day.

Got that? I didn't either. Every time I've tried to grow herbs on my balcony, they've lasted about three weeks. My shrivelled, dried-up herbs seem to me to encapsulate a broader problem. Because they are the very baseline minimum of the grow-your-own business, the entry-level stage. And even that doesn't seem to work. The glossy new food revolution that's advertised on our TV screens and in our beautiful recipe books purports to be democratic, accessible, available to everyone, but it's not. I'm fine with Heston Blumenthal and his baroque creations, his frog's leg blancmange and exploding cakes. He is not for a minute pretending that we should try this at home. And I've long been a fan of Nigel Slater, whose thirty-minute recipes are as good as their word. But if the others really wanted to come up with a quick and easy cookbook for 'hard-working families', they'd write one that only used the kind of ingredients I can buy at my local Costcutter: potatoes, tomatoes, onions and carrots. No pomegranate. No mirin. No Pecorino, young or old.

And yet there's an obsessive emphasis on teachability, on getting your hands dirty, on This Will Change Your Life. I remember recipe programmes on TV in the 1980s that paused, politely, while you grabbed a pen to note down the ingredients list. Now, supposedly real-time cookalongs are a frantic marathon, and full ingredients lists are only to be found in the accompanying book, priced at £19.99. And to me it's extraordinary that celebrity cookbooks rarely announce their gastronomical allegiance. I mean, I have a vague sense that Nigel likes comfort food and Nigella likes, well, lots of comfort food; that Gordon sets things on fire and Heston freezes things in liquid nitrogen; that Rick Stein likes fish and John Torode likes meat. But beyond that, a lot of celebrity cheffery kind of blends into a modern European, pan-Asian melange. It's beyond fusion. It's category meltdown. I find it really odd that for all today's flag-waving about the wonder of different cuisines, our modern chefs are so coy about their culinary brand. And for all the apparent kitchen-sink empowerment, I also find it somewhat patronising. These are often connoisseurs who've been trained to distinguish Spanish from Catalan tapas, or trace the genealogy of haute cuisine; but don't you worry your little heads about such finer points, they seem to say. It's the food equivalent of the modern post-ideological politician who gives speeches saying Right and Left are over, but back at Oxford made damn sure he mastered the taxonomy of political theory. Today's TV chefs claim to be making food accessible, but they don't give ordinary people the vocabulary, the building blocks, to get a handle on food. Just as art schools today don't teach much drawing, there's no going back to food-type basics, techniques or the elements of different cuisines: no culinary periodic table.

Now you might be thinking, what's wrong with a little recreational food porn? I'm not averse to a bit of Nigella myself. But while these fantasies may be fun, they are not harmless. We lap them up, but they ultimately leave us still more famished. Appearance is everything, and expectations are created daily which absorb us but cannot be fulfilled. Meanwhile, we carry on as normal, ordering yet another disappointing takeaway. The fastest-growing computer game of all time is FarmVille, which currently has fifty-six million active players. The game involves sowing, tending and reaping vegetables on a virtual farm. There are forty million farms, twenty million more than the number of actual farms in America. One of them is owned by McDonald's. Players sit at their desks at work, weeding their carrots and watering their potatoes, and then go out at lunchtime to buy a sandwich from Pret a Manger. Our obsession with food is overtaking our obsession with sex. But the more time we spend watching cookery programmes and reading restaurant reviews, the less we spend on actually cooking. According to the Food Standards Agency, in 1980 the average meal took an hour to prepare. By 1999, it took twenty minutes. And a 2002 Mintel report found that only one in five viewers try a recipe after watching a chef on TV and only one in seven buy new ingredients. A large proportion of apparently hand-made gastropub meals are actually trucked in by catering giants like Brakes or 3663 which provide microwaveable or boil-in-the bag versions of old-fashioned rustic classics such as venison and pork sausages 'infused with sloe gin and served in a rich and sweet bramble berry and red wine sauce', a 'mushroom, brie, rocket and redcurrant filo bundle' or, for dessert, an 'apricot, apple and stem ginger crumble … heaped with hand-placed golden oaty all-butter crumble'. The 'authenticity' of these dishes is a fib impossible to spot. We may be aware that there's been a huge rise in sales of ready meals, but now they're being disguised as real cooking. Instead of Pot Noodles and frozen lasagne, the discerning after-work shopper can choose tuna steaks coated in Asian marinade, a stir-fry kit, or a self-assembly fruit tart. Food culture is about more than simply what we eat: it's about a whole way of life. It brings with it dreams of trading the urban grind for a country idyll, of relaxed dinner parties, kitchen gardens and bread rising in the Aga. But those dreams remain tantalisingly out of reach.

My problem is not only the reality gap between wild venison and supermarket chicken. It's the general pretence that the gap isn't there. It's not only that Hugh went to Eton and lives on a country estate, it's that he emphasises his local-community involvement and Farmer Giles familiarity with farmyard muck. And it's not only that Jamie employs around 5,000 staff and is reportedly worth £65 million, it's that he foregrounds his lovely-jubbly persona and rapport with dinner ladies. TV executives try to get around these contradictions with the help of that weasel word, 'aspirational'. But it just doesn't wash. This is not just food. This is 100 per cent, mock-authentic, mock-egalitarian class hierarchy. Supermarket labels such as 'organic', 'finest' and 'taste the difference'; and 'economy', 'basics' and 'everyday' are euphemisms for food apartheid. As I may have mentioned, I am addicted to the genius TV series *Come Dine With Me*, but the butt of the jokes are the wannabe foodies in Luton who serve starters of 'microsalads', main courses in 'towers' on large square plates, and desserts which always come as a trio. *Jamie's Ministry of Food* claimed to bring home cooking to the ordinary British family, but the series was riddled with undeclared class dynamics. Those mothers who passed chips through the fence at Rawmarsh school in South Yorkshire after it started serving Jamie's healthy school dinners were protesting against paternalism. As one of them explained, 'This isn't about us against healthy food, like they've been saying … It's about how people change the rules.' I believe Jamie's gastronomical good intentions, but his outrage at seeing mothers bottle-feeding Coke to their babies has a class dimension that is never explicitly addressed. Because he himself doesn't sound posh, there's a sense that if he's made it good, so can they. Jamie raises the stakes for middle-class fans by presenting expensive, cheffy food as barrow-boy basics ('Tear up yer tarragon, drizzle yer top-quality olive oil'). And he raises the stakes for working-class mums by implying that there's no excuse for not pulling themselves up by their culinary bootstraps.

It's not only class inequality that lurks beneath the new food culture, it's gender inequality too. When Jamie debuted on British TV as *The Naked Chef* in 1998, he was credited with encouraging the most male-chauvinistic of oafs to try their hand at a fairy cake. And indeed, this has come to pass in some households. But very often it's the men who are flambéing the bananas at the Saturday-night dinner party, while the women are plotting how to stretch the Sunday-roast leftovers into day three. Female TV chefs are filmed in a cosy kitchen, male chefs in some kind of rustic outhouse or on a beach with an improvised barbecue. In 2010, Waitrose spent £10 million on an advertising campaign featuring two people: 'Britain's best chef' and 'Our best-loved cook'. No prizes for guessing which was Heston Blumenthal and which was Delia Smith. It's a new backlash sexism, I believe, that accounts for the fact that so many famous chefs' wives are prominent foodies themselves. Their role is to absorb the feminine connotations of their husbands' cookery. 'The trick to Christmas,' says *Tesco Magazine* Celebrity Mum of the Year Tana Ramsay, being interviewed for said magazine, 'is making things in advance as much as you can, such as chopping the vegetables on Christmas Eve.' Am I alone in finding it rather depressing that Tana Ramsay spends her Christmas Eves in this way? 'After the Ramsays have opened their stockings,' the article continues, 'Gordon and son Jack, eight, whizz off to Claridge's to wish his restaurant staff a merry Christmas. At home, under Tana's watchful guidance, daughters Megan, ten, Holly, eight, and Matilda, six, help their mum keep an eye on the turkey.' To go with the gendered division of labour, the family has two kitchens: his is equipped with a custom-made, £67,000 two-and-a-half-tonne industrial stove; hers is down in the basement. Tana does most of the cooking at home, and Gordon has apparently never wiped any of his four children's bottoms. The end result is that celebrity chefs and their wives – Tana 'n' Gordon,

Jamie 'n' Jools – end up modelling traditional gender stereotypes in the media that undercut the right-on rhetoric. In the introduction to *Tana's Kitchen Secrets*, Tana sets the domestic bar terrifyingly high: 'I now cook a variety of dishes every day. My four kids always have a homemade meal after school, and then I make something for Gordon and me later in the evening. And I love to plan weekends filled with nurturing, delicious food that we can all share.' Jools Oliver's *Minus Nine to One: The Diary of an Honest Mum* contains children's recipes that were serialised in the *Daily Telegraph*. 'A few months before our wedding,' she confides in the book, 'Jamie asked if I wanted to become his PA. I agreed, as it meant that I would get to see him every day and I thought it would be fun, plus I was never really a career girl anyway. (Who was I kidding? I wanted the babies, the baking and the roses round the door.)' For all the metrosexual class-busting bluster, it's this message that we are left with.

Consuming fictions

My local Waitrose offers a choice of four different kinds of salmon fillets. There are standard fillets, 'Wild Alaskan Sockeye' fillets 'caught in Alaska's well managed, sustainable fishery certified to Marine Stewardship Council standard', 'Select Farm' fillets from 'dedicated farms in locations carefully chosen for their highly oxygenated, fast-flowing tidal waters', and 'Duchy from Waitrose Organic' fillets, 'organically farmed to Soil Association standards on Shetland and Orkney'. It's a classic example of totally uninformative information. If I was a salmon, I think I'd appreciate highly oxygenated, fast-flowing tidal waters; so how come Duchy from Waitrose organic salmon don't get to swim in them? And how come wild Alaskan salmon are caught in a fishery? Reading these labels doesn't enable me to rank the salmon in order of either taste or green credentials. The first half of this chapter explored how the celebrity-chef media culture creates unrealistic culinary expectations using the rhetoric of ease and accessibility, and disguises pernicious class and gender politics with the trappings of right-on food revolution. This second half explores how the food industry offers tempting food choices to consumers which obscure the reality of what we're really eating. How governments let them get away with it. And how we, as consumers, swallow the fiction that buying food is a matter of informed choice, empowerment and personal responsibility. Much has been written about disturbing trends in modern industrial food production, by Felicity Lawrence, Joanna Blythman, Eric Schlosser and Michael Pollan, among others. They've shown how the interests of multinational food giants are being pursued to the detriment of our health, our wallets, Third World farmers, small businesses and the environment. But what really gets me are the false promises sold to us: of choice, high quality and accessibility. The thing about that shelf of salmon fillets was that it appeared to offer a diverse range of tasty, affordable, environmentally-friendly fish. But the reality of which kind of fillet would be best for me, best for fishermen and best for our oceans was simply impossible to make out. The same goes for seasonal fruit and veg. Seasonality is a virtue heavily promoted by Hugh, Jamie and the rest. It has the advantage of being an enjoyable virtue, too: I love summery, flavoursome tomatoes and cheap, sweet blackberries. But if I go to the supermarket or the local grocer's, it's just not that easy to work out what's on nature's menu. Seasonality is a matter of duty as well as desire, but we are not given the info we need to get either Brownie points or satisfaction.

Where the selling of food is concerned, appearance is now what counts. Don't get me wrong: my local farmers' market and my veg box are a weekly joy (even if I do palm off the swedes and turnips on my infant son). But in many cases, the transformation has been cosmetic as well as real. There are a lot of people buying ready-made burgers and pies at my farmers' market. And the dilution of so many great restaurant brands – from the Real Greek to Carluccio's – is a real sign of our times. Ninety-seven per cent of British food is sold in supermarkets; 76 per cent by the big four chains. Then there's organic food. The tech spec of organic food – the fact that nothing synthetic is used in its production – suggests flavour, nutritional value and agricultural ethics. But it's become a devalued, mass-market symbolic indicator.

In 2006, even Walmart pledged to become a provider of 'organics for everyone'. Last time I bit into an organic tomato, it was just as bland as a normal tomato. Organics are promoted as both available to all and a luxury treat, but often they're more expensive and they taste the same. And they're not even necessarily good for the environment, either. Increasing demand has led to organic meat being raised on vast industrial feed lots, and the scarcity of organic ingredients means they are flown around the world. Research sponsored by the Department for Environment, Food and Rural Affairs showed that producing a litre of organic milk requires 80 per cent more land than conventional milk. And that organically reared cows burp and fart twice as much methane as conventionally reared cattle, which would be amusing if it weren't for the fact that methane is twenty times more powerful a greenhouse gas than CO_2. Overall, the research on environmental impact is contradictory, which only makes it harder for consumers to work out what to do. The marketing of organic food taps into our innermost drives and ambitions: to be good, to be good to ourselves, to be worth the extra cost. But the only people it definitively seems to be good for are managers of multinationals. Ben & Jerry's is owned by Unilever. Coca-Cola has a majority stake in Innocent smoothies. Back to Nature is owned by Kraft. Supermarkets may display their organic food in rustic-looking baskets, and Starbucks may camouflage its corporate brand under local 'community personality'. But farmers in the developing world suffer from diminishing profits, and our soil, sea and atmosphere are ever more degraded.

I applaud the growing network of food activists, snapping at the heels of the food giants. There are campaigns for animal welfare, campaigns against GM crops, campaigns for proper fair trade. They make brilliant use of science to cut through commercial claims. But it's hard for them to make a lot of headway, because the food industry successfully hides its influence behind persuasive talk of the power of the individual. The industry and government alike argue that it's consumer choice and consumer demand that really drive change. The former chief executive of Tesco, Terry Leahy, hailed as the high point of the noughties 'the rise of the influence of consumers through improvements in communication'. Policy-makers and businesses, he claimed, have 'an unprecedented opportunity to listen as well as to lead'. In a speech in 2010 to launch the government's national food strategy for the next twenty years, the then environment secretary Hilary Benn called on 'people power' to 'help bring about a revolution in the way food is produced and sold'. Yet a Royal Society report published around the same time revealed that although consumers were consulted ten years previously about whether they wanted GM food, responding with a resounding 'no', GM has nevertheless thoroughly penetrated the food supply in the form of soya animal feed and cooking oil. Channel 4's 'Big Fish Fight' season attempted to shift British fish-eating habits towards more sustainable varieties: from haddock to hake, cod to coley. 'I wouldn't bother waiting for the politicians, guys,' Jamie Oliver said in his *Fish Suppers* series. 'You can really help from the comfort of your own kitchen.' But when I visited branches of Sainsbury's and Tesco three months later, the traditional selection (salmon, trout, cod and haddock) didn't seem to have changed. Consumers don't have power when the choices are set.

The notion that consumers are in control of the food industry is a myth, as is the notion that they are at liberty to make well-informed decisions about the food they buy. One of the Cornish pasty company Ginsters' favourite slogans is 'Keeping it local'. But its pasties are taken on a 250-mile round trip by lorry before being delivered to the Tesco next door to its Cornwall plant (they insist it's more efficient that way, but still). A slice of Cranks seeded farmhouse bread has twice the amount of salt as a packet of Walkers ready-salted crisps. McVitie's light digestive biscuits have less fat than McVitie's original digestives, but more sugar, so the difference between the biscuits is just four calories. But then, a 2009 article in the *New Scientist* pointed out that even calorie labelling is unhelpful, because the body digests different foods at different rates. 'Consumers aren't stupid' is the stock industry response when challenged on their campaigns of misdirection. Yet in her 2010 book *Green Gone Wrong*, the environmental writer Heather Rogers quotes the director of an organic conglomerate noting that 'Most consumers are simple minds [who] look at the label and nothing else.' But with labels that are this misleading, intelligence is a red herring.

The industry insists that in selling the sugary, fatty, salty foods that are contributing so much to rates of obesity, heart disease and type 2 diabetes, it is simply giving people what they want. In reality, of course, the industry doesn't just respond to desires: it shapes them. As Joel Salatin, the self-styled 'Christian-libertarian-environmentalist-lunatic farmer' writes in his book *Everything I Want to Do is Illegal*, the idea that Americans have the freedom to choose the food they grow, buy and eat is totally undermined by a car-crash of government regulations and industrial, globalised food production which ensures that shoppers are actually discouraged from buying local, environmentally-friendly food. But the myth of empowered free will seems credible, because the experience of shopping at a supermarket feels so much like exercising choice. And it chimes with our general sense of being modern, self-aware consumers. The voluminous small print on cereal boxes or tubs of chocolate mousse looks like a tool for effective consumer discernment. But it distracts from the fact that the food industry is busily leading us astray.

Richard Thaler and Cass Sunstein talk a lot about food choices in their book *Nudge: Improving Decisions About Health, Wealth and Happiness*. Their proposals, which include placing fruit at eye level in school canteens, are an acknowledgement that people aren't very good at choosing healthy food. They're an acknowledgement, in other words, of the fallacy of the notion of the rational consumer, although the governments that are in thrall to the politics of nudge seem untroubled by this contradiction. For all their good intentions, Thaler and Sunstein underestimate just how energetically the food industry is working to prevent healthy choices. Often what is needed is some basic information, some rudimentary transparency, rather than a nudge. A traffic-light system for labelling healthy and unhealthy food would be a start: research shows it's the most helpful one for consumers. But that would mean giving consumers real power to choose.

One of Tory health secretary Andrew Lansley's first moves in office was to promise that 'government and FSA promotion of traffic-light labelling will stop' as part of a big shake-up of public health. Out went regulation, legislation and 'top-down lectures'; in came voluntary corporate action and individual responsibility. Building on his Public Health Commission report 'We're All in This Together: Improving the Long-Term Health of the Nation', Lansley set up a series of 'responsibility deal networks', designed to get public-health officials to 'work with business'. The idea of McDonald's, KFC and Pepsi designing public-health policy outdoes Orwell's *Nineteen Eighty-Four*. And one of the networks, in charge of 'public health behaviour change', was to work with the government's newly set up 'nudge unit'. Its aim: to bring together experts in behavioural science with captains of industry. There it is again, the real payoff of nudge policy: to nudge us into buying from big corporations. Nudge is often not about helping us to make better choices, it's about deliberately withholding information. It's about nudging, not regulating, industry. And nudge is also corporate PR: Lansley said part of the FSA's new remit would be to 'highlight the continuing contribution made by business to improving diet by reformulating its products'. He chose as his special adviser on policy development one Bill Morgan, a former food PR executive. Never mind that there's a clear public-health conflict of interest: that too much alcohol and any amount of trans fats are unequivocally bad for you. Not to mention the fact that with all this emphasis on responsibility, we're not even allowed to get properly inebriated any more. There's neither proper regulation at the top nor proper freedom at the bottom.

There's a huge denial of inequality here: between consumers and corporations, and also between different kinds of consumers. In reality, there is one group of shoppers that can afford to be ethical, and another that can't. The fact is that people on low incomes are more likely to buy food that is bad for them and bad for the environment. But corporations and governments take advantage of the taboos of false consciousness and inequality in order to protest that they are simply letting consumers choose what they want. If we are unable to look this issue squarely in the face, then we are forced to accept that argument. We are labouring under the delusion not only of freely available, low-cost, great-quality, nutritional food, but also of a level playing field of money, power and information.

Grow your own PR

I live near a little field of allotments. I love to walk there with my son in his pushchair to look at the runner beans, the strawberry plants and the improbably large sunflowers. I fantasise about summer barbecues and distributing a bumper crop of squashes to my impressed neighbours. But I would happily steamroll the vegetable garden that Michelle Obama planted on the White House lawn in the spring of 2009. It's a perfect example of non-politics in action, of a piece with her gendered decision to give up a good career to become a perfect First Lady. Like Sarah Brown's Twittery philanthropy and Samantha Cameron's pre-election bump, this was a way for Michelle to do something visible while staying clear of her husband's public role. The garden was linked to her non-controversial 'Let's Move' campaign to combat childhood obesity, which was launched at the same time with a speech to the Grocery Manufacturers Association. 'We need you not just to tweak around the edges,' she told them, 'but to entirely rethink the products that you're offering, the information that you provide about these products, and how you market those products to our children.' The industry must have been relieved when she also said, 'We can't solve this problem by passing a bunch of laws in Washington.' It's that friendly self-regulation again. As Michael Pollan reported in the *New York Review of Books*, when CropLife America, a trade association representing pesticide makers, wrote a critical letter to Michelle Obama, the president appointed one of its executives to a high-level trade post. One of Barack Obama's first moves in office was to appoint Tom Vilsack as Agriculture Secretary; one of Vilsack's was to plant 'The People's Garden' at his departmental HQ. In a speech in 2009, Vilsack described how the garden was an 'opportunity to showcase what we do at USDA'. 'There are a lot of people who walk this mall from all over the country, and we thought if we had a statement garden that we would begin to get people's attention about this.' He encouraged people to plant similar gardens in their own neighbourhoods: 'You can help expand the message of our everyday everyway USDA by getting involved and participating. It doesn't have to be acres and acres of garden, it can be a flowerbox – just some indication, some awareness, some appreciation for the power of land to be able to produce and the connection that USDA has to it.' The candour is almost heart-warming. This is not about courgettes. This is about advertising. In reality, Tom Vilsack is a long-time supporter of intensive, genetically engineered industrial agriculture. He is a friend to the agribusiness giant Monsanto and has favoured the interests of heavily polluting factory farms.

These 'statement gardens' are spectacles which distract attention from disappointing domestic food habits and disastrous food-production practices. They embody that irresistible combination of attractiveness and apparent authenticity, escapism and down-to-earth reality that jams our scepticism radars. Ethical, environmentally-friendly food culture has been co-opted, producing empty rhetorical gestures which satisfy our imaginations and our consciences but achieve next to nothing. The spectacle of TV chefs and political figures going 'back to the land' creates the illusory impression that environmental problems are really being solved. It's facts on the ground … on TV. The soil clinging to the organic carrots on our supermarket shelves is the most effective PR of all. Just as the supposedly apolitical nature of food conceals inequalities of class and gender, that pesky soil is making it harder than ever to care for the real earth. It exemplifies yet another booby trap in ideology's undercover arsenal: to hide iniquities and intentions behind aspects of life that seem fundamental and basic.

The fact that we tolerate this delusional state of affairs does not speak well of us. It makes us seem passive, blinkered and bovine. The cheapness of food has provided us with a false sense of security, allowing us to believe we're getting the best of both worlds. But food prices are rising. In some ways that will make food choices more conscious, and more consciously political. But there's also a danger that we'll focus more attention on price alone. It's not really our fault. It's hard to make good choices when the marketing of products is so opaque and befuddling. It's hard to detect the silent promotion of inequality by mainstream food culture when the headlines are all about democratisation and demographic change. But we are becoming like orally fixated toddlers, transfixed by Nigella's cupcakey bosom, Starbucks' vanilla frappuccinos and Michelin-starred creamy, frothy sauces. We are focusing on the appearance, the rhetoric of food, rather than the taste, the reality. In an age of the most cynically industrialised food production, we are distracting ourselves with the comforting chimera of mother's meals like they used to taste, back in the olden days. We need to actively and consciously try to make the best food choices we can, difficult as that may be. We need to think about food in terms of ideas, of politics, of ideology; otherwise we'll be unconsciously consuming backward-looking prejudices. We need to put whatever pressure we can on our governments to regulate the suppliers and supermarkets that are making money at our own and our planet's expense. And then we can treat ourselves to a nice piece of independent-shop-bought cake.

TEN

Greenwash

On the night of Friday, 26 August 2005, as Hurricane Katrina crossed Florida and swept into the Gulf of Mexico, the New Orleans Saints played the Baltimore Ravens at the Louisiana Superdome. It was only after the game finished, at 11 p.m., that the stadium began to be prepared as a 'refuge of last resort'. An order of voluntary evacuation was made on the Saturday and mandatory evacuation, belatedly, on the Sunday; but what the authorities didn't realise was that 100,000 people were unable or unwilling to leave the city of New Orleans. By noon on Sunday, there were 14,000 people in line trying to get into the Superdome, but the Superdome wasn't ready for them. This despite the fact that it had been used as a refuge in 1998 during Hurricane Georges and in 2004 during Hurricane Ivan. Have you ever seen 14,000 scared, angry people waiting in line in the street? I haven't, but I've seen the pictures from New Orleans, and they are apocalyptic. To me, that football game encapsulates the delusions and denial at the heart of our attitude towards the environment. How could it have gone ahead, with disaster on the horizon? How could the fans have cheered and booed and munched away on their hotdogs?

According to climate scientists, storm surges of the kind that flooded New Orleans in 2005 will in the future become a regular occurrence, devastating coastal cities. We hear this kind of thing on the news all the time. But delusionalism on the subject of the environment goes right along the spectrum, from government apathy to the failure of everyday good intentions. This chapter is not only about denial, however: it's also about the symbolic green solutions peddled

189

by corporate vested interests and their multi-billion-pound lobbying machine, and which ordinary people, with their anxiety and their optimism, are only too glad to accept.

And yet there's a twist in the gloomy tale. I've chosen to end this book with the environment because despite the likely reality, this is one area in which the delusion-spotting that I've been championing in this book is already up and running. Green campaigners have their sights trained on denial and misdirection. They have their work cut out, because just as this grassroots activism is getting going, corporations are fighting back with astroturf and PR. As individuals we can get better at detecting this covert ideology. But it's only governments that can stop it being produced in the first place. That's why I'll be arguing that not only do we need to combat delusions, we also need to come together politically and press for change at the top. In order for that to happen, we need to rediscover our idealism. Because idealism, or overt ideology, is after all about changing the world not only as it is now, but as it could be in the future.

Be realistic

But first – deep breath – the stats. Climate scientists generally agree that the safe limit for the concentration of carbon dioxide in the atmosphere is 350 parts per million. As I write this, we're already at 390 ppm. During the nineties, CO_2 emissions rose by 0.9 per cent. Between 2000 and 2007, they rose by 3.5 per cent. According to the UN Development Programme, we need to cut emissions by 50 per cent worldwide by 2050, in comparison with 1990s levels, to prevent runaway climate change (I don't know about you, but I find that word 'runaway' particularly scary). But the International Energy Agency estimates that emissions will actually increase over the next fifty years, by up to 100 per cent. And that's before we really get into the feedback effects of warming producing yet more warming. So far, international attempts to control emissions have failed. The Kyoto Protocol, initially adopted in 1997, did nothing to stop them rising by the same amount as they were supposed to fall because of it. But Kyoto looks impressive alongside Copenhagen in 2009 and Cancún in 2010. The Intergovernmental Panel on Climate Change is not doing a very good job of coordinating things. The row in 2009 over errors in the IPCC's Fourth Assessment Report left many people thinking its predictions had been too alarmist. But the IPCC is actually as over-optimistic as it is weak. Its future projections rely on 60 per cent of emissions reductions happening spontaneously as the result of market-driven technological solutions. If only the market had a green conscience.

James Hansen of NASA's Goddard Institute, one of the most respected climate scientists, warns that if the use of coal as a source of energy isn't phased out in the developed world by 2020 and in the developing world by 2030, we'll face droughts, heatwaves and ferocious forest fires, an out-of-control sea-level rise, frequent extreme weather events, and the extinction of at least 20 per cent of earth's species. We are already going through a mass extinction of life, the worst since the disappearance of dinosaurs. But while sea ice is thinning, icebergs are calving, and glaciers are shrinking, a new coal-fired power station opens in China every week. Oh and also, the UN has said that with the world's population reaching between seven and nine billion by 2050, food production will need to double. Except that because of climate change, there will no longer be any agriculture in huge swathes of Asia, the Middle East, Africa and the Caribbean. There's also the small problem of 'peak oil', the point when oil production starts to decline, and prices start to rocket. Predictions vary, but this may well happen within the next ten years, and may well create huge worldwide disruption. Global warming, population explosion, peak oil, biodiversity in freefall: planet Earth is facing unprecedented and multiple crises. It's little wonder, therefore, that as the situation becomes more desperate, self-deception becomes more attractive. If the world is turning into a desert, it's tempting to put your head in the sand.

But denial about the environment is not just a matter of individual psychology. It's being orchestrated from above by energy corporations with a lot to lose. Take ExxonMobil, the most profitable corporation in the world, most of whose $1 billion-a-day profits come from oil.

Exxon spent more money on lobbying in the first half of 2009 (nearly $15 million) than the entire clean-energy industry. Or take Koch Industries, the second largest private company in the US, which runs crude-oil refineries and coal suppliers. It's provided undercover funding for the Tea Party movement and more than thirty American right-wing think tanks. According to Greenpeace, Koch Industries has since 1997 funded climate-change denial to the tune of nearly $50 million. They are not alone: in 2008 there were 2,340 energy lobbyists registered in Washington. A 2010 report by Common Cause, the non-partisan organisation monitoring money in politics, found that over the last decade the energy industry has spent nearly $3 billion lobbying and influencing politicians and lawmakers. Since 1990, donations to lawmakers from energy companies or their representatives have increased by 300 per cent.

And the very same astroturf-layers employed by tobacco companies in the 1990s are now sowing seeds of climate-change doubt for energy companies. It's just a different form of hot air. As the PR specialist James Hoggan and the author and activist Richard Littlemore note in *Climate Cover-up: The Crusade to Deny Global Warming*, corporate denialism takes on the guise of the little guy through astroturf campaigns that make out that scepticism about global warming is springing up from a diverse, unrelated array of individuals and organisations. Climate sceptics present themselves as plucky dissenters, speaking out in the face of the dominant ortho-doxy. They claim to be debunking environmentalist delusions, which is a great way for the real delusions to avoid detection. And they inaccurately claim that climate science is open to 'debate'. No peer-reviewed scientific journal article has ever challenged the evidence of man-made global warming. But the 'climategate' row of 2009–10 over hacked emails between scientists at the University of East Anglia provided an ideal opportunity for the denial industry to pretend it had 'sound' science on its side. Meanwhile, climate scientists and their supporters are portrayed as the purveyors of partisan ideology. 'Global warming is a socialist scam' read one 2010 Tea Party placard. This name-calling serves to obscure the covert ideology of the deniers:

as with the pro-smoking campaigns of the nineties, the underlying motivations are pro-corporate and anti-interventionist. These astroturf campaigns are proving effective at all levels of society. In 2007, nearly two thirds of Republican voters believed that there was clear evidence of climate change. Just two years later, only 35 per cent still believed in it. And a Gallup poll in 2011 found that a full 41 per cent of Americans believe the threat from global warming has been exaggerated, the highest amount of scepticism in the survey since it was first conducted in 1997.

Some time in the 1980s, the environmental activist Jay Westerveld read a notice in a hotel bathroom. 'Save Our Planet,' it began. 'Every day, millions of gallons of water are used to wash towels that have only been used once. You make the choice: A towel on the rack means, "I will use again." A towel on the floor means, "Please replace." Thank you for helping us conserve the earth's vital resources.' The notice prompted Westerveld to investigate how hotels save money on their laundry bills while wasting resources and polluting the environment in other ways – for example by using harmful laundry detergents. He wrote an influential 1986 essay in which he coined a neat term. 'Wash my towels please,' he argued, 'just don't "greenwash" me.'

Greenwash uses fake environmentalism as a cover for wrecking the environment. We'd be better off if energy companies went all out to fight the green movement openly. Instead they have courted the movement and co-opted its language. There are the ads for the General Motors Saturn Vue SUV that ran in *Newsweek* in 2002, featuring a big black SUV parked on a melting iceberg, the implication being that SUVs are themselves an endangered species (caption: 'At home in almost any environment'). There are less tongue-in-cheek but no less brazen examples such as the Airbus A380 airliner, advertised on its fuselage as 'a better environment inside and out' (during 2010, the same planes carried the official logo of the United Nations International Year of Biodiversity). There's the European Union's 'Ecolabel' on paper made partly from Indonesian rainforest timber. And the Poland Spring 'Eco-shape' bottle, slogan: 'A little natural does a lot of good' (bottled water is notoriously un-ecological). There are the 98 per cent of 'natural' and 'environmentally friendly' products on US supermarket shelves that an American organisation called TerraChoice has found to be making 'potentially false or misleading claims'. And the ads for a website called futurefriendly.co.uk featuring 'a range of well-known products' and asking: 'Wouldn't it be nice if we could all do our bit for the environment – without changing our everyday lives?', with no mention of the fact that all these products are made by Procter & Gamble, the multinational household-chemicals giant renowned for promoting disposable nappies to the developing world. There's Edinburgh airport – an airport, mind – announcing with great media fanfare that it will sponsor schoolchildren to plant five hundred trees in nearby Perthshire: 'a great example of how we can all play a part, however small, in safeguarding the natural environment' ('small' being the operative word). And there are the new breed of 'green' motorway service stations with timber-framed cafés serving home-made local food and a vegetable patch beside the coach park. There's the commercial catering giant, 3663, which makes a meal out of the fact that it washes its trucks in nice fresh rainwater. And there's the Strata tower in London's Elephant and Castle, whose prominent wind turbines produce less than 8 per cent of its energy.

That's before we even get on to the really juicy examples of energy company greenwash. Those would include BP's 'Beyond Petroleum' ad campaign, the prelude to a $3 billion investment in drilling the Alberta tar sands in the Canadian wilderness. And Chevron's well-publicised installation of solar panels to run pumps and pipelines at one of the dirtiest oilfields on the planet. And the Shell ads about the development of new low-carbon technologies with images of a butterfly net catching CO_2, its 'Profits or Principles' campaign which announced a commitment to renewable energy with photos of green forests, and its slogan 'Let's build a better energy future'. Less well advertised was Shell's 2009 admission to reporters, asking about its future plans for wind and solar power, that 'We do not expect material amounts of investment going forward.' Greenwash speaks the language of wish fulfilment, oxymoron, and the squaring of logical circles. It conjures a world of 'hybrid SUVs', 'carbon credits', 'sustainable development' and 'clean coal'; a topsy-turvy world in which oil companies trumpet their enthusiasm for alternative energy and gas guzzlers are pictured in the company of polar bears. With the rampant corporate co-option of environmentalism, it's harder than ever before for consumers to be truly green.

If corporate greenwash is bad enough, it's the government variety that I find really scary, because they're the ones who are supposed to be taking care of things. NASA's James Hansen has convincingly argued that when our political leaders refer to new power plants as 'carbon capture ready', and when they use words like 'goal', 'cap' and 'targets', they're leading us up the garden path. In 2008, it emerged that UK government claims that greenhouse-gas emissions had been falling since the 1990s had left out the small matter of emissions from aviation, shipping and imported goods. In December of that year, Ed Miliband, then minister for climate change, called for a 'modern suffragette movement' to tackle the threat of global warming. Pressure for change, he declared, must come from below. But when, on the very same day, the campaigning group Plane Stupid established a 'fort' on the runway at Stansted airport, they were promptly arrested and charged with aggravated trespass. In the light of the spectacular failure of governments to reach an agreement in Copenhagen one year later, Miliband's proclamation seemed doubly hypocritical. Copenhagen failed because governments – particularly in rich Northern countries – don't want to tackle climate change enough. While apparently sanctioning bottom-up protest, Miliband's government was also busily approving the expansion of Stansted and Heathrow airports. The coalition government that took over in 2010 promised to be 'the greenest ever', but one of its first moves was to abandon the regulation of coal-fired power stations. In the summer of that year, readers of newspapers around the world could enjoy the sight of Barack Obama frolicking in the Gulf of Mexico with his nine-year-old daughter Sasha. He was sporting a wide grin; she seemed not so sure. The picture was released during a well-publicised twenty-six-hour 'vacation' designed to prove that despite the 4.9 million barrels of crude oil leaked by the BP oil spill, Florida's beaches were 'clean, safe and … open for business'. Also open for business were the oilfields under the Gulf Coast seabed, where drilling soon quietly resumed.

Instead of reining in corporate environmental destruction, governments around the world approach regulation in the spirit of a Victorian gentlemen's agreement. It's all about 'corporate social responsibility', 'voluntary codes of conduct' and 'win–win partnerships', a strategy about as effective as putting an arsonist in charge of a petrol station. It's government that should be taking responsibility for making sure that companies don't pursue profits at the cost of all our futures. But right now, nobody is holding them to account. The UK government's Department for Environment, Food and Rural Affairs issues guidance to companies about being up-front about their activities, but it's all carrot and no stick. Like volatile, pampered teenagers, companies cannot be told what to do; they must be cajoled via corporate self-interest. As the guidance admits, 'There is no mandatory requirement for companies to provide information about environmental credentials,' since 'Defra does not have an enforcement role in relation to self-declared claims.' Likewise, in the US, the Federal Trade Commission provides guidelines for companies and marketers, but these are all voluntary. Greenwash complements 'self-regulation' perfectly, producing an empty performance of piety and PR. Corporate executives now bypass government and aim their charm offensives directly at green bloggers and brand consultants. Governments' faith in corporate environmentalism is just like their faith in consumers' green antennae: totally unrealistic.

This familiar nexus of voluntarism, a lack of enforcement and the advertisement of symbolic achievement produces an attractive world of pretty green illusions. I love online greenwash guides with their tips on how to decode 'fluffy language' or 'suggestive pictures', but many of them are run by green communications companies. These companies are doing some great work to 'incentivise' (I swore I'd never use that word) corporations to be more environmentally responsible, but there's a risk that projecting a green message is a substitute for actually doing anything. Take for example Coca-Cola's PlantBottle, launched at the Copenhagen summit in December 2009 and conspicuously showcased at events around the world, including the 2010 Vancouver Winter Olympics. It was touted as an alternative to the traditional petroleum-based plastic bottle, as 'up to 30 per cent' (read 15–30 per cent) is made from 'plant-based material'. Coca-Cola said it would produce two billion PlantBottles by the end of 2010, which sounds a lot until you realise that it sells 580 billion drinks a year. Now I know Coca-Cola is a cliché corporate target, but what's new about this kind of thing is the widely publicised sense that the corporations are really changing. When *The Times* asked Coke why it wasn't making more of its bottles out of plants, Lisa Manley, director of 'sustainability communications', blamed consumers' suspicion about greenwash. 'There is a great deal of scepticism in some markets about green communications,' she said. 'We are working hard to make sure that the communications of the benefits of the bottle are done credibly.' How bizarre to justify a tokenistic marketing gimmick by referring to consumer scepticism. It's as if greenwash is being sold as the antidote to greenwash. It's truly mind-boggling.

The PlantBottle was hailed as 'a revolutionary solution' by The Climate Group, an 'independent, not-for-profit' organisation calling for a cut in greenhouse-gas emissions. This seemed to me to be something of an overstatement, so I did a bit of digging to try to work out just how green The Climate Group really is. It was pretty hard to find out. Its Wikipedia page has been under dispute, since chunks of it appeared to have been copied and pasted from the Group's own website. Its 'Together' campaign, launched in 2007 by eight 'leading British firms' including Tesco, Barclaycard and HSBC to 'help shoppers cut carbon emissions', was reported on favourably by the *Guardian* newspaper among others, and was referred to as 'the best inoculation against greenwash' – but how do we know that it's not just a vehicle for greenwash in disguise? The Climate Group has after all fifty large corporate members, including Cathay Pacific Airways, PSA Peugeot Citroën, and several energy companies. It's increasingly difficult to distinguish the 'good' PR of green communications from the 'bad' PR of corporate and government greenwash. Meanwhile the real world is being invisibly and mortally wounded.

There's a similar problem with the eco-porn that's filling our cinemas and TV screens. The fact that *Avatar* is the highest-grossing film ever may be down to its green message as well as its spectacular special effects. But what if seeing *Avatar* was actually bad for the environment? Let's recap the story. A disabled ex-soldier is sent on a mission to a distant planet inhabited by a race of giant blue-skinned natives, the Na'vi, to enable a greedy corporation to plunder their homeland's natural resources. But the hero falls in love with the Na'vi's princess, and switches sides to help them save their planet. So far, so green. But as Slavoj Žižek and Caleb Crain have argued, what *Avatar* really ends up doing is undermining the ostensible moral of its own story. It's the very 3D realism of the film that is so mendacious: its vividness is the cover for its sleight of hand. Because it has its cake and eats it by making the Na'vi's planet, Pandora, seem both like a place on earth (it resembles a dream-like Venezuelan rainforest) and an alternative to earth. This allows it to play with the fantasy of saving our own planet while also inventing an imaginary alternative that we don't in reality have: a planet B. *Avatar* escapism isn't much help as far as our environmental reality is concerned. The Na'vi themselves are portrayed as natural creatures, but they are also kind of half computer. They are hippy/hi-tech oxymorons, braided, beaded products of CGI animation. They can commune with trees and animals by plugging their USB-esque tails into them. The Disney-Pixar-animated post-apocalyptic sci-fi film *WALL-E* was praised for its audacious portrayal of environmental disaster. But it's actually a covertly reassuring and optimistic film, not only because it ends with a fantasy of eco-renewal, but also because its robot protagonists have cosily human attributes, like the ability to fall in love. Similarly, *Avatar*'s granola automatons legitimate our tampering with the environment by suggesting that a future man-made world will be all natural, just as ads for broadband always seem to feature utopian images of green countryside under an empty blue sky.

If *Avatar* delivers cathartic complacency in faux eco-warrior packaging, what about films that don't offload their environmental dilemmas onto a different CGI world: *Deep Impact*, *The Day After Tomorrow* and *2012*? What about Al Gore's *An Inconvenient Truth* or Franny Armstrong's cautionary 'documentary' set in 2055, *The Age of Stupid*? Or Fate of the World, a computer game designed to educate its players about climate change? Does watching these films and playing these games produce a net result of doing more or less to curb climate change? Do they allow us to imagine that we have discharged our environmental duties for the year? Some of them are not your average escapist fantasy, it's true: there's that apocalyptic scene in *The Day After Tomorrow* when Jake Gyllenhaal and his new friend Emmy Rossum are camping out in a storm-battered New York Public Library, burning books to stay warm. And that moment in *Deep Impact* when you realise that even the main heroine is not going to make it out alive. Those films are disturbing because they break traditional rules of cinematic genre. In the dystopian future, they seem to say, things will be so bad that not only will books no longer be considered sacred, neither will those precious audience expectations that mainstream cinema normally satisfies so punctiliously. The situation will be too existential for the budding romance between Gyllenhaal and Rossum to really flourish, as it would have done in the Brat Pack movies of the eighties. But despite this dramatic shift, I'm just not sure whether watching these films is genuinely galvanising. It's not even clear to me whether it's better for them to be alarming or redemptive, pessimistic or optimistic, because in the end they are an ersatz experience, a spectacle. The more real they feel, the more easily they replace real action.

I know I'm being hard on those film-makers and campaigners who are trying their best to be creative and work their persuasive magic on our ostrich-like apathy. But the problem with the green imagination is that it can provide us with a mental experience that complements, rather than combats, the psychology of denial. The environmental problems that lie ahead are tediously concrete: there will probably come a point when we won't even be able to employ the phrase 'There are plenty more fish in the sea.' But since that's not our reality just yet, it's hard to summon up the energy to do anything about it. We're unlikely to do anything that really makes a difference until we're actually seeing the full-scale effects of climate change, and by then it'll be too late. It's a sad but true fact that the snow that accompanied the Copenhagen summit in 2009 eroded public belief in global warming, because that snow was more immediately real. Green consumerism, green PR, green internet campaigns, the consumption of eco-themed films and computer games, carbon credits circulating in a self-contained fantasy economy: many of these initiatives exist in a virtual realm that has little connection with reality. And we end up epitomising the final ploy in ideology's cunning campaign: to create the appearance of action while actually doing nothing at all.

Be idealistic

It's true that skewering greenwash, exposing eco-porn and turning the spotlight on denial *is* taking action. Environmentalists have been doing my work for me, delusion-spotting all over the place. There are those greenwashing blogs where you can send in juicy examples and rate them on a scale from authentic to suspect to bogus. There are the Greenwash Academy Awards, whose 2002 winners included Enron for 'Best Make Up' and Arthur Andersen for 'Best Documentary Destruction' (specially commended for 'Excellence in Shredding'). There are articles and books on the subject by journalists George Monbiot and Heather Rogers, the activist Ross Gelbspan, PR Watch's John Stauber and the aforementioned James Hoggan. The greenwash-hounds are hot on the heels of the vested interests doing their damnedest to mislead the public. The game is on.

But that's not the whole story. Modern environmentalism is awash with the rhetoric of grassroots, internet-fuelled activism. I'm all for ordinary citizens cycling more and flying less. And it should be obvious if you've read this far that I'm passionately in favour of green-wash-spotting. But that ubiquitous rhetoric contains another delusion: that bottom-up action is enough on its own. Because far from being empowered to make savvy green decisions, consumers are blundering about in the dark. Report after report reveals irrational behaviour and mistaken assumptions: that people think turning off lights saves more energy than buying more efficient lightbulbs, for example, or that line-drying clothes saves more energy than washing them at a lower temperature. And there are commercial interests – energy, automobile, construction and agriculture – which stand to profit directly from these errors. So many environmental actions are symbolic mitigations, like paying a carbon-offset tax when you buy a long-haul flight: they are little green cherries on a big bad cake.

If this book is about the power of individuals to spot illusions, it's also about recognising the useful function that those illusions perform for us. Rationally, we would do anything to avert environmental disaster. But in practice, we are busily absorbing ourselves with long-hours work culture or playing Pokemon on our iPhones. And the other day, as I was idly flicking between the razzle-dazzle of *Strictly Come Dancing* and a remake of the classic seventies drama *Upstairs, Downstairs*, I was struck by just how obsessed we've become with old-fashioned nostalgia and period dramas, as if we're scared to look the future in the face. We'll be quite happy rearranging the 'Keep Calm and Carry On' themed deckchairs as our *Titanic* goes down, and we'd rather work or entertain ourselves to death than face the likely reality. Technological gadgets have provided us with the perfect compound of illusory progress and handy distraction. We are living in a strange moment: there's a window of opportunity, but also a sense that effective action is impossible. Because even though the chance is there to save the world, it's as though everyone has been caught under a spell of paralysis. Of course, it doesn't help that effective action would involve real sacrifice. As *The Age of Stupid* predicts, future generations may well look back in astonishment that we remained pathetically irresolute in the face of impending disaster. But it's not the case that we're all just stupid, or selfish. The collective delusion we are living under is totally paradoxical: it's both gobsmackingly insane and utterly understandable. And it's not only ordinary citizens who are deluded. Governments may think they don't need to worry about the long term, but they do. Energy company executives may believe their profits are infinite, but they're not. But although there's self-deception at every level, there are massive differences in power.

And that's why this has got to be about politics, about overt ideology, as well as about spotting covert forms of ideology such as greenwash. The grassroots green movement is incredibly inspiring, but it
needs to engage with accountability in order to really get things done.
We still need our bullshit-binoculars, but we also need to restore the
old-style 'isms' that set out a blueprint for concerted action. Because
otherwise, nothing significant will come of all that smart suspicion.
James Hansen maintains that the only way to halt runaway climate
change is to impose a fee on fossil-fuel use. Individual action will not
be enough, he says: we need formally-imposed economic levers. I
don't agree with Anthony Giddens, one of the architects of New
Labour, very often. But in his book *The Politics of Climate Change*, he
argues that the radical decentralisation that characterises today's
green activism will not produce the coordinated action we need; that
governments have to take a bigger role. Political authorities need to
take the advice of scientists, to analyse the risks and to make the best
choices possible. Call me wide-eyed, call me authoritarian, but they
need to make business behave.

We still have a vital role to play in this, but it's about bottom-up
lobbying for top-down enforcement. Most governments, even
progressive ones, don't think it's politically worthwhile to make the
environment a priority. Investment in alternative-energy technology
is dwindling. Climate-change science is ludicrously underfunded.
Responsibility is constantly deflected – onto corporations, and onto
individuals; but when individuals do take action, they are subjected
to surveillance and stamped with a criminal record. State denialism
has almost reached the point of totalitarian repression: news images
of riot police breaking up environmental protests look like really
clunky Leftist student theatre. Governments and private companies
cooperate in infiltrating protest groups as if we were living under
Stalin. At some point in our future, it's going to be seen as surreal that
attempts to avert catastrophe were treated as 'extremist'. It all seems
very pathological. But right now, governments can quite reasonably
claim that there's little pressure to place environmentalism at the
centre of their electoral remit; and that serious green protesters are

therefore beyond the pale. We can do our democratic bit – through our political representatives, in focus groups and surveys, and in the polling booth – to try to halt that vicious circle. But there needs to be a new form of long-termist global governance that has more teeth than the IPCC.

For me, though, there is hope in the fact that the environmental emergency is a chance for idealism to make a comeback, an opportunity to rescue the overt ideology that we so scornfully chucked away in the early 1990s. It's a chance to remember that politics is the business of how we decide as a society what our priorities are and then set about achieving them. What could be more idealistic, after all, than defending planet Earth? But since this is a new and unprecedented situation, it calls for old-style ideology with a new twist. It's got to address a problem that is global, all-encompassing and existential. This new kind of idealism, this new kind of 'ism', needs to be both more general and more practical than before: paradoxically, a think-outside-the-box belief system that's about down-to-earth concrete reality. I feel sorry in a way for today's young green activists that the issues they're fighting for are frankly pretty dull; at least compared to 1968. They have to spend their time talking about concentrations of CO_2 and the technology of nuclear power stations rather than class dynamics or the question of whether marriage is a form of patriarchal subjection. It's all got rather basic. So today's young environmentalists are right in a way when they say they've moved beyond the age of Right and Left. But if environmentalism doesn't come in different flavours, as the old-style ideologies traditionally did, it is at least a *cause*. And as William Golding's *Lord of the Flies* amply illustrated, there are power dynamics in even the most basic of situations. Although ultimately we're all in this together, some people have more to lose than others. Prospects are bleaker in Sierra Leone than in Sweden.

It is hard to be idealistic in the face of such anxiety. But idealism is also undermined by our automatic belief in the inevitability of progress. This belief has been an integral aspect of human culture from the Enlightenment through D:Ream's 1994 hit 'Things Can Only Get Better'; and like Rupert Murdoch's Sky TV, we continue to

Believe in Better. But that secretly cherished belief is now coming up against some awkward evidence. It seems that not only is the idea of necessary human progress something of a delusion, but the human race is in some ways actually going into reverse. There were those employees of bankrupt bank Lehman Brothers, walking out with their cardboard boxes in 2008; the unsold luxury apartments languishing in the Dubai sun; the gaping holes in bank balance sheets revealed by the shrinking tide of liquidity. The past seemed to follow a linear forward path, rather like art history's journey from Classicism to Modernism to Post-modernism. But now it's all got a bit messy. We live in an age when iPads rest on retro kitchen tables, when the *Twilight* saga romanticises Victorian abstinence, when the teeny-boppers at gigs by tribute rock band the Darkness don't get why half the audience are in their fifties. Global warming and peak oil conjure the spectre of abandoned coastal cities, potatoes planted in parking lots, and a renewal of interest in the horse as a mode of transport. The West is in decline, and sub-Saharan Africa is regressing. We are faced with a new and disturbing predicament: a post-progress future. Of course, in some ways this may be a better kind of progress, a move in the direction of living ethically, locally, on a modest human scale. But it's hard to get our heads around nonetheless.

It's perhaps for this reason that the neo-Darwinians are oddly silent on the subject of global warming. The fact that the human race is busily destroying the conditions of its own survival doesn't disprove Darwin – there's no reason why cockroaches should not inherit the world. But it does place the mantra of 'survival of the fittest' in a somewhat different light. It means we might have to stick a picture of a cockroach on the end of that classic illustration of the Ascent of Man. Humans may have dominated all other species, but we are ourselves vulnerable. We may seem like the fittest, but that doesn't mean we're going to survive. Is it natural that humans should destroy their environment? Well, it must be, because we are as natural as other animals. That's why the environmentalists' fencing off of an idea of 'nature' is not exactly right. Even really artificial things like shopping malls and six-lane highways are technically natural.

But if the human race is unprecedentedly stupid enough to modify its own habitat to destruction, it is also unprecedentedly clever enough to stop that process in its tracks. The scientism that is so prevalent in our culture downplays our unique human agency, portraying us as just another species, governed by instinctual natural forces. It's a way of shooting ourselves in the foot on a grand scale. Science isn't just about modelling the likely future, it's about choosing to avoid a future determined by arbitrary human choices which are portrayed as unavoidable.

Perpetual economic growth, the greedy exploitation of resources, and food production on an industrial scale: these are particular *ideological* ways for humans to organise the world. They are not, as the neo-Darwinists would have us believe, the only way, the necessary consequence of greedy, competitive 'human nature'. We've become mired in contradictory illusions of inevitability: both the inevitability of human progress, and the inevitability of catastrophic events taking their course. These illusions are responsible for both the false confidence and the false despair that are causing all this paralysing denial. Progress isn't inevitable, but it is perfectly possible. The environmental challenge encapsulates both meanings of the word ideology that I've explored in this book. It's about unmasking the deceptions of vested interests. And it's about embracing a better vested interest: namely, our interest in saving the world.

AFTERWORD

While I was writing this book, my son was born and my father died. These two events were like opposite poles of hope and despair, bookending the project. I felt pulled between optimism and pessimism. Some days I felt that the whole world was excitingly up for grabs. Public opinion was forcing policy U-turns. Election campaign posters were getting online makeovers. Protesters were risking their lives in Tahrir Square. My local farmers' market was like heaven on earth. But then other days I'd feel as if everything was sewn up. Politicians were using *mea culpa* speeches to regain the advantage. A topless Lady Gaga was being hailed as a feminist icon. Crowds of morons were filming gigs on their mobile phones. A thirty-minute meal by Jamie Oliver was taking the entire evening.

I kept thinking: can things really change? In twenty years' time, is my adult son going to be walking around in a world full of corruption disguised as transparency and elite interests disguised as the popular will? Is optimism ever going to win over pessimism?

But then it dawned on me that optimism and pessimism are not opposites after all. Critique requires pessimism – being suspicious of motives and the appearance of progress – but it also provides the grounds for optimism, since it's the only way to identify problems that need to be solved. It's critique, rather than cheerleading, that enables us to distinguish progress from PR.

That's why so many literary utopias contain elements of dystopia – Jonathan Swift's *Gulliver's Travels*, for example, where the gentle, rational Houyhnhnms are presented alongside other distinctly unattractive societies; or Aldous Huxley's *Island*, his counterpart to *Brave New World*, in which an idyllic island society is under threat from Western oil companies. Utopias are combined with dystopias because they're actually addressing the problems of the here and now. They're recognising that it's satirical critique – rather than flights of fancy – that has the potential to change the world we live in.

That's also why I get so tired of people saying, 'It's all very well knocking the status quo, but what are you going to put in its place?' Critique keeps inequalities under scrutiny. It stops elites automatically having their interests served. It prevents fake panaceas pre-empting genuine improvements. Identifying the rules of the covert ideological game can help us to avoid being played. And we need to keep on exposing power's ruses and tactics, otherwise they will spring back up again.

In our culture critique is really underrated. The authority of the professional critic is under attack from the cult of the amateur and internet 'democratisation'. The humanities, the academic training grounds for critique, are suffering a crisis of legitimacy. And newspapers, its journalistic home, are fighting for their lives. Everyone's into celebration, storytelling and personal journeys – which are lovely, but not very incisive. Critique is constructive because it's about debunking delusions, but also because it's about identifying hidden agendas and buried projects; about resurrecting overt ideologies, the building blocks of change.

Like millenarian Christians, whose ecstatic vision of Christ's Second Coming is bound up with the apocalyptic destruction of the universe, our post-millennial culture ricochets between hype about world-changing revolution and catastrophic anxiety about health scares or climate change. And that is how ideals have slid into illusions. Rather than roll up our sleeves and see what's possible, it's tempting to indulge in pipe dreams. And rather than face real problems, it's easier to go into deluded denial. John Gray argues in his brilliant book *Black Mass: Apocalyptic Religion and the Death of Utopia* that it's dystopian not utopian thinking that we need. And not dystopias that imagine an unthinkable disaster, but rather dystopias that take realistic elements of our world and spool them out a little further, to see what's down the road. As in the creepy but recognisable fictional worlds of William Burroughs and J.G. Ballard. I think he's right. But – call me demanding – I want realistic utopianism as well. And that starts with taking a look at the world around us, raising a sceptical eyebrow, and telling it to get real.

ACKNOWLEDGEMENTS

I'm grateful to Louise Haines at Fourth Estate for her astute advice and wholehearted enthusiasm for the project, and to Robert Lacey for his scrupulous and efficient editing. To Tracy Bohan at the Wylie Agency for being a brilliant agent and friend. To Michelle Levene, Emma Satyamurti and David Schneider for reading the manuscript and providing valuable reality checks (we all need them). To my dad, with whom I was able to share many illuminating kitchen-table discussions before he died in January 2011, and to my mum for her generosity and curiosity. To my son Ezra for teaching me to type with one hand, and for banging on the keyboard when it was time to pack it in for the day. And above all I'm grateful to Adam for letting me rant about ideology before he'd had his first sip of morning coffee, and for everything else.

FURTHER READING

To those trusty readers who have come this far and still want more, I offer a little smorgasbord of books which may be of interest. This is not by any means a comprehensive list, and it's biased towards recent books I've been reading over the last few years, but it'll certainly provide further food for thought. I'll list them in the order of my chapter themes, and I've chosen the most readily available editions.

If you like my take on contemporary politics and culture in general (Introduction), you'll probably also like *Heresies: Against Progress and Other Illusions* by John Gray (Granta, 2004), *Capitalist Realism* by Mark Fisher (Zero, 2009), *44 Letters from the Liquid Modern World* by Zygmunt Bauman (Polity, 2010) and *The Age of Absurdity: How Modern Life Makes it Hard to be Happy* by Michael Foley (Simon & Schuster, 2010). All four provide astute analysis of our weird world.

For more on the history of PR, advertising and commercial manipulation (Chapter 1), I'd recommend three classics: *The Hidden Persuaders* by Vance Packard (reissued by Ig Publishing in 2007), *PR!: A Social History of Spin* by Stuart Ewen (Basic, 1998) and *No Logo* by Naomi Klein (reissued in 2010 by Fourth Estate). From the mini-genre rather inelegantly titled 'bullshit studies', you might sample *On Bullshit* by Harry Frankfurt (Princeton, 2005) or the entertaining *Your Call is Important to Us: The Truth About Bullshit* by Laura Penny (Crown, 2005).

On ideology in general, the charismatic star of Marxist-Lacanian theory Slavoj Žižek is a dense but exhilarating read. He's written a whole stack of books, but you could start with a wide-ranging

211

collection of essays entitled *In Defence of Lost Causes* (Verso, 2008) or his analysis of our current economic and environmental predicament, *Living in the End Times* (Verso, 2010). If you're up for more hardcore digging around in the theoretical aspects of this book, there's *Ideology: An Introduction* by Terry Eagleton (reissued by Verso, 2007) and *How to Read Marx* by Peter Osborne (Granta, 2005). If you really want to get your hands dirty, try *Dialectic of Enlightenment* by Theodor Adorno and Max Horkheimer (Continuum, 1997), *Postmodernism: Or, the Cultural Logic of Late Capitalism* by Fredric Jameson (Verso, 1992) or *One-Dimensional Man* by Herbert Marcuse (reissued by Routledge, 2002).

For those with a penchant for politics (Chapter 2), Thomas Frank's *What's the Matter with America?: The Resistible Rise of the American Right* (Secker & Warburg, 2004) is notable for tackling the thorny issue of political false consciousness. David Runciman's *Political Hypocrisy: The Mask of Power, from Hobbes to Orwell and Beyond* (Princeton, 2008) is good on the pitfalls of political authenticity, that great con trick of our times. The essays in *What Orwell Didn't Know: Propaganda and the New Face of American Politics*, edited by András Szántó (PublicAffairs, 2008), update Orwell's critique for a postmodern world. Steven Poole's *Unspeak: Words are Weapons* (Abacus, 2007) is a super-smart unmasking of contemporary political language. And both *Shock Doctrine: The Rise of Disaster Capitalism* by Naomi Klein (Penguin, 2008) and *Zombie Economics: How Dead Ideas Still Walk Among Us* by John Quiggin (Princeton, 2010) pinpoint the shifty ways in which capitalism dominates our politics.

On inequality and its concealment in contemporary society (Chapter 3), Ferdinand Mount's *Mind the Gap: Class in Britain Now* (Short, 2004) is elegant and perceptive, and Richard Wilkinson and Kate Pickett's *The Spirit Level: Why Equality is Better for Everyone* (Penguin, 2010) is to be credited with reigniting the public debate. *One Dimensional Woman* by Nina Power (Zero, 2009) and *The Equality Illusion: The Truth About Women and Men Today* by Kat Banyard (Faber, 2011) both show that what passes for feminism these days is often not really feminism at all. *Shattered: Modern Motherhood and the Illusion of Equality* by Rebecca Asher (Harvill Secker, 2011) adds a dose of reality to perceptions of parenting.

To the techno-sceptics among you (Chapter 4), I highly recommend the extraordinary manifesto *You are Not a Gadget* by Jaron Lanier (Penguin, 2011), as well as the following three critiques of internet utopianism: *Technopoly: The Surrender of Culture to Technology* by Neil Postman (San Val, 1993), *The Net Delusion: How Not to Liberate the World* by Evgeny Morozov (Allen Lane, 2011) and *The Cult of the Amateur: How Blogs, MySpace, YouTube and the Rest of Today's User-Generated Media are Killing Our Culture and Economy* by Andrew Keen (Nicholas Brealey, 2008).

Flat Earth News: An Award-Winning Reporter Exposes Falsehood, Distortion and Propaganda in the Global Media by Nick Davies (Chatto & Windus, 2008) and *Manufacturing Consent: The Political Economy of the Mass Media* by Noam Chomsky and Edward Herman (Vintage, 2006) skewer journalistic delusions and the infrastructure that sustains them (Chapter 5). *Perpetual Euphoria: On the Duty to be Happy* by Pascal Bruckner and Steven Rendall (Princeton, 2011), and Barbara Ehrenreich's *Smile or Die: How Positive Thinking Fooled America and the World* (Granta, 2010) identify the media's bad habit of bombarding us with stress-inducing happy-clappy imagery. For more on our culture's love–hate relationship with reality, see *Storytelling: Bewitching the Modern Mind* by Christian Salmon (Verso, 2010) and *Authenticity: Brands, Fakes, Spin and the Lust for Real Life* by David Boyle (Harper Perennial, 2004). And if you're after more theoretical books on reality today, you could do worse than peruse *Ways of Seeing* by John Berger (reissued by Penguin Classics, 2008), *The Perfect Crime* by Jean Baudrillard (reissued by Verso, 2008) and *The Society of the Spectacle* by Guy Debord (reissued by Rebel, 1992).

Considering how much of our lives is spent working, it's surprising there are so few prominent books about it (Chapter 6). But there is *Willing Slaves: How the Overwork Culture is Ruling our Lives* by Madeleine Bunting (Harper Perennial, 2005) and Alain de Botton's more meditative *The Pleasures and Sorrows of Work* (Penguin, 2010). Matthew Crawford's *The Case for Working with Your Hands: Or Why*

Office Work is Bad for Us and Fixing Things Feels Good (Penguin, 2010) critiques modern work's unreality and arbitrariness. *Work's Intimacy* by Melissa Gregg (Polity, 2011) is good on how new technology lets work bleed into our private life. And Matthew Stewart's *The Management Myth: Debunking Modern Business Philosophy* (W. W. Norton, 2010) is a much-needed corrective to the self-justifying rhetoric coming down the management hierarchy.

If you'd like to explore the meaning of 'free' time as well as the nine to five (Chapter 7), you could start with *The Labour of Leisure: The Culture of Free Time* by Chris Rojek (Sage, 2009). Three books which reveal the limits of our apparently radical and free counterculture are *The Conquest of Cool: Business Culture, Counterculture and the Rise of Hip Consumerism* by Thomas Frank (Chicago, 1997), *The Rebel Sell: How the Counter Culture Became Consumer Culture* by Joseph Heath and Andrew Potter (Capstone, 2006) and *Retromania: Pop Culture's Addiction to its Own Past* by Simon Reynolds (Faber, 2011).

For sterling pseudoscientific myth-busting (Chapter 8) see Ben Goldacre's *Bad Science* (Fourth Estate, 2008). And for our culture's growing obsession with reductive neuroscience see the excellent *Absence of Mind: The Dispelling of Inwardness from the Modern Myth of the Self* by Marilynne Robinson (Yale, 2010) and *Aping Mankind: Neuromania, Darwinitis and the Misrepresentation of Humanity* by Raymond Tallis (Acumen, 2011). *Delusions of Gender: The Real Science Behind Sex Differences* by Cordelia Fine (Icon, 2011) unpicks the new scientific justifications of patriarchy, as does Natasha Walter's *Living Dolls: The Return of Sexism* (Virago, 2011).

On the secrets and lies of the global food industry (Chapter 9), I would recommend three books for starters: *Not on the Label: What Really Goes into the Food on Your Plate* by Felicity Lawrence (Penguin, 2004), *Shopped: The Shocking Power of British Supermarkets* by Joanna Blythman (Harper Perennial, 2007) and *Fast Food Nation: What the All-American Meal is Doing to the World* by Eric Schlosser (Penguin, 2002). And bravely fighting the disinformation that's getting in the way of saving the world (Chapter 10) are *Heat: How We Can Stop the Planet Burning* by George Monbiot (Penguin, 2007), *Climate*

Cover-up: The Crusade to Deny Global Warming by James Hoggan and Richard Littlemore (Greystone, 2009), *Green Gone Wrong: How Our Economy is Undermining the Environmental Revolution* by Heather Rogers (Verso, 2010) and *Boiling Point: How Politicians, Big Oil and Coal, Journalists and Activists are Fuelling the Climate Crisis – and What We Can Do to Avert Disaster* by Ross Gelbspan (Basic, 2005).

INDEX

Abramović, Marina 136
Absence of Mind (Robinson) 155, 214
'accommodating authoritarianism' 73–4
Adorno, Theodor 25, 135, 212
advertising: xiii, 87, 102, 115; people power
  and xii, 16, 71; subliminal deception in 14,
  15–21, 23–9, 71, 127–30; 'depth boys' 17;
  images of freedom and counterculture
  used to sell symbolic forms of escape
  18–19, 127–30; product placement 29,
  109; online 81; 'outdoor' 106, 137; ironic
  127–8; viral 18–19, 20–1, 25, 127–8, 135;
  environment and 193–4, 198 *see also*
  marketing *and under individual company*
  or product name
Advertising Age 29, 37
Advertising Standards Authority 23
Afghanistan 39, 99, 106
Age of Stupid, The (film) 199, 201
'Al Gore's Penguin Army' (YouTube video)
  50, 127–8
Allen, Woody 102, 134
Allsopp, Kirstie 57, 173
Althusser, Louis 25, 144
American dream 11, 49, 55, 68, 168
Americans for Prosperity (AFP) 49, 80
Anderson, Chris 73, 75, 77, 79, 85
Aping Mankind (Tallis) 155, 214
Apple xv, 10, 70–1, 76, 83, 86, 92, 115, 130,
  136, 166, 201
Apprentice, The (TV show) 56, 99, 101, 119
Arab Spring xii, xiii, 4, 43, 45, 74
Armstrong, Fanny 199
Art of Immersion, The (Rose) 109
Arthur Andersen 200
Assange, Julian 75
Astonishing Hypothesis, The (Crick) 150
'astroturf' campaigns 46–51, 80, 190, 192,
  193
AT&T 72

Authenticity (Boyle) 91, 213
Autumn in New York (film) 103
avant-garde culture 42, 87, 138
Avatar (film) 198
Axelrod, David 48

Baby and Child Care (Spock) 163
'back to basics' 19, 98
Bacon, Francis 158–9
Bad Science (Goldacre) 151, 153, 214
bankers 8, 28, 35, 41, 43, 48, 56, 58, 59, 118,
  119, 120
Banksy 137
Barclays Bank 118, 128
Baron-Cohen, Simon 152, 153
Barroso, José Manuel 1–2
Barthes, Roland 93, 98
Baudrillard, Jean 106, 213
Ben & Jerry's 182
Benn, Hilary 183
Berkeley, Bishop George 105
Berlusconi, Silvio 28
Bernays, Edward 15–16, 19, 24
Berry, Halle 61
Big Breakfast, The (TV show) 95
Big Brother (TV show) 93, 99
bin Laden, Osama 91
Black Mass (Gray) 208–9
Black Swan, The (Taleb) 9
Blair, Tony 1, 21, 22, 30, 36, 55, 59, 65, 107
Blank Slate, The (Pinker) 149
bloggers 92–3, 103, 117, 161, 196, 200, 213
Blumenthal, Heston 176, 179
Blythman, Joanna 181
BNP Paribas 44
Boehner, John 37
Bogdanor, Vernon 38
Bonner & Associates 49, 50
Bookchin, Murray 113
Bourdieu, Pierre 12, 141–2

Boyd, Danah 76, 134
Boyle, David 113
Boyle, Susan 42, 56, 101
BP xi, 7, 194–6
brands xiv, 20–4, 37, 70, 71, 78, 114, 123,
   124, 127, 128, 176, 181, 182, 196, 213
Bridget Jones's Diary (film) 115
Brin, Sergey 70
Bristow, Jennie 163
Britain's got Talent (TV show) 56, 98, 101
Brooke, Heather 58, 69
Brooks, David 23, 55, 56
Brown, Gordon 36, 37, 39, 60, 65, 73
Brown, Sarah 186
Brown, Scott 47, 54–5, 59
BSkyB 41
Bunting, Madeleine 113, 149, 213
Burson, Harold 19
Burson-Marsteller 47
Bush, George W. 2–3, 6, 14, 49, 55, 90, 91
buskers, London 136–7

Cage, John 138
camera obscura 10, 11, 73
Cameron, David xi, xv, 1, 13, 19, 30, 36, 38,
   39, 40, 41, 42, 43, 48, 54, 59–60, 65
Cameron, Samantha 186
Campbell, Alastair 48
Cancún Climate Summit (2010) 191
capitalism: near-collapse of (2008) xiii, 8–9;
   'capitalist realism' 7; ideology of 8–10, 12,
   168; Marx/Engels outlook on 12, 27, 116;
   'back to basics' politics and 19, 98; leads
   working classes to unwittingly conspire in
   their own subjection 27–8, 116; sovereign
   debt crisis (2011) and 45; people power
   and 46; cyber-utopianism mirrors
   language of 72; Luddites and 84–5; work
   and 116, 117, 120, 127, 135; sex and 133
Capitalist Realism (Fisher) 101, 211
Case for Working with Your Hands, The
   (Crawford) 77, 122
Century of Self, The (TV series) 16
Certeau, Michel de 141–2
Chevron 194
Childbirth Without Fear (Dick-Read) 162–3
China 73, 74, 99, 191
'choice' 62–4
Civilising Process, The (Elias) 141
class 12, 27–8, 55–7, 59–60, 62, 64, 66, 69,
   76, 84–5, 99, 108, 119–21, 138, 160, 161,
   164, 173–4, 178–81, 187, 203, 212
Clear Skies Act, US (2003) 14
Clegg, Nick 2, 19, 37–8, 39
climate change 39, 48–50, 129, 142–3, 168,
   189–205

Climate Cover-up (Hoggan/Littlemore) 192
Clinton, Bill 1, 22, 64, 73
Clinton, Hillary 71, 72
coalition government, UK (2010) 3, 7, 19,
   44, 58, 195
Coca-Cola: Honest Tea and 37; Burn energy
   drink 78; 'Open Happiness Global
   Platform' 129–30; Innocent smoothies
   and 182; PlantBottle 196–7
coffee chains 23–4
Cohen, Jared 72
Colao, Vittorio 71
Cold War xiv, 11, 125
Come Dine With Me (TV show) 95, 178
Communism 3, 4, 10, 33, 45–6
comparethemarket.com 20–1, 128
Conquest of Cool, The (Frank) 18, 125, 214
Conservative Party xi, 8, 10, 13–14, 21, 35,
   38, 54, 60, 136
Copenhagen Climate Summit (2009) 191,
   195, 196–7, 200
covert ideology xvi, 54, 86, 101, 167, 190,
   208; theory of 11–15; politics and 13–17,
   21, 31; evolution of 15–34; science and
   151; climate change and 190, 192–3
Cowell, Simon xv, 98, 99
Cox, Brian 147
Craftsman, The (Sennett) 122
Crain, Caleb 198
Crewe and Nantwich by-election (2008) 60
'cross-ownership rule' 80
'crowd-sourcing' 58
Cult of the Amateur, The (Keen) 78–9
'culture-jamming' 127
'culture wars' 8, 9, 55, 56
Curb Your Enthusiasm (TV show) 141
Cybernetic Culture Research Unit, Warwick
   University 69–70
'Cyberspace and the American Dream'
   (Progress and Freedom Foundation) 68, 84

Daily Mail 61, 64, 140
D'Alessandro, David 20
Dances with Wolves (film) 103
Darwin, Charles/Darwinism 9, 149–50, 155,
   167–9, 204, 205, 215
David, Larry 141
Davies, John 47, 50
Dawkins, Richard 147, 148, 149–50
Day After Tomorrow, The (film) 198, 199
DCI Group 50, 128
de Botton, Alain 116
Dean, Howard 39
Debord, Guy 90, 213
Decisive Moment, The (Lehrer) 150, 154,
   155–6

Deep Impact (film) 198, 199
Democratic Party, US 49, 55
Dennett, Daniel 149
Department for Environment, Food and Rural Affairs (DEFRA) 182, 196
Department of Agriculture, US (USDA) 186–7
'depth boys' 17
Derrida, Jacques 25, 105
Desert Storm, Operation 104
Devil Wears Prada, The (film) 115
Diageo 44
Dichter, Ernest 17
Diderot, Denis 97, 122
Digital Destiny (Chester) 80
Douglas, Michael 115
Downes, Lawrence 130
Downton Abbey (TV show) 57, 138
Drew, Robert 94
du Sautoy, Marcus 147
Duffy, Gillian 39
Durkan, Mark 43
Dworkin, Andrea 63, 103
Dyson, Esther 84

'Economic Possibilities for our Grandchildren' (Keynes) 113
Economist, The 1–2, 112
Edelman, Richard 107
Edelman Digital 81
Edinburgh airport 194
Edinburgh Television Festival (2008) 9
Efficient Market Hypothesis 69
Egypt, revolution in xii, 74
elites, power of xii, xiv, xvi, 9, 10–11, 14, 28, 29, 31–3, 44, 49, 70, 71, 75, 136, 142, 207, 208
Ellroy, James 101
email 49, 67, 74, 84, 115, 135, 192
'Energy Citizen' rallies 49
Engels, Friedrich 10, 11, 12, 27, 90, 116
'Engineering of Consent, The' (Bernays) 16–17
Enron 10, 200
equality: of opportunity 28, 55, 65; gender 53, 54, 60, 64, 151, 153–4, 166, 169, 179–80, 186, 187, 214; racial 60–2, 64, 65, 66
eroticism in popular culture 130–6
Esquire (magazine) 90, 107
Essential First Year, The (Leach) 164
European Union 50, 193
Everything I Want to Do is Illegal (Salatin) 184
Evidence-Based Care for Normal Labour and Birth (Walsh) 161

expenses crisis, UK MPs 6, 38, 58–9
ExxonMobil 50, 128, 191–2

Facebook 5, 20, 25, 42, 45, 47, 49, 70, 72, 73, 74, 76, 81, 134, 142, 159
Falling Down (film) 115
false consciousness xiv, 26–30, 32, 33, 63, 120, 185, 212
FarmVille 177
Fear of Freedom, The (Fromm) 145
Fearnley-Whittingstall, Hugh xi, 57, 95–6, 171, 173, 178
Feather Larson & Synhorst (FLS) 47, 50
Federal Communications Commission (FCC) 80
Federal Trade Commission (FTC) 196
Fellowes, Julian 57
Femfresh 'natural balance' 17–18, 19
feminism 63–4, 70, 102–3, 123, 131, 143, 153, 161, 163, 168, 207, 212
Fey, Tina 103
Fine, Cordelia 153
Fisher, Mark 7, 101, 211
Flat Earth News (Davies) 99
focus groups 15, 17, 21–3, 30, 31, 38, 44, 108, 203
food 171–88; choice 171–2; celebrity chefs 171, 173–4;, 176–7 'reality'/accessibility and 174–80; class inequality and 174–9; gender inequality and 179–80; selling of 180–8; organic 181–2; activists 182–3; GM 182, 183; local 172, 181, 183, 184, 194, 204; labels 31–2, 172, 173, 178, 180, 183–5, 214; nudge theory and 184, 185; 'statement gardens' 186–8; price 187–8
Food Standards Agency (FSA) 32, 177, 184–5
Ford, Gina 163
Frank, Lone 150, 154
Frank, Thomas 18, 29, 48–9, 125, 212, 214
freedom: ideology of 3, 63; internet 72, 76; technology and 72, 76, 86–7; work and idea of 125–30; sex and 130–6; culture and 136–9; of speech 136; laws and 139–46; self-control and 139–46; unspoken rules and 141; true 145; food and 184
FreedomWorks 49
Freud, Sigmund/Freudian psychoanalysis 15, 17, 18, 21, 24, 26–7, 30, 32, 33, 133, 141, 149
Fukuyama, Francis xiv, 4, 45
Future Sex (magazine) 133

G20 28
Gamechanger 48
gaming 87, 96, 129, 130

Gelbspan, Ross 200
gender equality 53, 54, 60, 64, 151, 153–4, 166, 169, 179–80, 186, 187, 214
general elections, UK: (1992) 35; (2005) 21; (2010) 36, 38–9, 59–60, 91
General Motors Saturn SUV 193
Gere, Richard 103, 114–15
Gilder, George 84
Glassman, James 71–2
Glee (TV show) 101, 103
Global Business Network 85
God is Not Great (Hitchens) 148–9
Gok Wan 62
Goldin, Nan 136
Goodwin, Fred 41
Google xii–xiii, 10, 28, 70–4, 83, 112, 172
Gorbachev, Mikhail 42
Gore, Al 50, 55, 127–8, 199
Gormley, Antony 42, 139
Gould, Stephen Jay 154
Graham, Mark 76
Gramsci, Antonio 12–13, 25
Grand Theft Auto (video game) 101
Gray, John xiii, 169, 208–9, 211
Green Gone Wrong (Rogers) 183–4
Greenblatt, Stephen 41–2
Greenpeace 192
greenwash 189–205
Guardian 43, 50, 58, 75, 79, 149, 152, 153, 197
Guns, Germs and Steel (Diamond) 158

Habermas, Jürgen 33
habitus (second nature) 141, 142
Halpern, David 30, 31
Hansen, James 191, 195, 202
Harris, Josh 69
Harry Potter Alliance 128
Hatwell, Lynne 42
Hawking, Stephen 148, 157
Haynes, Dave 79
healthcare, US 2, 4–5, 49
Heathrow airport 195
Heidegger, Martin 105
Heider, Fritz 19
Here Comes Everybody (Shirky) 72
Hidden Persuaders, The (Packard) 25
Hilton, Steve 30
Hitchens, Christopher 3, 148–9
Hoggan, James 192, 200, 215
Hollywood 16–17, 61, 95, 103, 114–15, 131
Honest Leadership and Open Government Act (2007) 50
Honest Tea 37, 91
Horkheimer, Max 135
Hornby, Andy 41

Hotmail: 'The New Busy' 115–16
How It Is (Bałka) 138
Howard, Russell 102
HTC Smartphone 127, 134
Hughes, Karen 90
Hume, David 23, 71
Hunt, Jeremy 38
Hurricane Katrina 189
Husserl, Edmund 105

ideology: second life of xiv–xv, xvi, 1–34; death of xiv–xv, xvi, 1–10, 45–6, 125, 176–7; Marx and Engels' theory of 10, 11, 12, 90; as hegemony 12–13; covert xvi, 10–15, 17, 21, 25, 26–7, 31, 32, 33, 34, 45, 54, 86, 101, 124, 151, 167, 190, 192–3, 208; 'choice' and 62, 63; women and 62, 63; of freedom 63; fairness and 66; internet and 71, 72; technology and 86, 87; distorting reality with realism 98; ideological effect of media on our imaginations 102, 104; of work 112, 113–14, 116, 117, 119, 120, 123, 124, 126; advertising and 128, 130; sex and 133; external expectations passing as our own liberated desires/of hedonistic liberty 126, 128, 130, 133, 139–40, 142–3; seductiveness of 144–5; science and 151, 160, 167; to hide inequities 187–8; food and 187, 188; climate change and 192–3; be idealistic 200–5; environmental 200–5
'immersive' guerrilla marketing 21; immersiveness 96, 97, 99, 109, 130
Inconvenient Truth, An (film) 50, 127–8, 199
Independent 160
inequality 4, 9, 11, 46, 53–8, 60, 66, 76–7, 117–20, 179, 185–8, 208, 212
Infotopia (Sunstein) 82
Institute for Fiscal Studies (IFS) 7, 19
Institute of Chicago 139
internet xiii, 5, 19, 20, 21, 25, 38–41, 42, 45, 47–8, 61, 67–84, 88, 89, 92, 96, 106, 109, 111, 112, 123, 130, 134, 142, 159, 167, 186, 200, 208, 213
'Invisible Bullets' (Greenblatt) 41–2
Invisible Gorilla, The (Chabris/Simons) 156
IPCC (Intergovernmental Panel on Climate Change) 191, 203
iPhone 76, 115, 130, 136, 166, 201; apps xiii, xv, 70–1, 83, 92
Iran 40–1, 73, 74
Iraq 36, 44, 104, 106, 107
Ireland 43, 160
Islam 2–3, 64–6, 136, 148

Jackson, Andrew 57
Jobs, Steve 29, 70, 71, 86, 134

Johnson, Alan 2
Johnson, Boris 142
Johnson, Samuel 105
Jones, Steve 167–8
Joseph Rowntree Foundation 56
journalism 77–80, 92–4, 99
Jowell, Tessa 60

Kant, Immanuel 105
Keynes, John Maynard 8, 113, 124
Keyworth, George 84
Khamenei, Ayatollah Ali 40–1
King's Speech, The (film) 57
Klein, Melanie 21–2
Klein, Naomi 20, 37, 127, 211, 212
Knocked Up (film) 115
Koch, Charles 49
Koch, David 49, 50
Koch Industries 192
Kraft 44, 182
Kyoto Protocol 190–1

L'Oréal xiii, 47, 62
Labour Party 1, 6, 21–2, 30, 35, 36, 38, 48,
    54, 55, 60, 202
Lacan, Jacques 144, 145, 211
Lane, Anthony 102–3
Lansley, Andrew 184–5
Lawrence, Felicity 181
Lawson, Mark 136
Lawson, Nigella 63, 174, 176, 177, 188
Leadbeater, Charles 69
Leahy, Terry 182–3
Lee, Ellie 163
Lee, Ivy 16
Leroi, Armand 150
Levi's 127
Levy, Jeffrey 40
Lewis PR 50
Liberal Democrats 37–8, 49
licensing laws, UK twenty-four-hour 140
Lieberman, Joe 2, 6
Life and Death of Democracy, The (Keane)
    38
Lobbying Disclosure Act, US (1995) 50
Logue, Lionel 57
Long Tail, The (Brand) 85
Lucas, George 93
Luddites 84–5

McDermott, Nancy 164–5
McDonald's 10, 172, 177, 185
Mackey, John 47
MacKinnon, Catharine 63
McQueen, Lee 101
'machismo of demythologization' 101

Major, John 6, 19, 35, 55
Making of the English Working Class, The
    (Thompson) 84
Mandelson, Peter 36
'March for the Alternative' (2011) 4
Marcuse, Herbert 113
marketing xii, xiv, 14, 15–23; psychological
    15–23, 24; viral 18–19, 47–9, 127–8
Marx, Karl/Marxism 8, 10–12, 27, 33, 73,
    77, 90, 96–7, 103, 113, 116, 121, 124, 211,
    212
'meat puppets' 47
Merkel, Angela 2, 6
Michele, Lea 103
Microsoft xii, xiii, 70, 71, 82, 115–16
Miliband, Ed 195
Mindfield (Frank) 150
Mindspace (Cabinet Office Paper) 30, 31
mobile phones xv, 18–19, 67, 79, 102, 145,
    207
models xii, 62, 154
Monbiot, George 100
Monderman, Hans 143
Monsanto 176
Morgan, Bill 185
Morgan, Piers 56
mothers, working 63–4, 122, 123, 152, 153,
    161, 165, 178
movies 57, 72, 93, 95, 102–4, 114–15, 198,
    199
Mugabe, Robert 28
multiculturalism 7, 65
Mumsnet 163
Murdoch, James 9
Murdoch, Rupert 41, 98, 203
music industry 78–9
Myners, Lord 43
Myspace 76, 213

NASA 191, 195
NASDAQ crash (2001) 69
NCT (National Childbirth Trust) 160–2
Nelson, Fraser 60
Net Delusion, The (Morozov) 73
'network neutrality' 80
neuroscience 24, 30, 32, 149–51, 154–9, 165,
    214
Never Pure (Shapin) 151
New America Foundation 71–2
New Economics Foundation 113
New Nation 61
New Orleans 189
New Republic 73
New Rules of Marketing and PR, The
    (Meerman Scott) 20
New York Review of Books 186

New York Sun 64
New York Times 75, 90, 130, 152
News Corporation 75
News of the World 41, 60
Newsweek 154, 193
NHS, coalition government reorganisation of 41, 44
Nike 20, 127
9/11 2–3, 65, 79–80
Nineteen Eighty-Four (Orwell) 14–15, 108
No Logo (Klein) 20, 127, 211
Noel's House Party (TV show) 95, 96
Nudge (Thaler/Sunstein) 30–1, 184
'nudge' theory xiv, xv, 29–34, 184, 185
Nye, Joseph 13

Obama, Barack xiii, 2, 4–5, 30, 36, 37, 40, 48, 61, 64, 91, 128, 150–1, 195–6
Obama, Michelle 36, 53, 186
Observer 64, 161
oil companies xi, 6–7, 191–2, 194–6, 204, 208, 215
oil spill, Gulf of Mexico (2010) 6–7
Oliver, Jamie 174, 175, 178–9, 180, 183, 207
One & Other (Gormley) 139
Open Government Initiative, US government 40
optimism and pessimism 207–8
Outliers (Gladwell) 154–5

Packard, Vance 25, 29
Page, Larry 70
Palin, Sarah 36
Parker, Sarah Jessica 64, 102
participation, myth of 18, 20, 21, 22, 96, 97, 98, 109, 138–9
Peckham Finishing School for Girls (TV show) 98
pedestal paradox 58
'people power' xii, xv, 27, 36–46, 51, 58, 69, 70, 73, 81, 183
Perfect Crime, The (Baudrillard) 106
Perpetual Euphoria (Bruckner) 102
'personal responsibility' 32, 181
Pfeiffer, Daniel 40
phenomenology 105
Philip Morris 47
Phillips, Adam 135–6
Phipps, Belinda 161
phone-hacking xii, 42, 44
Pickles, Eric 59
Pink, Daniel 75
Pinker, Steven 149
Plane Stupid 195
Plant, Sadie 69
Poland Spring 'Eco-shape' bottle 193

Political Mind, The (Lakoff) 149
Politics of Climate Change, The (Giddens) 202
politics: 'nudge' theory xiv, xv, 29–34, 184, 185; Right and Left xiv, 1, 7, 8, 54, 176–7, 203; ideology, death of xiv–xv, 1–15, 19, 54, 176–7, 203; 'back to basics' 19, 98; focus groups 17, 21–3; outsourcing 20; identity 25, 60–2; false consciousness and 27, 30; conviction 35–7; fake authenticity 35–7; 'people power' and 37–46; 'astroturf' and 46–51; equality and 53–60; model politicians 57–60; 'choice' 62–4; respect and 64–6; internet and 71, 73–7, 83; work and 120, 124, 127–8; liberty and 143–4; science and 151, 153, 154, 156, 168, 169; food and 173, 176–7, 180, 183, 184, 187, 188; climate change and 189–205
Pollan, Michael 181, 186
Polling Report, The 22
pollution xi, 14, 84
Poole, Steven 135
post-materialistic age 79
'post-scarcity economics' 113
Power, Nina 138
'Power of Us, The' (*Business Week*) 82
PR (public relations) xiv, 12, 14–16, 19–20, 24, 25, 27, 30, 33, 36, 40, 47–50, 61, 66, 76, 81, 104, 107, 109, 128, 185–8, 190, 192, 197, 200, 207
PR! (Ewen) 16
PR Power (Barry) 19–20
PR Watch 47, 200
Prahalad, C.K. 82
Prescott, David 48
Prescott, John 48, 59
presidential campaign, US (2000) 55
Pretty Woman (film) 114–15
Primark 63, 131
Prince, Richard 136
Proctor & Gamble 194
Promise Corp 21–2
Propaganda (Bernays) 15–16
public apologies, vogue for 41
Public Opinion (Lippmann) 16–17
public-spending cuts, UK xi, 4, 7, 13–14, 19, 43, 44

Queer Eye for the Straight Guy (TV show) 95
Quiet: We Live in Public (experiment) 69

race, equality and 60–2, 64, 65, 66
Raese, John 49
Rampton, Sheldon 47

Ramsay, Gordon 95, 174, 176, 179–80
Ramsay, Tana 179–80
reaction formations 131–2
Reagan, Ronald 73
reality: inverted xii–xiv, 10–12; appeal to
 19; effect 19–20, 91–8; ideology and 25;
 bytes 73–4; internet 74–84; television 89,
 93–104; tampering with 90–1;
 'augmented' 92; 'virtual' 7, 73, 92, 107;
 representing 105–9; philosophy of 105–7;
 food and 174, 178, 181, 184, 185, 187,
 188
Reality is Broken (McGonigal) 129
Rebel Sell, The (Potter/Heath) 127
regulation: 'light touch' 32; self- 186, 196
religion 11–12, 53, 64–6, 148, 157
Republican Party, US 10, 37, 54–5, 48–9,
 193
'respect' 64–6
'responsibility deal networks' 32
Retromania (Reynolds) 138
Revolution Will Not be Televised, The
 (Trippi) 39
riots, English (August 2011) 4, 127
Roberts, Julia 115
Rogen, Seth 72
Rogers, Desirée 37
Rogers, Heather 200
role models 53–4, 59, 61–2, 66, 99, 103
Ronseal 19, 106
Rose, Frank 109
Rove, Karl 90–1
Roy, Arundhati 27
Royal Society 30, 183
Royal Society of Arts 149, 155, 165
royal wedding (2011) 43, 57, 62, 104
Rubel, Steve 81
Rushdie, Salman ix, 136
Russia 2, 15, 74, 102

Saatchi & Saatchi 18–19, 133, 174
Saenz, Mike 133
Sainsbury's 172, 183
Sakharov, Andrei 73
Salmon, Christian 20, 21
Schindler's List (film) 103
Schlosser, Eric 181
Schmidt, Eric 70
science 147–69; faith in facts 147–52;
 wonder of/religious nature of worship
 147–52, 157–8; 'new Enlightenment'
 148–9; evolution/genetics 149–50, 152–8,
 167–9, 204, 205; neuroscience 24, 30, 32,
 149–51, 154–9, 165, 214; stem-cell
 research 150–1; covert ideologies 150–2;
 evolutionary psychology 152–8; gender
 difference and 152–4; 'neuro-realism' 154;
 conflating nature with 158–66; childbirth
 and 160–3; bringing up children 163–5;
 tomorrow's world 166–9
Sears, Martha 165
Sears, William 165
Secret Millionaire, The (TV show) 56–7, 96,
 98
Seinfeld (TV show) 141
sex 130–6
Sex and the City (TV show) 63, 64, 102–3
'Shaping Public Opinion' (1994 conference)
 47
Shell 194
Shirky, Clay 72, 73
Simms, Andrew 113
Sisley, Justin 93
Skilton, Brian 174
Sky News 41, 91
'slacktivism' 74–5
Smart Mobs (Rheingold) 82
'smart power' 71
Smile or Die (Ehrenreich) 56, 102
Smith, Delia 179
social mobility xi, 53–60
Social Network, The (film) 72
Society of Spectacle, The (Dubord) 90
Sociobiology (Wilson) 149
'sock puppets' 47
soft power xiv, xv, 13, 35–51, 71, 126
Sony 47, 127, 128, 133
Sourcewatch 49
Spectator 60
Spent (Miller) 168
spin xiv, 16, 19–20, 22, 25, 35, 91, 98, 106,
 211, 213
Spock, Dr Benjamin 163
Stanford Center for Biomedical Ethics 154
Stansted airport 195
Star Wars (film) 93
Starbucks 24, 182, 188
Stauber, John 47, 200
Stein, Joel 95
Stein, Rick 176
Stevenson, Lord 41
Stewart, Martha 173
Stolorow, Robert 5
Storytelling (Salmon) 20, 21
Strategy of Desire, The (Dichter) 17
Straw, Jack 36
student protests against tuition fees, UK
 (2010) 43
subversion and containment 41–2
Sugar, Alan 53, 71, 101
Sunday Telegraph 153
Sunstein, Cass 30–1, 82

surveillance society 139, 142, 143–4, 202
Suskind, Ron 90

Tarantino, Quentin 101
Taylor, Matthew 149, 155, 165
Tea Party 36, 37, 46, 48, 49, 50, 192
technology xii, xv, xvi, 4, 31, 48; people
    power and 39–40, 51; seductive promises
    of 67–88, 100, 112–13, 133–6, 142;
    internet 68–84, 133–6; Luddites and 84–5;
    visual echoes of manual ancestors in 92;
    blurs distinction between work and
    non-work 115–16, 129, 130; sex and
    133–6; scientific justifications for 159;
    Tomorrow's World/future of 166–7; climate
    change and 191, 194, 201–3
Technopoly (Postman) 82
television: talent shows xi; 3D 25; product
    placement 29; politicians on 36; class and
    57; internet 69; advertising 29, 80; reality
    89, 93–104; popularity of 89–90; lack of
    quality 108; interactive 135, 141; retro and
    nostalgic 138; science on 147, 150, 157,
    163, 166; food shows 174–80
TerraChoice 194
Tesco 21, 131, 179, 182, 183, 197
TFI Friday (TV show) 95
Thatcher, Margaret 1, 28, 57, 61, 120, 168
3663 (catering company) 194
Time (magazine) 24
Time Machine, The (Wells) 135
Times, The xi, 152–3, 197
Timpson, Edward 60
T-Mobile 18–19, 135
Toffler, Alvin 78, 84, 88
Torode, John 176
Tower Block of Commons (TV show) 98
Trippi, Joe 39
Truman Show, The (film) 95
tuition fees, UK (2010) 2, 43, 113
21st Century Enlightenment (Royal Society
    of Arts) 165
Twitter 21, 25, 40, 42, 47–9, 61, 69, 73, 74,
    79, 112, 134, 186
'Twitter Power: How Social Networking is
    Revolutionising the Music Business'
    (*Guardian* article) 79
'Two Cultures, The' (Snow) 157

Ugly Betty (TV show) 103
Ulay 136
United Nations 62, 190, 191, 193
Unilever 182
Up (TV series) 95
'user-generated content' xiv, 80, 99, 100,
    213

Vahidnia, Mahmoud 40–1
Vancouver Winter Olympics (2010) 197
'veil of obviousness' 19
Vilsack, Tom 186–7
viral advertising/marketing 18–21, 25, 47–9,
    127–8, 135
'virtual reality' 7, 73, 92, 107
Vodafone 'Our Power' ad xii, 16, 71

Wall Street Journal 37, 50
WALL-E (film) 198
Walmart 47, 182
Walsh, Denis 161
Walter, Natasha 153
Ways of Seeing (Berger) 78, 108
We the Media (Gillmor) 80
Web 2.0 69–73, 81
Westerveld, Jay 193
What's the Matter with Kansas? (Frank) 29
Which? (website) 83
Whole Foods 9, 47
Wii 87, 135
WikiLeaks xii, 72, 75
Wikipedia 75–6
Wilde, Oscar 145
Willing Slaves (Bunting) 113–14
Windfall (TV show) 98
Windows, Microsoft, 70; Explorer xii, xiii
Wired (magazine) 68, 73, 75, 85, 109
Wisdom of Crowds, The (Surowiecki) 82
women: liberation of 45; choice and 62–4,
    66; media representation of 102–3, 115;
    work and 122, 123; liberty and 131;
    science and 152–4, 160–5, 168; childbirth/
    child-rearing and 160–5; food and 173,
    179
work 111–24; 'no-collar' employees 112;
    technology and 112–13; ideology of
    113–14, 116–17; workers as 'internal
    customers' 114; 'dress-down Fridays' 114;
    in movies 114–15; freedom and 127–30;
    falling in love with 127–30; retail and
    127–30
'Work of Art in the Age of Mechanical
    Production, The' (Benjamin) 77

X Factor (TV show) xv, 5, 39, 100

Yahoo 71, 82
You are Not a Gadget (Lanier) 78–9
YouTube 5, 19, 40, 50, 73, 76, 81, 86, 127–8,
    134, 213

Žižek, Slavoj 131, 132, 198, 211
Zombie Economics (Quiggin) 68–9
Zuckerberg, Mark 70, 134, 159